Praise
First Edition of

CARROTY NELL

"One of the best Ripper books of 2010."

—*Ripperologist*

"He (John Keefe) relates her final days and hours on earth in such minute detail, and examines the aftermath of her murder in such a well-written way, that he succeeds in making what may be a familiar tale to most of us, compelling once again."

—*Casebook Examiner*

"It's an excellent book in which a lot is skillfully weaved from very little core material."

—Paul Begg
  Author of:
    Jack the Ripper, Jack the Ripper: The Definitive History, Jack the Ripper: The Uncensored Facts
  Co-Author of:
    The Complete Jack the Ripper A to Z, Great Crimes and Trials of the Twentieth Century

CARROTY NELL

Frances Coles

Lloyd's Illustrated Newspaper, March 1, 1891

© The British Library Board
Used with Permission

Carroty Nell

The Last Victim of Jack the Ripper

John E. Keefe

CARROTY NELL

The Last Victim of Jack the Ripper

All rights reserved.
No portion of this book may be transmitted
or reproduced in any form, or by any means,
without the prior written permission of the
publisher and copyright holder.

SECOND EDITION

Copyright © 2012 by John E. Keefe

ISBN-10: 1-4751-2565-8
ISBN-13: 978-1-4751-2565-8

Menotomy Publishing
Arlington, MA
www.menotomypublishing.com

For Rose Marie

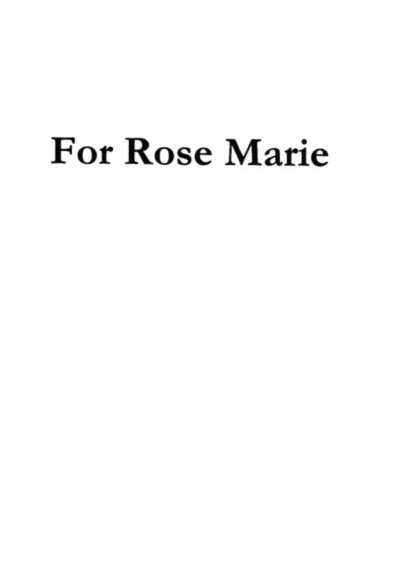

CONTENTS

Preface   xiii
Foreword   xv

Part One – The Whitechapel Murders

1   Swallow Gardens   3
2   A Gruesome Discovery in George Yard   8
3   Buck's Row, Whitechapel   17
4   "I Won't Be Long"   25
5   The Double Event   35
6   "Don't Look in There"   53
7   Castle Alley   63

Part Two – The Final Victim

8   "She's Known As Carroty Nell"   73
9   Rumors, Hearsay, and Misinformation   86

10	Frances Coles	95
11	Friday, the 13th	119
12	"You Are Hereby Charged ..."	134
13	Mr. Baxter's Inquest	150
14	Rest In Peace	182
15	Upon Closer Examination	187

Part Three – The Aftermath

16	Total Disagreement	197
17	The Suspects	214
18	Was it Jack, or Someone Else?	234
	Epilogue	239

Appendix

The Witnesses	247
The Statement	250
The Interview	255
Notes and Sources	267
Bibliography	275
Index	277

PREFACE

Frances Coles was the last, and the most misunderstood of the Whitechapel murder victims. For over one hundred and twenty years, since her untimely death in a desolate underpass beneath some railway tracks, she has been the subject of more errors, more misconceptions, and more mistaken speculation that any of the other victims. Until the publication of *Carroty Nell* in 2010, every book, every magazine article, every reference to her invariably stated that she was twenty-six when she died. They were wrong. *Carroty Nell* revealed that she was thirty-one. It also disclosed that she was born and raised in abject poverty in one of the poorest slums in London—a far cry from the rose-colored but unidentified respectable suroundings that other sources usually associate with her childhood. It was the first book to mention the correct age for Ernest Thompson, the constable who discovered her body. To the best of my knowledge, it was also the first to correctly identify the birthplace of suspect Severin Klosowski. Other publications often confuse it with a similarly-spelled village one hundred and seventy miles away.

The new edition contains additional information that wasn't known when the first edition came out—and it debunks more of the myths that continue to surround her, like the oft-repeated claim that she sometimes called herself

CARROTY NELL

Hawkins. It discloses new information about her last employment with a wholesale druggist company, and reveals for the first time details of her prior employment with a soap and toiletries manufacturer. And, thanks to the kind courtesy of the Gilbert and Sullivan Archive, it includes Sir W. S. Gilbert's original comic sketch of *Carrotty Nell* [sic]. Gilbert coined the name and brought it into popular use almost twenty years before anyone thought of applying it to an impoverished East End streetwalker. I believe this is the first time Gilbert's sketch has appeared in print since the 1870s.

I have always felt that the best prefaces are the shortest ones. So, with that in mind, it's time bring this one to a close and move on to *Carroty Nell*.

FOREWORD

My grandmother could remember her parents talking about the *Yellow Days*—days of strange, copper-tinted skies and eerie, multi-colored haloes surrounding the hazy, midday sun; days that invariably ended with spectacular, blazing sunsets. The unusual phenomena were caused by microscopic dust particles that were blown skyward when a cataclysmic explosion in the far-off Indian Ocean vaporized two-thirds of a volcanic island called Krakatoa, sending five cubic miles of dirt into the stratosphere. The thin blanket of dust slowly encircled the globe, dimming the sunlight. That, in turn, caused temperatures to drop and weather patterns to change, sometimes dramatically. Those effects lingered for several years. The dust particles may or may not have had a hand in the chaotic weather conditions that summer but, regardless of the cause, the summer of 1888, with its seemingly-endless onslaught of dull gray clouds and drizzle, went down in British weather journals as one of the coolest and wettest ever recorded.

Many of London's four and a half million residents had awaited its arrival with some apprehension, worried that the city might see a repeat of the previous fall's rioting that broke out when thousands of desperately poor East Enders marched on Trafalgar Square to press their demands for higher wages and better living conditions.

CARROTY NELL

In June, Queen Victoria celebrated the fifty-first anniversary of her ascension to the throne. She was already Great Britain's third-longest reigning monarch. A few weeks earlier the directors of a French construction company had announced their plan to link England and France with a railway bridge over the English Channel. The project stood little chance of gaining approval, especially since Lord Randolph, Winston Churchill's father, was leading a spirited Parliamentary campaign to block a proposed tunnel under the channel. Opponents feared an invading army could use it in wartime.

In July, fourteen hundred women went on strike at London's Bryant & May Match Co. after three "match girls" were dismissed for leaking information to the press about the unhealthy working conditions and the punitive fines management imposed for minor offences such as coming in late, or talking during work hours. The company held out for three weeks before they gave in and agreed to eliminate the fines and reinstate the fired employees. It was the first time unskilled women had successfully banded together to gain such concessions, and it was considered by many to be a watershed in unions' attempts at organization.

One night in early August, as the summer was just beginning to wane, a twenty-four-year-old cab driver ended his shift and headed home to Whitechapel, the poorest and most infamous slum district in London. It was nearly three thirty in the morning when he started climbing the pitch-black stairs to his room. While carefully making his way up the steps in the darkness, he nearly stumbled over someone sprawled across a landing. It didn't surprise him since derelicts often slept in the stairway, and he continued his ascent without giving the incident further thought.

When the first rays of sunlight began to creep across the walls of the dingy stairwell, they revealed that the "derelict" was a woman's blood-soaked body. She had been stabbed so many times even hardened police investigators winced as they looked down upon her.

Foreword

A few weeks later another body was discovered, and then another. Before long a strange blend of fear and fascination began to grip the residents of London. A diabolical killer, someone who could seemingly blend into the shadows, was at large and prowling the dim, gas-lit streets of the poorest ghetto in the world's largest city. His target—the prostitutes of Whitechapel.

The killer's *modus operandi* was unmistakable. He slashed his victims' throats so deep they were nearly decapitated. For some, the violence didn't end there. He cut their lifeless bodies open and made off with some of their internal organs, leaving the mutilated corpses with their hideous incisions in plain sight to be discovered by the first person who happened along.

The bloody rampage finally came to an end in February 1891 with the brutal murder of a young, attractive, and surprisingly reserved *unfortunate*, the Victorian term for an impoverished woman who turned to prostitution for survival. On the squalid streets of Whitechapel where she plied her trade, people often knew her only by her street name, *Carroty Nell*.

Her real name was Frances Coles. This is the story of her all too brief life, and tragic death.

CARROTY NELL

Part One

The Whitechapel Murders

CARROTY NELL

Chapter 1

Swallow Gardens

Ernest Thompson, or to use his proper title, Metropolitan Police Constable Ernest William Thompson – Badge 240H, glanced at the clock over the front door of the Cooperative Stores on Leman Street. It was twelve minutes past two on Friday morning, February 13, 1891. The twenty-two-year-old policeman had to be the proudest, most excited man on the force that night. He had just completed a six-week training course, and was walking a beat alone for the very first time.

If the person who handed him his first assignment had a sense of humor, admittedly something rather unlikely, they could have told him they had good news, and bad news. The good news was that his beat was close to the Leman Street Police Station—surely a comforting thought for someone about to spend his first night walking one alone. That bad news was that it was in the Metropolitan Police Department's H, or Whitechapel, Division. It was the most squalid, crime-ridden section of London.

The easiest way to describe that beat is to say that he walked around the block, a block bounded by Leman, Chamber, Mansell, and Prescott Streets. Every time he came to an intersection he turned right. But the block Thompson patrolled wasn't quite that simple. Leman and

CARROTY NELL

Mansell Streets were almost a thousand feet apart. To reach Mansell Street he had to walk the length of Chamber Street; to return he had to walk the length of Prescott Street. Chamber Street was the more unpleasant of the two.

To begin with, it was dark. But so were most of the back streets in Whitechapel. Gaslights were often spaced so far apart that they were little more than small islands of light in a sea of shadows. Silent, mostly empty buildings lined the narrow roadway—some old warehouses, a four story building that housed the Tower Hill Catholic School, a few rundown private homes, and the stables of the Great Northern Railway. From Leman Street, where it began, it ran in a straight line for about eight hundred feet, and then made an abrupt, forty-five degree turn to the right.

A massive, twenty-foot-high, brick-faced viaduct that carried the tracks of the Great Eastern Railway ran behind the pavement along much of the left hand side of the street, and right along side it for the last few hundred feet before the bend. Sandwiched between the viaduct on one side and the buildings on the other, that section of the street resembled a small canyon.

There were three tunnel-like passageways, or archways, through the viaduct that allowed pedestrians and wagons to pass under the tracks. Each one was over a hundred feet long. They were the only means of reaching Royal Mint Street, on the other side of the viaduct, without going all the way down to the end of the street. Although they were heavily traveled during daylight hours, only the bravest pedestrians dared venture through them alone once the sun went down. Thompson was supposed to walk through each one as he made his way along Chamber Street. Including the time spent checking the passageways, it took him between fifteen and twenty minutes to complete one walk around the beat.

Twelve minutes past two. He was just about on schedule. He had already walked the complete beat thirteen, maybe

Swallow Gardens

fourteen times, and nothing out of the ordinary had happened. Unbeknownst to Thompson, his luck was about to change. He continued down Leman Street and once again turned into Chamber Street. Only this time he wasn't the only one there. He could hear someone else walking along the dimly-lit street. Thompson strained his eyes, but couldn't see anyone. Whoever the person was, they had apparently already passed beyond the bend up ahead.

Few people were up and about at that hour in the mostly-commercial district. The streets had become noticeably quieter after midnight, and for the last hour or so they were practically deserted. Perhaps some loiterer had thought it better to move on rather than face questioning. Maybe someone had emerged from one of the passageways that ran through the viaduct.

Thompson checked the first one, then the second. A lone gas lamp illuminated the street in front of the last passageway, and while some of its light penetrated a short way inside the one hundred and twelve ft. long tunnel, it quickly gave way to deep shadows. Locals called the passageway Swallow Gardens, a corruption of *Swallow's Garden*, the name of the neighborhood that formerly occupied the site before it was demolished in the early 1840s when the railway came through.

The name sounds a bit cynical. It conjures up images of fresh air and sunshine; it calls to mind the scent of fragrant blossoms and the cheerful twitter of chirping birds. But there wasn't any fresh air, or sunshine, or anything of the sort in the inner reaches of Swallow Gardens—only a damp, musty smell and the ever-present darkness.

Thompson flashed his lantern into the passageway and saw someone lying on the ground, about forty feet in from the street. His first thought was that it was probably a drunk, and he started inside to investigate. It wasn't until he got close that he realized it was a woman lying on her back. Then he saw the blood, and the deep cut in her throat. It extended almost from one ear to the other. Blood was still

CARROTY NELL

Interior of a Railway Passage

There are no known photos depicting the interior of Swallow Gardens at the time of the murder. This picture of a nearby archway suggests how it would have looked.

Swallow Gardens

oozing from the wound. While he was looking at her, she opened and closed one of her eyes. He crouched down beside her, took hold of her wrist, and detected a slight pulse.

The young constable hesitated, unsure of what to do. Metropolitan Police procedures were quite clear—if there were signs of life, he was to remain with the victim, and yet the assailant had just left and might still be apprehended.

Thompson decided to stay with the victim, and blew his police whistle three times in rapid succession—the signal that an officer needed assistance. That decision would trouble him for the rest of his life. For had he pursued those fading footsteps Thompson, on his very first night on the beat, might have managed to achieve something that had eluded his fellow officers for two and a half years. He might have caught the infamous Jack the Ripper.

Chapter 2

A Gruesome Discovery in George Yard

Jack the Ripper! He was already well on his way to becoming something of a legend. Two and a half years had passed since he claimed his first victim, and the police still had no idea who he was, or even what he looked like.

During the late summer and fall of 1888 he held London in a vice-like grip of terror, killing five women in a two-month span. Then the bloodbath stopped. Six months, seven months, eight months went by. It seemed that he had vanished, or at least it did until a constable walking through a dark alley early one morning came upon a woman's body that bore many of the telltale signs of his previous victims. That was in July 1889. Since then there had been no indication that he was still in the area, or, for that matter, that he was still alive. And then Ernest Thompson walked into a deserted underpass at quarter past two in the morning and found a woman with her throat cut. Could the diabolical killer have resurfaced? Had he struck once more? Those questions reverberated through the world's newspapers, through the halls of government, and through the minds of local residents for weeks and weeks afterward. They are questions that some feel have yet to be answered.

A Gruesome Discovery in George Yard

To get a better understanding of the infamous killer, a person has to go back to the beginning—to a dingy tenement project in Whitechapel called the George Yard Buildings at quarter of five in the morning on Tuesday, August 7, 1888. That was when a twenty-three-year-old resident named John Reeves left his small room and began walking toward the stairs.

The building that Reeves called home, although still rather new, was already starting to show the first signs of neglect. At its dedication only thirteen years earlier it was hailed as a model dwelling, the first of what was hoped would eventually be several similar projects that would replace decaying, overcrowded slum structures with affordable, cooperative housing for the working class. On paper, the concept looked good; in the hardscrabble world of Whitechapel, it proved to be a complete failure.

The former residents who were displaced when their ancient, crumbling homes were torn down couldn't afford the higher rents in the new building. Neither could the thousands who routinely sought shelter in four-pence-a-night common lodging houses. The equivalent of today's flophouses, they rented beds by the night in overcrowded, foul-smelling, bug-ridden dormitory rooms. The beds were usually crammed together so close that it was difficult to squeeze between them. Sheets and pillowcases were changed only once a week, and it wasn't uncommon for several people to sleep on the same bedclothes. It goes without saying that the hundreds and hundreds who weren't able to come up with four pence, and had to sleep in stables, doorways, or on the sidewalk couldn't even consider the thought of living there. On the other hand, the skilled workmen who earned enough money that they could afford the George Yard rents usually had no desire to relocate their families into the heart of London's worst slum. No one could blame them.

Here's how Jacob Adler, the acclaimed Yiddish actor who lived in Whitechapel for a short time after he fled his

CARROTY NELL

native Russia, later described it:

> *"The further we penetrated into Whitechapel, the more our hearts sank. Never in Russia, never later in the worst slums of New York, were we to see such poverty."*

In 1889, researcher Charles Booth reported that thousands in Whitechapel belonged to:

> *"The lowest class, which consists of some occasional labourers, street sellers, loafers, criminals and semi-criminals. Their life is the life of savages, with vicissitudes of extreme hardship and their only luxury is drink."*

To attract tenants, the directors of George Yard eventually had to lower the rents to the point where even casual, or day laborers, could move in. "People of the poorest description," was how the *East London Observer* described the occupants in 1888. John Reeves was one of those "people of the poorest description".

His destination that morning was the nearby waterfront where, with a little luck, he might get a day's work on the docks. Experienced day laborers always arrived early to get a place in front, near the gate. Those in the rear stood little chance of being selected. Reeves knew his chance of success was still rather slim. On a good day, perhaps one man in four would be hired; on a slow day, the number could drop below one in ten. The lucky ones who were able to find work would receive relatively little for their toil. It was a matter of simple economics. The demand for unskilled help had been on a steady decline for several years throughout all of London's East End as mechanization continued to replace labor-intensive tasks. At the same time, the number of people who depended on that type of work continued to rise. Like Reeves, a large number of Whitechapel's eighty thousand residents were day laborers.

He reached the stairs and began to walk down—one

A Gruesome Discovery in George Yard

flight, a landing, and then another flight. As he started to descend once more, he glanced down toward the landing below. A body was sprawled across the cold stone floor—a woman's body—lying on her back, her fists clenched tight. Her dark green skirt and brown petticoat were raised well above her knees, as if she had been struggling with someone. From waist to shoulders, the body was punctured with stab wounds.

Reeves stood there stunned, not sure if he should shout for help or go outside and try to find a policeman. He decided on the latter, and he slowly approached the blood-soaked body, keeping as far away as possible. Once he had passed it, he raced down the rest of the stairs and into the street where he spotted Constable Thomas Barrett of the Metropolitan Police.

Barrett ran back to the building, took one look, then rushed outside and frantically blew his whistle for assistance. He told the first constable who responded to hurry to nearby Brick Lane and fetch Dr. Timothy Killeen.

Dr. Killeen counted thirty-nine stab wounds, almost all of them on the upper torso. One had shattered the chest bone, leaving him to believe the killer used two different weapons. While an ordinary knife could have inflicted most of the wounds, it would have taken a larger weapon, such as a dagger, to break through the chest bone. The stab wounds certainly weren't superficial. The left lung was punctured five times; the right lung twice. Killeen also found a wound to the heart, five to the liver, two to the spleen, and six to the stomach. He placed the time of death about three hours earlier.

Barrett told his superiors he noticed a soldier loitering in the neighborhood about two o'clock. The man told him he was waiting for a friend who had "gone away with a girl". Barrett was certain he could identify him. A detective arranged for Barrett to visit the Grenadier Guards barracks the next day and see every private and corporal who had been on leave the night of the murder. The men were lined up in formation as Barrett walked past. He pointed to one man, hesitated, and then selected another. Both men looked like the soldier he had seen in George Yard, he explained, but the first one had more medals on his uniform.

Detectives questioned both soldiers and quickly ruled out the first. The other, a private named John Leary, told them he and a fellow soldier had spent the night drinking in Brixton. The two had separated for a while but met again about four thirty and returned to their barracks an hour and a half later. Investigators questioned the second man who told essentially the same story as Leary. Neither man could furnish the name of any witness.

The possibility that a soldier might be involved led some to suggest that a bayonet may have been the larger of the two weapons Dr. Killeen thought were used. Even if it was a bayonet, however, it wouldn't necessarily implicate a soldier. Scrap metal dealers on Petticoat Lane sold used bayonets for as little as a penny apiece. Children often used them as playthings.

Investigators learned someone else had walked past the body. A cab driver spotted it when he returned home from work at three thirty that morning. The stairs were dark, and he assumed it was someone sleeping. He told the police it was a common occurrence. The stairwell lights were always extinguished at eleven o'clock to keep costs down, but the front doors had to be left unlocked all night because many tenants worked irregular hours.

From the start, investigators realized they were dealing with no ordinary murder. Fatal wounds or blows were almost always delivered in anger. In George Yard, however, the only sign that any type of struggle may have taken place was the victim's disarranged skirt and petticoat. There was no indication she had tried to fight off her assailant. Moreover, if she or her killer had even spoken to one another, they did so in a whisper as the body was found a mere twelve ft. from the superintendent's door. Neither he nor his wife

A Gruesome Discovery in George Yard

heard anything unusual during the night. Someone, however, had flown into such a blinding rage on the stairway that they plunged a knife into a defenseless woman time and time again—thirty-nine savage, deliberate thrusts—still flailing away long after their victim's last tenuous grip on life had slipped away.

George Collier, the Deputy Coroner for South Eastern Middlesex, conducted the coroner's inquest on the still-unidentified body. He described the murder as, "one of the most terrible cases that anyone can possibly imagine. The man must have been a perfect savage to have attacked the woman in that way."

The body remained in the Whitechapel mortuary for a week before the police made a positive identification. The victim was thirty-nine-year-old Martha Tabram, a suspected prostitute. She was five ft. three in. tall, somewhat overweight, and had dark brown hair. She also had a long history of alcohol abuse.

Martha was born on May 10, 1849 in Southwark, on the south side of the Thames. Her parents separated when she was sixteen and her father died a few months later. On Christmas Day 1869 she married Henry Tabram, a thirty-three-year-old widower with an eight-year-old son. Tabram worked as a foreman in a furniture warehouse. A year later they moved into a new home on Marshall Place in Southwark, close to Martha's girlhood home. Martha bore Henry two more sons before the couple separated in 1875. Henry just couldn't tolerate her heavy drinking.

For the next few years he sent her twelve shillings a week, but cut the payments back to two shillings, sixpence when she continued to badger him for more money. In retaliation, she had him arrested and jailed for nonsupport. Henry wasn't the only target of Martha's abuse—she also pestered his sister, Ann Norris. Mrs. Norris became so annoyed she finally went to the police. Martha was brought before a magistrate and sentenced to seven days in jail.

CARROTY NELL

Henry Tabram stopped sending money altogether when he learned Martha was living with another man—a carpenter named William Turner.

Martha and Turner lived together for nearly nine years in a stormy relationship that was sometimes strained almost to the breaking point by her heavy drinking. During that time she occasionally resorted to prostitution to supplement Turner's meager earnings.

Turner lost his job early in the year and by the end of June he and Martha had fallen six weeks behind in their rent. They skipped out without paying. Martha must have felt some twinge of conscience; she returned to the rooming house a few nights later and managed to leave the key without being seen by the landlady.

The couple separated soon afterward, and Martha took to selling cheap jewelry on the street. The last time Turner saw her was two days before her death when he gave her a little money to buy more trinkets to sell.

A few days after the murder a prostitute named Mary Ann Connolly told the police she and Martha (whom she knew as Emma Turner) had been drinking with two soldiers in Whitechapel on the night of the murder. They parted company shortly before midnight, each woman leaving with a different man. Connolly saw Martha and her companion head into George Yard, a narrow alley off Whitechapel High Street. The George Yard Buildings faced one side of that alley.

If Connolly's description of their uniform caps was correct, the soldiers belonged to the Coldstream Guards, not the Grenadier Guards whom Constable Barrett had seen. Investigators arranged for Connolly to view every soldier in the nearby Wellington Barracks who had been on leave the night of the murder. She picked out two men and said they were the ones she and Martha had met. Both men had airtight alibis. One had already returned to the barracks before the murder; the other had spent the night with his family.

A Gruesome Discovery in George Yard

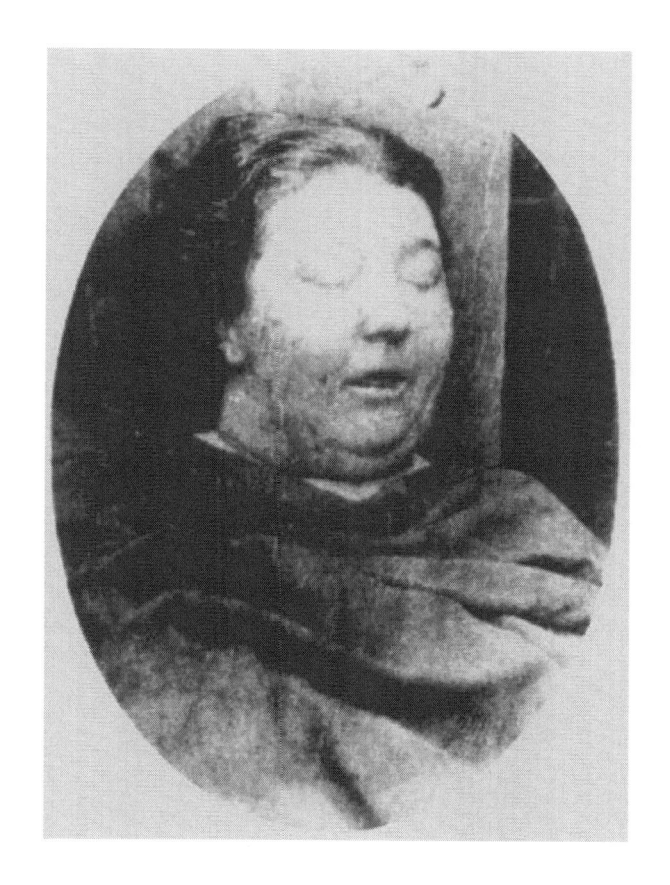

Martha Tabram

Mortuary photo

Courtesy of Stewart P. Evans

CARROTY NELL

The Metropolitan Police continued to press their investigation, but most detectives realized that, for all practical purposes, they had little hope of making an arrest. Victorian police had only the most fundamental investigative tools at their disposal, and they relied on informants, witnesses, and their probes into a victim's lifestyle and background. A killer who managed to escape detection for only a few days could begin to breath easy.

Although most newspapers eagerly printed every dramatic detail of Martha Tabram's murder, none of them bothered to make any mention of her funeral. Researchers have no idea where or when she was buried.

No one realized at the time that her death was but the first in a series of grisly slayings that came to be known as *the Whitechapel murders*.

Chapter 3

Buck's Row, Whitechapel

Charles Cross couldn't help but notice it—something out of place on the pavement up ahead. It looked like it might be a piece of heavy fabric—maybe a tarpaulin, or perhaps a torn canvas sail, but he couldn't be sure. The street was just too dark. The nearest gas lamp was back at the intersection of Brady Street, too far away to provide much light. Cross always felt a bit apprehensive when he walked along Buck's Row in the early morning hours. The gas lamps were few and far-between on the narrow, warehouse-district street, and there was always the chance that some unseen peril might be lurking in the deep shadows. But cutting through Buck's Row was the quickest way to get from his home in Mile End Old Town to Broad Street, where he worked as a wagon driver.

As he drew closer to the mysterious object that had caught his attention, he realized it wasn't a piece of canvas; it was a woman lying on her back just outside a heavy wooden gate. He could see that her skirt was raised above her knees, but the street was so dark he couldn't make out her facial features.

It was twenty minutes to four on Friday morning, August 31, 1888—three weeks and three days after the discovery of Martha Tabram's body only a half mile away.

CARROTY NELL

Cross was still trying to decide what he should do when he heard footsteps approaching. Someone else was turning into Buck's Row. He looked back toward the intersection of Brady Street and saw a man pass under the gaslight. The newcomer turned out to be another wagon driver named Robert Paul. Cross waited until he got closer, and then asked him to come over and take a look.

Paul put his hand on the woman's chest and thought he felt some movement. "I think she is still breathing," he said. Cross bent down and touched her hand. It was cold, and he told Paul he believed she was dead.

Both drivers were supposed to start work at four o'clock, and they decided to continue on their way and tell the first constable they saw. Before leaving, Paul tried to pull the woman's skirt down to her knees but it seemed to be stuck. A few minutes later they spotted Constable Jonas Mizen on Hanbury Street and told him of their discovery. Mizen hurried to Buck's Row only to find another policeman already there.

Metropolitan Police Constable John Neil had spotted the woman at three forty-five when he walked through Buck's Row on his regular beat. He missed bumping into the two wagon drivers by about two minutes. Neil had a lantern, and he could see that the woman's throat was cut, and her eyes were wide open. As he crouched over the body, he noticed another policeman pass by the end of the street, and he swung his lantern back and forth to attract his attention. Constable John Thain came running, and Neil told him to hurry and fetch Dr. Rees Llewellyn, a police physician who lived a few blocks away on Whitechapel Road. Thain returned with the doctor about ten minutes later.

Dr. Llewellyn made a superficial examination and determined that the woman had probably died about thirty minutes earlier. When he finished, he gave permission to move the body to the Whitechapel Mortuary where he planned to perform a postmortem examination later in the

Buck's Row, Whitechapel

day. At the time, the mortuary was nothing more than a wooden shed in the yard behind the Whitechapel Workhouse.

Llewellyn returned home and went back to bed. An hour later another constable was pounding on his door. He told the drowsy doctor that Inspector John Spratling wanted him to come to the mortuary right away. Spratling had gone there to make a more detailed examination of the body. The September 8 edition of the *Illustrated Police News* detailed the horrible sight that awaited him when he lifted the victim's skirt.

> *"In addition to the gash in her throat, which had nearly severed the head from the body, the lower part of the abdomen had been ripped up, and the bowels were protruding. The abdominal wall, the whole length of the body, had been cut open, and on either side were two incised wounds almost as severe as the central one. They reached from the lower part of the abdomen to the breast-bone. The instrument with which the wounds were inflicted must have been not only of the sharpness of a razor, but used with considerable ferocity."*

It was so dark at the scene of the murder that no one observed those injuries.

Spratling thought the victim was about forty-five years old. She was five ft. two in. tall, with brown eyes and dark brown hair streaked with gray. She had a laceration on her tongue and a bruise on her lower jaw. Three of her teeth were missing. A search of her pockets produced a comb, a handkerchief, and a broken piece of a mirror. Investigators soon learned she was a forty-three-year-old derelict named Mary Ann Nichols. Most of her friends called her Polly. Her background was surprisingly similar to Martha Tabram's.

Mary Ann was born in London on August 26, 1845, the

CARROTY NELL

daughter of Edward and Caroline Walker. Her father was a blacksmith. At eighteen, she married a printer named William Nichols and they moved in with her father. That arrangement lasted for nearly ten years.

She and Nichols had five children before their marriage faltered. In 1881, after several temporary separations, she walked out on her husband and children for good. Her youngest child was just a year old. William Nichols claimed his wife's heavy drinking was the cause of the rift. Her father had a different story. He said his daughter left Nichols when she discovered he was having an affair with the woman he hired to help with the housework after the last child was born. Nichols continued to send his wife a small weekly allowance, but he stopped making payments two years later when he found out she was living with another man, and supplementing his allowance from time to time through prostitution.

Mary Ann's new boyfriend was named Thomas Drew. Like her father, he too was a blacksmith. After living together for about four years, they separated in the summer of 1887. The breakup left Mary Ann with no income, and she began shuffling from one workhouse to another. She was at the Lambeth Workhouse for about a month, and left there on May 12, 1888 when the matron found her a job working as a servant in a private home in Wandsworth. It looked promising at first. Shortly after starting her new job she wrote to her father:

> *"I just right [sic] to say you will be glad to know that I am settled in my new place, and going all right up to now. My people went out yesterday and have not returned, so I am left in charge. It is a grand place inside, with trees and gardens back and front. All has been newly done up. They are teetotalers and religious so I ought to get on. They are very nice people, and I have not too much to do."*

Two months later she left without giving notice. Her

Buck's Row, Whitechapel

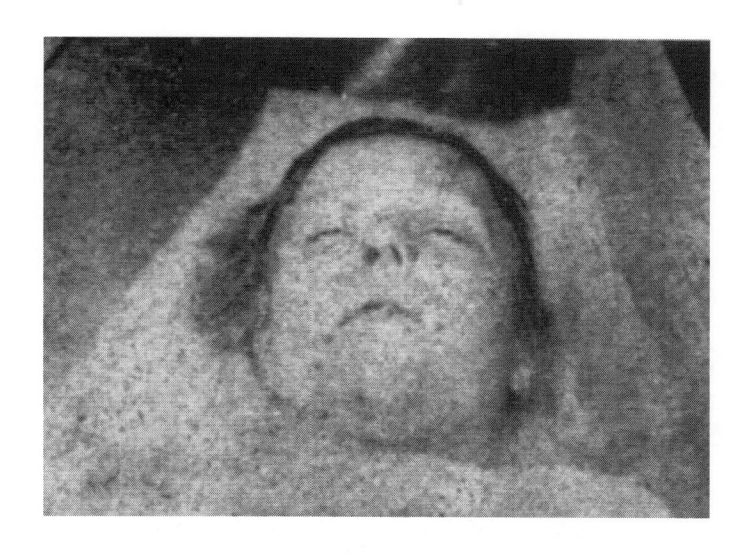

Mary Ann Nichols

Mortuary photo

Courtesy of Stewart P. Evans

CARROTY NELL

employers discovered soon afterward that several expensive items of women's clothing were missing. It wasn't long before she was back in Whitechapel and earning her bed and drink money from casual prostitution.

The police were now dealing with their second horrific murder in less than a month—two brutal, savage slayings within a half mile of each other. If Martha Tabram's murder had provided them with precious little to go on, the latest one gave them even less. Detectives were stymied.

Nichols was penniless when she left a common lodging house, or "doss house" as they were often called, about one forty in the morning to try and earn the four pence she needed for a bed. At two thirty that morning a woman named Ellen Holland was walking home after watching firefighters battle a spectacular fire on the nearby waterfront. She came upon Nichols on Whitechapel Road. The two were casual acquaintances, and she asked Nichols if she were going home. Nichols said she had already earned the money for a bed three times that day, but had spent it on gin each time. She was going to try to earn it one more time. Ellen Holland watched her friend stumble away, so drunk she was staggering against a wall. It was the last known sighting of Mary Ann Nichols.

Investigators had no idea how Nichols spent the last hour before her death. To compound matters, no one living on Buck's Row had heard any sound of a scuffle or any cry for help. Among those who were nearby were a widow and her three grown children, asleep in a small house less than twenty ft. from the spot where Nichols was killed, and a warehouse watchman and his wife who lived on the premises almost directly across the street.

On Saturday, September 1, Northeast Middlesex County Coroner Wynne Baxter opened his inquest into Mary Ann Nichols's death. Dr. Llewellyn was one of the many witnesses whom he called. Llewellyn testified that he found

Buck's Row, Whitechapel

two deep cuts on victim's throat that had reached the vertebrae. One was four inches long, the other eight. Both were made in a left-to-right direction by a knife "moderately sharp, and used with great violence." He also described the wound to the abdomen in detail, and told Baxter no internal organs were missing. Llewellyn said the man must have had "some rough anatomical knowledge" since he chose vital parts of the body to attack.

A few days later it appeared that there had finally been a break in the case. On September 5 the popular evening newspaper *The Star* told its readers a man known by the nickname "Leather Apron" had been extorting protection money from local prostitutes and assaulting those who refused to pay. The article claimed he was never seen without his trademark leather apron, and he always carried a razor-sharp knife.

The Star had made its debut only four months earlier and, in that short time, it had already become the largest selling evening newspaper in London. That was largely due to the sensational tone of its news coverage. The article on Leather Apron was true to form. It painted him as "a more ghoulish and devilish brute than can be found in all the pages of shocking history", and claimed he "kicked, bruised, and terrified" more than a hundred of the unfortunate women who plied their trade on the streets of Whitechapel. *The Star* went on to describe him, claiming the details were gathered from interviews with at least fifty Whitechapel prostitutes: "His name nobody knows, but all are united in the belief that he is a Jew or of Jewish parentage, his face being of a marked Hebrew type." The article ended with a question: why hadn't the police taken him into custody?

A follow-up article the next day was even more inflammatory. It described him as a "crazy Jew" and claimed he "would go to a public house and peep in through the window to see if a particular woman was there. He would then

CARROTY NELL

vanish, lying in wait for his victim at some convenient corner, hidden from view."

Detective Sergeant William Thick of the Whitechapel Division knew that Leather Apron was a thirty-eight-year-old boot maker named John Pizer. He couldn't locate him, however—Pizer had gone into hiding. When Thick finally tracked him down at his brother's house and brought him in for questioning, Pizer told Thick he had seen the piece in *The Star* and was afraid to venture outside. After convincing investigators he was nowhere near the scene when either of the murders was committed, Pizer was cleared of any involvement and released. He was never charged with any of the accusations brought by *The Star*.

The funeral service for Mary Ann Nichols was held on Thursday afternoon, September 6, at the City of London Cemetery at Manor Park. Nichols's father and two of her children accompanied the hearse to the cemetery where, according to newspapers accounts, a large number of spectators were already on hand. Her father, her estranged husband, and one of her sons shared the expense of the funeral.

Chapter 4

"I Won't Be Long"

Like many of its neighbors, the house at 29 Hanbury Street was built in the early eighteenth century as a combination home and workshop for Huguenot silk weavers—Protestants who had fled their native France after the punitive Edict of Fontainebleau took away their right to attend religious services. The weavers prospered for almost a hundred years until the Industrial Revolution, with its textile mills and machine looms, made hand weaving obsolete. By 1832 the weavers were long gone, and their homes and workshops had been converted into rooming houses for the poor. Here's how a report described the neighborhood that year:

> *"The low houses are all huddled together in close and dark lanes and alleys, presenting at first sight an appearance of non-habitation, so dilapidated are the doors and windows. In every room of the houses, whole families, parents, children and aged grandfathers swarm together."*

Fifty-six years later, in 1888, most of those houses remained in essentially the same condition.

John Davis was one of the hundreds of people who were

CARROTY NELL

drawn to Hanbury Street by its low rents. He and his family lived in a small front room on the top floor of number 29. For Davis, the location held an added attraction—it was close to the Spitalfields Market, an area of covered stalls where he worked as a porter.

Daylight was already streaming into his little room when Davis woke up shortly after five thirty on Saturday morning, September 8, two days after Mary Ann Nichols's funeral. He looked about and saw that his wife and three sons were still asleep. He got up, dressed quietly, then had a cup of tea before he gently closed the door behind him and started down the narrow, steep stairs. The only sound he heard was the creaking of the ancient stair treads. The other sixteen residents of the building were still asleep.

The stairs ended at a ground floor hallway that ran the length of the house. Davis noticed that the front door was wide open. It didn't surprise him—the door was often left open. He turned around, walked to the back door, unlatched it, and stood in the doorway for a few moments, gazing out into the small, dingy back yard. By chance he happened to glance down at the two stone steps below the door, and he instantly recoiled in horror. A woman's body, lying on her back with her dress pulled above her knees, was right below him, her lifeless eyes staring across the vacant yard. Her head was only a few inches from the bottom step. There was a deep cut in her throat and her abdomen was torn open. Some of her intestines were draped over her shoulder. Blood still trickled from the two wounds. Davis snapped to his senses, turned around, and raced out the front door seeking help.

Inspector Joseph Chandler was the first detective to respond, and he immediately sent a constable to fetch veteran police physician Dr. George Bagster Phillips from his nearby home in Spital Square. Phillips was fifty-five, and had been a police physician for twenty-two years. He had a reputation for being extremely competent, courteous, and

"I Won't Be Long"

polite. He also had one peculiarity—his choice of attire was decidedly out-of-date. Walter Dew, who was a constable in Whitechapel at the time, later remarked on Phillips's penchant for wearing old-fashioned clothing, "He used to look for all the world as though he had stepped out of a century-old painting." Dew added that he was "charming".

It was twenty minutes past six when Phillips arrived at Hanbury Street. He saw right away that the victim's face and tongue were swollen—indications that she had been suffocated. A deep jagged cut ran across the neck, and the abdomen was terribly mutilated. He didn't see any indication that a struggle has taken place.

At two o'clock that afternoon he went to the Whitechapel Mortuary to perform a postmortem examination. He had barely begun when he made a startling discovery—the killer had surgically removed the victim's uterus. Since it wasn't found at the murder scene, he must have taken it with him. Phillips was surprised to find the cut was skillfully made. Whoever removed the uterus had a good knowledge of anatomy.

Phillips also observed an abrasion on the victim's finger where a ring or rings had been pulled off by force. Detectives later learned she always wore two cheap brass rings—her wedding ring and a keeper—a wide band that kept the wedding ring from slipping off. Neither was found at the scene. Apparently the killer had taken the rings, along with her uterus, as gruesome souvenirs. The victim suffered from advanced tuberculosis along with a disease that affected the membranes of her brain. Phillips didn't identify it, but he was almost certainly referring to syphilis. Neither condition played a part in her death.

Investigators first thought that her name was Annie Sivvey, but soon learned that Sivvey was an alias taken from a former live-in boyfriend. Her real name was Annie Chapman. She was a forty-six-year-old widow, five ft. tall, heavyset, with dark brown curly hair. She was also known to be a casual prostitute. Born Annie Eliza Smith in September 1841, she was the oldest of five children. On May 1, 1869 she married a coachman named John Chapman in Westminster. They moved to Windsor several years later.

Annie and her husband both drank heavily, and they eventually separated, apparently by mutual consent. Their oldest daughter had died of meningitis at age twelve a few years before, and their only son was in a home for crippled children. John Chapman remained in Windsor, and sent Annie ten shillings every week, presumably unaware that she had taken up with another man and was living with him in a Spitalfields lodging house. That money, plus the small amount she made selling flowers, allowed Annie to get by. The weekly payments came to an abrupt end when Chapman died of cirrhosis on Christmas Day, 1886. He was forty-four years old. Soon afterward the man Annie was living with walked out, leaving her in decidedly desperate straits.

For a while she spent her weekends in another doss house with a man most people called "The Pensioner", believing him to be a retired military man. A guaranteed income like a monthly pension would have set him apart from many of his Whitechapel neighbors. Sadly, Edward Stanley's pension claims weren't true. Later, while testifying under oath at the coroner's inquest into Chapman's death, he had to admit that he had never served in the armed forces.

It was her lack of the four pence she needed for a bed that forced a desperate Annie Chapman onto the streets a few hours before her death. Investigators learned she had left a doss house on Dorset Street shortly before two that morning after telling the deputy she didn't have any money. "I won't be long," she told John Evans, the night watchman, as she was leaving. "See that Tim (Donovan, the lodging house deputy) keeps a bed for me." Evans later told investi-

"I Won't Be Long"

gators she was drunk.

The police had no idea where she went after she left the lodging house, or whom she may have encountered. The next reported sighting of her was some three and a half hours later at five thirty when a woman named Elizabeth Long, who was walking down Hanbury Street on her way to the Spitalfields Market, saw someone who looked like Chapman talking to a man in front of no. 29. The man had his back toward her and she couldn't see his face, but she said he looked like a foreigner and had a "shabby-genteel" appearance. As she passed by, she overheard the man ask, "Will you?", and the woman who looked like Chapman answer, "Yes." People in the East End often used the word "foreigner" when referring to someone who looked Jewish.

A man who lived next door happened to be in his back yard about the same time. Few houses in Whitechapel had indoor plumbing, and Albert Cadosch had stepped outside to use the outhouse. He overheard two people talking on the other side of the five-and-a-half ft. high wooden fence that separated the two back yards, but the only part he could remember was a woman saying "No." A few moments later he heard a thud as something fell against the fence. Cadosch went back inside without bothering to investigate what was going on next door.

While the police were combing the scene for clues, a man named John Richardson arrived at the house and demanded to be let in. Like Davis, Richardson was a porter at the Spitalfields Market. He told a constable the whole market area was abuzz with talk of a murder at 29 Hanbury Street, and he wanted to make sure that his mother, who lived there, was all right. He then casually mentioned that he had walked through the hallway earlier that morning, and had ventured out into the back yard as well.

Richardson's mother lived in a room by herself, and also rented space in the cellar where she ran a small business making packing cases. Someone had broken into her cellar workshop a few months earlier and stolen some tools. Since then Richardson had been in the habit of checking the premises every morning while on his way to work. More than once, he told the police, he had come upon strangers "acting immorally" in the hallway.

He stopped by at twenty minutes to five that morning. After making sure the cellar door was secure, he opened the back door and stepped down onto the stairs. One of his boots was rubbing against his foot, he said, so he took it off and cut away a small piece of leather. The place where he stood was only inches from where the body was found.

To say that detectives were completely frustrated would be an understatement. Once again, the killer had managed to strike and then make his escape without attracting anyone's attention. This time darkness wasn't a factor. The sun rose at five twenty-five that morning and the sky was already beginning to brighten by the time of the attack. The back steps at 29 Hanbury Street were visible from several neighboring buildings, and if anyone had chanced to look out their window at the time, the police would have finally had a witness.

What was particularly puzzling was the fact that some early risers were already up and about in the neighborhood—most of them on their way to the Spitalfields Market—and even though the killer must have had bloodstains on his hands and clothes, no one apparently took any particular notice of him as he slipped away.

Newspapers covered Chapman's murder with headlines like "Ghastly Murder in the East End". After several days went by without an arrest, some editors turned their attention to the horrific slum conditions of the East End and voiced their outrage at what they perceived to be inadequate police protection for the East End poor. A few newspapers like *The Star* began calling for the resignation of Sir Charles Warren, the head of the Metropolitan Police. Those demands intensified in the coming weeks.

"I Won't Be Long"

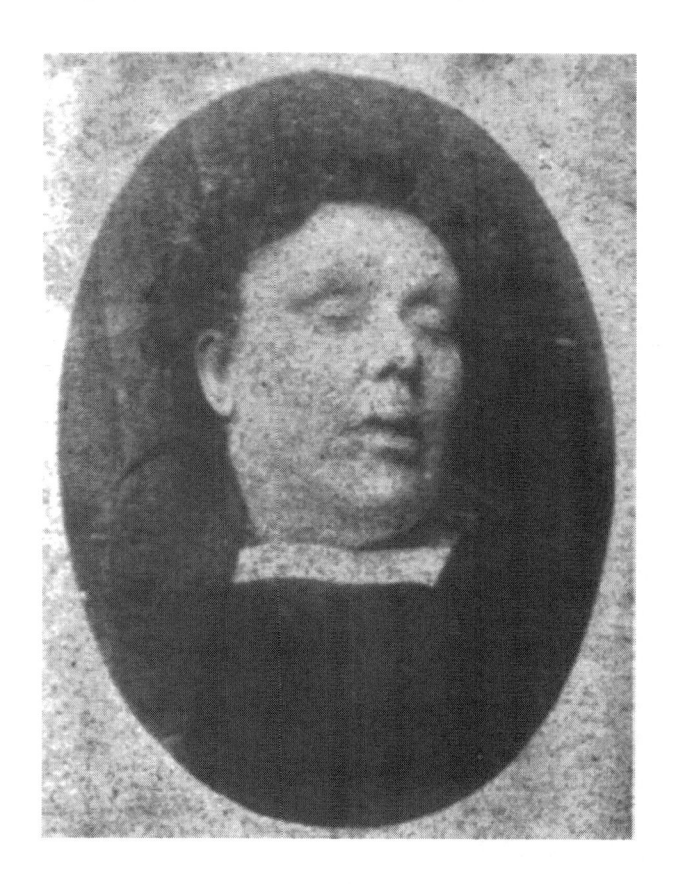

Annie Chapman

Mortuary photo

Courtesy of Stewart P. Evans

CARROTY NELL

Coroner Wynne Baxter, who had conducted the inquest on Mary Ann Nichols's death, convened an inquiry into Chapman's death on September 10. It would be adjourned and reconvened several times during the following two weeks. Dr. Phillips, the police surgeon, was the principal witness. He testified that there were two distinct, clean cuts on the victim's neck, a half-inch apart. Both were made from left-to-right. Death resulted from loss of blood. When asked to describe the mutilations on the victim's abdomen, Phillips stunned the coroner by refusing to answer. He told Baxter the injuries didn't cause the victim's death, and he didn't feel their details should be made public. Baxter was flabbergasted. Never during his entire career had he heard of evidence being kept from a coroner. The two finally reached a compromise. After the room was cleared of women and children, Phillips described the mutilations.

The abdomen had been ripped open and the uterus, the upper portion of the vagina, and two-thirds of the bladder were removed; no trace of them was found at the scene. The small intestines, while still attached, were pulled from the body and placed over the victim's right shoulder. Part of the wall of the abdomen was found on the other shoulder. The victim had been at least partially suffocated, but she was still alive when her throat was cut. Those cuts were very deep, and were made from left to right. The abdominal incisions were cleanly cut, avoiding the rectum and dividing the vagina low enough to avoid damage to the cervix uteri. The same knife inflicted the wounds on the throat and the abdomen. It was very sharp, with a thin narrow blade at least five inches long. Dr. Phillips said the mutilations "could only have been effected by a practiced hand". He was sure that it took the killer at least a quarter of an hour to remove the organs.

None of the newspaper reports mentioned the uterus by name. It was merely described as "the missing organ." One newspaper, for example, reported:

"I Won't Be Long"

"There were no meaningless cuts. The organ had been removed by someone who knew where to find it, and how to remove it without injury to it. No mere slaughterer of animals could have carried out these operations. It must have been someone accustomed to the postmortem room."

The coroner created something of a furor while he was delivering his summation to the jurors. He told them the curator of the pathological museum at one of London's most prestigious medical schools had contacted him shortly after reading that Chapman's killer had taken one of her organs. The man suspected the missing organ was a uterus, and he told Baxter a prominent American doctor had visited the museum a few months earlier and told the curator that he was interested in buying as many as he could, and offered to pay £20 apiece for them. He said he wanted to provide an actual specimen of a uterus with each copy of a medical book he was writing. The curator was dumbfounded, and told the doctor the museum couldn't possibly help him.

Baxter went on to suggest that perhaps some deranged individual who had a good knowledge of anatomy and had somehow learned of the potential market might have killed Chapman and removed her uterus for the £20. People in the medical profession were stunned by his comments. Even the respected medical journal *The Lancet* jumped into the fray, calling the coroner's theory highly improbable, and questioning why the curator hadn't contacted the police. The idea of someone providing a specimen with every copy of a book, they added, was "too grotesque and horrible to be entertained."

Annie Chapman was buried in Manor Park Cemetery in Forest Gate on Friday, September 14. The funeral plans were kept secret at her family's request, and only a few close relatives were in attendance.

The police continued to hunt for her killer, but their

efforts ultimately ended in failure. Annie Chapman's murder, like the two that preceded it, remains unsolved.

Chapter 5

The Double Event

On Saturday, September 29, 1888, a letter arrived at Metropolitan Police headquarters. It was from a reporter named Tom Bulling. Bulling was with the Central News Agency, a wire service similar to the Associated Press, and he said the news agency had received a strange letter in the mail a few days earlier. Several of his colleagues dismissed it as a practical joke, but he thought the police might want to see it. He enclosed an envelope addressed to Central News, with a letter inside. The letter read:

25 Sept: 1888

Dear Boss

I keep on hearing the police have caught me but they won't fix me just yet. I have laughed when they look so clever and talk about being on the right track. That joke about Leather Apron gave me real fits. I am down on whores and I shan't quit ripping them till I do get buckled. Grand work the last job was. I gave the lady no time to squeal. How can they catch me now. I love my work and want to start again. You will soon hear of me with my funny little games. I saved some of the proper red stuff in a ginger beer bottle over the last job to write with but it

CARROTY NELL

went thick like glue and I can't use it. Red ink is fit enough I hope ha ha. The next job I do I shall clip the lady's ears off and send to the police officers just for jolly wouldn't you. Keep this letter back until I do a bit more work then give it out straight. My knife's so nice and sharp I want to get to work right away if I get a chance. Good luck.

Yours truly
Jack the Ripper
Dont mind me giving the trade name

The police thought it was probably just a hoax. Most people would have sent the letter to their favorite newspaper, not to a wire service. The fact that Central News also stood to make some money by circulating it to their subscribers added to the suspicion. Hoax or not, the letter marked the first appearance of the name "Jack the Ripper". If it was a hoax, its timing was strangely coincidental for several hours after the Metropolitan Police received the letter, the dreaded killer struck twice.

*   *   *

The International Working Men's Educational Club was a socialist organization whose members were, for the most part, recent Jewish arrivals from Eastern Europe. Since 1885, the year it was founded, it had a clubhouse on Berner Street, and it was there that the club hosted a debate titled *Why Jews Should be Socialists* on Saturday evening, September 29. Approximately ninety people attended, and several of them decided to stay for the refreshments after the debate ended about eleven thirty.

Around one o'clock Louis Diemschutz, the club's twenty-six-year-old steward, was approaching the clubhouse in his little pony cart after having spent much of the day peddling cheap jewelry in South London. He and his wife

The Double Event

lived at the club—it was one of the perks that came with being the steward. It had rained earlier in the evening, but the skies cleared shortly after midnight and the temperature was beginning to drop. When he turned into Berner Street, Diemschutz noticed that the two six-foot-wide wooden gates that extended from the front of the club building to the one next door were open. He drove past them and started into the pitch-black passageway between the two buildings. Inside the clubhouse, someone was singing a plaintive Russian ballad. The pony pulled sharply to the left and wouldn't go near the right hand wall.

Diemschutz looked down and saw something on the ground, but he couldn't make out what it was. He prodded it with his whip, but it didn't move. Curiosity got the better of him, and he stepped down from the cart and struck a match. By the flickering light he saw what appeared to be a woman lying on her side.

He inched his way carefully through the darkness toward the side door of the clubhouse, and returned a few moments later with another member—and a candle. With the help of the stronger light they could see that it was a woman's body lying in a pool of blood. The two men ran out onto the street looking for a policeman.

About forty minutes later, as police officers and spectators swarmed about the club on Berner Street, Constable Edward Watkins of the London City Police began walking across silent and deserted Mitre Square. The secluded little quadrangle, only seventy feet across, was poorly lit and almost completely surrounded by tall, imposing warehouses. There were only three means of entry, and two of them were little more than alleyways. At one time it had been a bustling residential neighborhood, but most of the old houses were long gone, and the few that remained were, for the most past, dilapidated and vacant. The only people living in Mitre Square were a City policeman and his family, and a caretaker who lived above his employer's store with his invalid wife and her elderly nurse. While it was a beehive of activity during working hours, very few people had reason to venture through it after dark. Even though it was close to several busy streets, *The Daily News* thought it was "as dull and lonely a spot as can be found anywhere in London".

Watkins glanced about as he crossed the square, and he noticed something lying on the sidewalk in the far corner, deep in the shadows. When he got closer he saw it was a woman's body—a horribly mutilated body. The neck was nearly severed by a deep gash, and a jagged incision ran from the bottom of the abdomen up to the chest. Some of the intestines had been torn from the body and were draped over one of the shoulders. The face was slashed and disfigured, and covered with blood.

Watkins raced across the Square to the Kearley and Tonge Co. warehouse—the only one patrolled by a night watchman. The man was sweeping the stairs when he burst in.

"For God's sake, mate, come to my assistance," the constable shouted. "There's another woman cut to pieces."

The watchman happened to be a retired policeman. He ran outside, took one look at the body, then raced down Mitre Street, blowing his whistle and shouting for help.

* * *

Two constables rushed to Berner Street as soon as they heard of the murder. Henry Lamb, the first one on the scene, found some twenty to thirty people already gathered around the body. He ordered everyone to keep back, and sent the other constable to fetch Dr. Frederick Blackwell, who lived nearby. He also told one of the bystanders to hurry to the Leman Street Police Station and let them know what had happened.

It took Dr. Blackwell about ten minutes to get to Berner Street. The victim was lying on her left side with her left

The Double Event

arm extended. She was still gripping a package of breath lozenges in her left hand. Her right arm was resting on her stomach and her knees were drawn up. Her throat was cut open, almost from one ear to the other.

Blackwell placed the time of death about thirty minutes earlier. He thought the victim was about forty-two. She was five ft., two in. tall, with a pale complexion and had brown, curly hair. She was wearing an old black skirt, white stockings, an old, worn pair of boots, an old black jacket trimmed with fur, and a check silk scarf. Her clothing had not been disturbed.

Many investigators thought that Diemschutz interrupted the killer when he unexpectedly turned into the passageway. If that were the case, the man could have been standing in the darkness only a few feet away, perhaps still holding his knife, when the club steward stepped down from his cart to light the match.

The inquest into the death on Berner Street began on Monday, October 1, even though the body had yet to be identified. Once again, Coroner Wynne Baxter presided. After Louis Diemschutz and a few other members of the social club gave their testimony, a woman named Mary Malcolm told the coroner she had seen the body in the mortuary and she was sure it was her sister, Elizabeth Watts. She claimed Watts had visited her at work a few days before the murder, begging for some assistance. Malcolm went on to describe Watts as a drunk whose husband had left her after catching her with another man. She said her sister had a long history of arrests for public drunkenness and had once even abandoned a small child on her (Malcolm's) doorstep. The coroner then adjourned the inquest for a few days to await further developments. Reporters rushed to get Malcolm's revelation into print.

Elizabeth Watts wasn't the slightest bit amused when she read of her supposedly sordid life and sudden demise in the next day's newspapers. She and her sister hadn't seen each other in years, and she claimed Malcolm's story was nothing but a mean-spirited fabrication. Shortly afterward the police were able to establish the victim's true identity. She was a forty-four-year-old, part-time prostitute named Elizabeth Stride.

She was born Elisabeth Gustafsdotter in Torslanda, Sweden on November 27, 1843. When she was seventeen she began working as a servant in nearby Gothenburg. Four years later she became a prostitute and, to comply with Swedish law, she notified the Gothenburg police. She sought treatment for venereal disease twice that year.

In 1865 she moved to London and found work as a servant. Four years later she married a carpenter named John Stride. For the next few years she and her husband ran a small coffee shop in Poplar, then sold it in 1875. The couple separated soon afterward and by 1877 Elizabeth was living in a local workhouse.

Stride had a reputation for embellishing her stories, and it's often difficult to determine where the truth ends and imagination takes over. Her claim of having nine children is highly suspect; the story that her husband drowned when the steamship *Princess Alice* sank in the Thames on September 3, 1878 was a complete fabrication. John Stride died of heart failure in Bromley on October 24, 1884.

Stride claimed that she too was aboard the *Princess Alice* the night it sank with the loss of six hundred and seventy people, and said she was able to escape drowning by climbing up a rope. She used the incident to explain the five missing teeth in her lower left jaw. According to Stride, a man above her on the rope accidentally kicked her in the mouth, knocking out her teeth. The passenger list for the last, ill-fated voyage of the *Princess Alice* doesn't include anyone named Stride.

Dr. Blackwell took the stand when the inquest was reconvened a few days later. He told the jurors that, since the carotid artery wasn't completely severed, Stride had bled to

The Double Event

Elizabeth Stride

Mortuary photo

Courtesy of Stewart P. Evans

CARROTY NELL

death rather slowly. Her windpipe had been cut through, however, so even if she were still conscious, she couldn't have made any sound.

Curiosity seekers continued to visit the murder scene, and many onlookers taunted the police for failing to protect the residents. Officials knew they had to regain the public's confidence, and do so quickly. The last thing the police needed was to have *The Evening News*, a popular London newspaper, accuse them of bumbling incompetence.

The man responsible for the allegation was Matthew Packer. The fifty-eight-year-old Berner Street resident peddled fruit from the window of his ground floor room, only two doors from the social club. On Sunday morning, several hours after the murder, Sergeant Stephen White was questioning people who lived near the club, and he knocked on Packer's door. Packer told him he had closed at twelve thirty that morning because of the rain, and hadn't noticed anything out of the ordinary.

Two private detectives working for the Whitechapel Vigilance Committee visited Packer a few days later. During the course of the conversation they mentioned the £500 reward that the Committee was offering for information leading to the apprehension of the killer. Packer suddenly remembered something he had neglected to tell Sergeant White—he had not only seen a woman who resembled the victim that night, but had sold some grapes to the man who accompanied her. According to Packer, the couple stood opposite the club for the next thirty minutes while they ate the grapes and listened to the people inside singing. They were still standing there when he closed. The next day, when a reporter from *The Evening News* called upon him with some questions, Packer was able to recollect even more details about the woman's companion. They were almost identical to a description that appeared in many of that morning's newspapers of a suspicious looking man seen in the neighborhood shortly before the murder.

The Double Event

On October 4, *The Evening News* published a blistering attack on the Metropolitan Police for their alleged mishandling of the Berner Street investigation. The article painted the police as completely incompetent. Matthew Packer's statements played a pivotal role.

> *"Their (Mr. & Mrs. Packer's) unpretending premises are situated just two doors from the scene of the murder, and the presumption of any mind of ordinary intelligence would be that it was the very first place at which the detectives and the police would have made their inquiries. They did nothing of the sort, as the man's simple, straightforward narrative will show.*
>
> *"Well, Mr. Packer, I suppose the police came at once to ask you and your wife what you knew about the affair as soon as the body was discovered?" the reporter asked.*
>
> *"The police? No. They haven't asked me a word about it yet. A young man in plain-clothes came here on Monday and asked if he might look at the yard at the back of our house, so as to see if anybody had climbed over. My missus lent him some steps. But he didn't put any questions to us about the man and the woman."*

Metropolitan Police officials were livid when they read the article, and immediately launched an internal investigation. They wasted no time summoning Packer to police headquarters where he admitted he could have been mistaken about the time. It might have been as early as eleven o'clock when he sold the grapes. Packer's story soon began to unravel. Chief Inspector Swanson later described his information as "valueless." Packer's sudden recollection was apparently motivated solely by the hope of collecting some of the reward money.

Elizabeth Stride was buried in a pauper's grave at the East London Cemetery in Plaistow on Saturday, October 6. Surprisingly few people were in attendance. The cemetery was

CARROTY NELL

a four-mile walk from Whitechapel, and the weather forecasts in that morning's newspapers had called for a chance of rain developing during the afternoon. The thought of walking eight miles in the rain probably discouraged many of her friends from attending.

Later that night, an enterprising journalist caused quite a commotion when he was caught walking through a South London neighborhood while dressed in women's clothing. Supposedly, he was trying to get a first hand look at the plight of street women. He had managed to walk about undetected for some time before one woman became suspicious. She alerted some of her friends, and the reporter soon found himself surrounded. The crowd continued to grow until it reached the point where he had to seek refuge at the nearby Southwark Police Station.

* * *

The grisly discovery in Mitre Square brought a new police department into the search, for the killer had crossed an unmarked but very significant boundary on his fifteen-minute walk from Berner Street. He had passed the spot where an ancient, twenty-foot-high wall once stood. The Romans had built it toward the end of the second century to protect their little settlement from invasion by northern Scots. By the latter part of the nineteenth century only scattered traces of the old wall remained, and the former enclosed area was virtually indistinguishable from its nearby surroundings. It was still distinct in one respect—it retained a separate administrative government and police force. It was, and still is, known officially as the *City of London*. The area beyond the old walls was termed Metropolitan London, and patrolled by the Metropolitan Police—a separate police force. In 1888 many people thought the City Police were the more professional of the two.

Two police officers rushed to Mitre Square after hearing

The Double Event

the night watchman's frantic cries for help. They stood aghast as they looked down at the mutilated body of the small, frail, middle-aged woman lying on the pavement. Once again, the *Illustrated Police News* gives a description of the victim's injuries, this time from the October 5 edition:

> *"Her head was inclined to the left side, her left leg being extended, whilst the right was flex. Both arms were extended. The throat was cut half-way round, revealing a dreadful wound, from which blood had flowed in great quantity, staining the pavement for some distance round. Across the right cheek to the nose was another gash, and a part of the right ear had been cut off. Following the plan in the Whitechapel murders the miscreant was not content with merely killing his victim. The poor woman's clothes had been pulled up over her chest, the abdomen ripped completely open, and part of the intestines laid on her neck."*

The newspaper neglected to mention that the killer also slashed her eyelids, cheeks, and mouth, and that another two-foot-long piece of her intestines was lying on the ground alongside her body.

The victim was clad in an old, shabby black jacket trimmed with fur. Her black straw hat had fallen from the back of her head. She was wearing three skirts—a telltale sign she was a street person who carried or wore all of her possessions. She also had on a man's vest and a pair of men's boots, as well as a dirty white apron. Part of the apron had been torn off. Two pawnshop receipts were on the ground next to the body. One was for a pair of boots and the other was for a man's shirt. The names on the receipts were Emily Birell and Anne Kelly.

City Police detectives immediately contacted their counterparts at the Metropolitan Police and told them of the murder. About an hour later, a Metropolitan Police constable named Alfred Long was walking down Goulston

CARROTY NELL

Street in Whitechapel when he spotted a bloodstained piece of a white apron in a doorway. On the wall above it someone had written in white chalk:

The Juwes are the men that Will not be Blamed for Nothing.

Long took the piece of the apron to the Commercial Street Police Station. City Police detectives borrowed it and brought it to the mortuary where it proved to be the piece cut from the victim's apron. The killer had apparently used it to wipe the blood from his knife.

Goulston Street fell within the jurisdiction of the Metropolitan Police and the neighborhood had a sizable Jewish population. Superintendent Thomas Arnold of the Metropolitan Police was afraid a riot might break out if people passing by saw the message, and he wanted it wiped off. Detective Daniel Halse of the City Police wanted to have the message photographed before it was obliterated. A heated dispute broke out. Commissioner Charles Warren of the Metropolitan Police arrived while the two men were arguing. He took a look at the writing and concurred with his subordinate's decision. Halse pleaded for a little more time—the photographer was already on his way. Warren wouldn't agree. In desperation, Halse urged the men to wipe out only the words "The Juwes" and leave the rest of the message intact until it could be photographed. Warren again refused. The chalk message was completely obliterated before the City Police had a chance to photograph it. Many people regard that incident as the biggest blunder in the search for Jack the Ripper.

Dr. Frederick Gordon Brown, the City Police physician, examined the body at the scene, and then conducted a postmortem examination on Sunday afternoon. While recording the victim's injuries, he made a startling discovery. The killer had removed and taken away her uterus and her left kidney.

The Double Event

The Central News Agency received a card in the mail on October 1. The handwriting looked suspiciously similar to the handwriting of the person who crafted the Jack the Ripper letter. It read:

> *I was not codding dear old Boss when I gave you the tip, you'll hear about Saucy Jackys work tomorrow double event this time number one squealed a bit couldn't finish straight off. had not the time to get ears for police thanks for keeping last letter back till I got to work again.*
>
> *Jack the Ripper*

The card was postmarked *before* newspaper accounts of the two murders had hit the streets, but not before the first details were known at the Central News Agency. Many investigators were convinced that the postcard was also a hoax, sent by the same prankster.

At ten o'clock Tuesday night, almost three days after the murder, a forty-year-old day laborer named John Kelly walked into the Bishopsgate Street Police Station. Kelly's voice was probably trembling as he told the station sergeant "the missus" hadn't been home for three days, and he was beginning to worry she might be the Mitre Square victim. A police sergeant took him to the City Mortuary on Golden Lane. Kelly was nearly overcome with grief as he identified the victim as Catherine Conway. He explained that the two weren't actually married, but had lived together for the past seven years. It turned out later that the victim's name wasn't Conway, it was Eddowes. Conway was the name of her former common law husband.

Catherine Eddowes was born in Wolverhampton on April 14, 1842, one of eleven children of George and Catherine Eddowes. For a number of years she lived with an army pensioner named Thomas Conway. Although they had three children, the couple never married. Conway didn't drink, and he grew increasingly upset as Eddowes's drinking spiraled out of control. He also began to hear rumors she was working as a prostitute to earn money to support her drinking. The two finally separated, and a short time later she moved in with Kelly.

Eddowes and Kelly had spent most of September in Kent, working as itinerant hop pickers, and had returned to London only two days before Eddowes was killed. Whatever money their hop picking efforts may have earned had disappeared by the time of their return. The two were so desperate Kelly pawned his boots on Saturday morning so they could buy breakfast. A few hours later Eddowes decided to walk over to Bermondsey, on the other side of the Thames, and try to get some money from her married daughter. She told Kelly she would be back by late afternoon.

Eddowes had been estranged from her children for some time. All three had become fed up with her heavy drinking and frequent appeals for money. If she did go to Bermondsey that afternoon, she never got a chance to plead with her daughter. Annie Phillips had moved away two years earlier without leaving a forwarding address. She told the police she had done so to keep her mother from finding her. Eddowes's two sons had also taken similar precautions.

About nine o'clock that night Kelly met two women who told him they had seen a constable taking Eddowes into the Bishopsgate Street Police Station fifteen minutes earlier. She was drunk, they added. Kelly returned to the doss house at 55 Flower and Dean Street where he and Eddowes usually stayed. He told the deputy he only needed a single bed. There was no need to pay an extra four pence for a double bed if "Kate" was spending the night in jail.

Kelly heard about the murder the next day and, like many others in the East End, he went over to Mitre Square and saw the dried bloodstains that were still visible on the

The Double Event

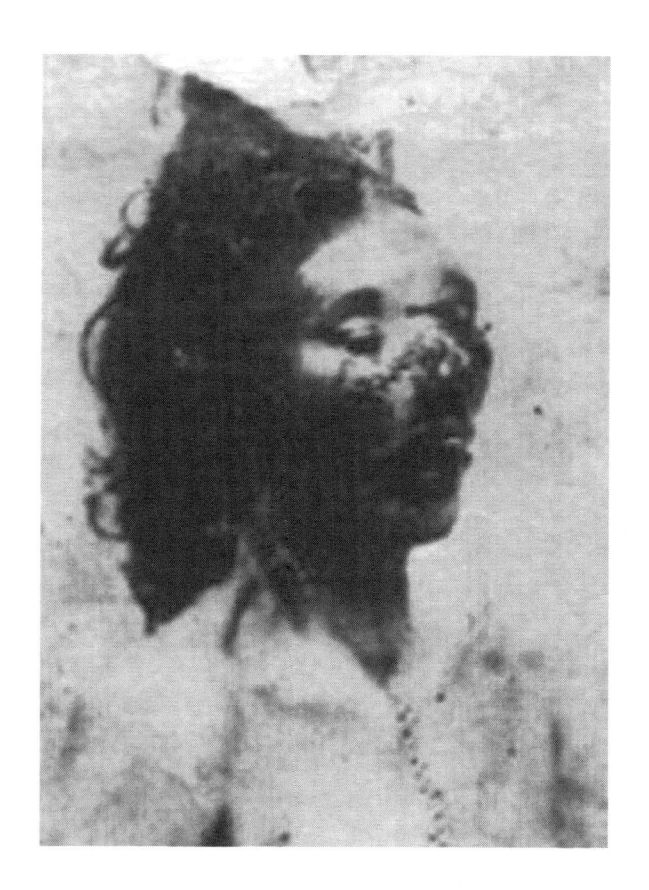

Catherine Eddowes

Mortuary photo

Courtesy of Stewart P. Evans

CARROTY NELL

sidewalk. The thought that his longtime companion might be the victim never occurred to him. As far as he knew, she had safely spent the night in police custody. It wasn't until he heard of the pawnshop receipts found next to the body that he began to worry.

The City Police had indeed held Catherine Eddowes in protective custody until less than an hour before her death. A constable patrolling Aldgate High Street had found a woman sound asleep on the sidewalk at about eight thirty Saturday evening. She was obviously drunk, and he brought her to the Bishopsgate Street Police Station. When the station sergeant asked for her name, she mumbled, "Nothing." The sergeant told a constable to place her in a cell. At one o'clock she was sober enough to be released. Since she hadn't identified herself when she was brought in, Constable George Hutt, the city jailer, again asked for her name. "Mary Anne Kelly," she answered. She also said she lived on Fashion Street in Spitalfields.

"I'll get a damned fine hiding when I get home," she told Hutt.

"Serves you right. You have no right to get drunk," he replied.

Hutt noticed that instead of walking towards Spitalfields when she left the police station, she headed in the opposite direction, towards Houndsditch and Mitre Square.

The inquest into Catherine Eddowes's death began on October 4, 1888 and ended a week later. Mr. S.F. Langham, the City Coroner, presided. Some twenty-two witnesses were called over the course of two sessions. Among them were Eliza Gold, the victim's sister, and Dr. Brown, the City Police Physician. Brown described the victim's wounds in detail and said Eddowes' throat was severed so quickly she couldn't have made any cry. He was certain it took the killer at least five minutes to perform the extensive mutilations.

The Double Event

Catherine Eddowes was buried on Monday afternoon, October 8, at the City of London Cemetery at Manor Park, the same cemetery where Ripper-victim Mary Ann Nichols had been laid to rest a month earlier. An unexpectedly large crowd of spectators—some estimates placed the number at more than a thousand—had gathered at the mortuary on Golden Lane to watch the procession leave, and many of them chose vantage points in the windows or on the roofs of adjoining buildings. According to *The East London Advertiser*, a large wagon filled with women followed the funeral procession to the cemetery. The majority of them, the newspaper added, were dressed in a style "not at all befitting the occasion." Several hundred mourners had already gathered around the grave when the procession reached its destination. The cemetery chaplain conducted the brief service without incident.

A week later, on October 15, a girl named Emily Marsh glanced up when she heard someone open the door of her father's leather goods shop on Mile End Road. A tall, thin man was walking toward her, his dark beard and moustache in sharp contrast with his ashen, almost-bloodless complexion. He was wearing a long black overcoat and a black felt hat pulled low over his forehead. It was his collar—a clergyman's Roman collar—that struck Miss Marsh as being wrong. He didn't look like a cleric. She was glad John Cormack, the shop assistant, was also in the store.

When the man spoke, she thought she could detect a trace of an Irish brogue. He asked if she knew where George Lusk, the chairman of the Whitechapel Vigilance Committee, lived. Marsh's shop, like most others in the neighborhood, had a Vigilance Committee poster in the window offering a reward for information about the recent murders. Miss Marsh was puzzled. The poster urged anyone with information to contact the Committee's treasurer, a man named Joseph Aarons, who owned a pub called The Crown. It was at the corner of Jubilee Street, less than a hundred ft. away. She told the stranger he should walk over and see Mr. Aarons.

"I'll speak to no one but Lusk," the man replied.

Emily Marsh could only tell him that Mr. Lusk lived on Alderney Road; she didn't know the number. When the man left the shop she stepped outside and watched him. He walked right past the treasurer's pub without stopping.

George Lusk received a strange package in the mail the next day. It was addressed to him on Alderney Road—there was no street number. When he opened it, he made a gruesome discovery. It contained half of a kidney along with a diabolical note:

From hell

Mr. Lusk
Sir
I send you half the Kidne I took from one woman prasarved it for you. tother piece I fried and ate it was very nise. I may send you the bloody knif that took it out if you only wate a while longer

Catch me when you can Mishter Lusk

Doctors who examined the kidney were certain it was human, but since Catherine Eddowes had been buried a week earlier, they couldn't compare it with her remaining kidney without exhuming the body. Lusk told investigators he didn't know anyone resembling the stranger who spoke to Emily Marsh, and no one matching the description ever contacted him to furnish information. Whether the kidney sent to Lusk was a macabre memento from Jack the Ripper or just a sick practical joke remains a mystery.

Chapter 6

"Don't Look in There"

The area that falls within the boundaries of the ancient City walls was, and still is, governed by the Lord Mayor of London. The one-year, elected position dates back to the year 1189. On Friday, November 9, 1888 the City was set to celebrate the inauguration of James Whitehead as its six hundred and thirty-fifth Lord Mayor, and the people who planned the event had done their best to ensure that it would be a memorable occasion. The daylong festivities featured a traditional parade, plus a special treat for the poorest residents of the East End. Three thousand of them enjoyed a complimentary meal that evening at a special banquet.

Thomas Bowyer probably would have been much happier if he were heading over to watch the Lord Mayor's parade that morning instead of hearing his employer, John McCarthy, tell him to go around to Mary Jane Kelly's room and collect the past due rent. McCarthy owned a chandler's shop, similar to today's convenience store, and he rented out a few sparsely-furnished rooms at the back of the building. They were called "McCarthy's Rents", and they opened onto Miller's Court, a small enclosure that could only be reached by passing through a three-foot-wide walk-

CARROTY NELL

way between numbers 26 and 27 Dorset Street. Like most of McCarthy's other tenants, Kelly was a prostitute. She hadn't paid her rent in almost six weeks.

When his knocks at Kelly's door went unanswered, Bowyer walked to the side of the building where he noticed that one of the two windows in her ground floor room was broken. He reached through the jagged hole and carefully pulled back a man's coat that served as a curtain. It took a few moments for his eyes to become acclimated to the darkness inside Kelly's room. Bowyer suddenly recoiled in horror. The naked body of Mary Jane Kelly was lying on top of a blood-soaked mattress, mutilated and butchered beyond recognition.

Bowyer raced back to his employer's store. "Governor, I knocked at the door but couldn't make anyone answer," he told McCarthy. "I looked through the window and saw a lot of blood."

McCarthy went to the back of the building with Bowyer to see for himself. He took one look, and then told Bowyer, "Don't say anything about this. Let's go and fetch the police." The two men hurried to the nearby Commercial Street Police Station.

Inspector Walter Beck summoned a few constables, and the men accompanied McCarthy and Bowyer to Miller's Court. They couldn't enter Kelly's room, however. Commissioner Charles Warren had issued strict orders prohibiting anyone from disturbing the next suspected Ripper murder site until the two bloodhounds his office had rented could be brought to the scene. Beck walked over to the broken window, peered inside, and immediately turned away. "For God's sake, don't look in there," he told the others.

The police milled about outside Kelly's room for two and a half hours, unaware that the bloodhounds they were awaiting had already been sent back to their owner. Finally, Superintendent Thomas Arnold told McCarthy to break down the door. The carnage that greeted their eyes stunned

"Don't Look in There"

even the most hardened homicide detectives.

Kelly's room was just under twelve ft. square. A small table stood to the right of the doorway, so close that the door banged into it when opened all the way. Beyond the table, a bed was pushed almost into the corner. There wasn't much else in the way of furnishings...a small cupboard that contained a basin, a few empty beer bottles, and a stale piece of bread...an old wooden chair...a cheap framed print entitled *The Fisherman's Widow* on the wall above the tiny fireplace. There were two windows, both on the left-hand wall. The one closest to the door had the broken pane.

Most of those details were only noticed afterward, for everyone's attention was riveted on the bloody, mutilated remains of twenty-five-year-old Mary Jane Kelly. Excerpts from Dr. Thomas Bond's report of his examination of the body show what the horrified detectives encountered:

> *"The body was lying naked in the middle of the bed...*
>
> *"The whole surface of the abdomen and thighs was removed...*
>
> *"The arms mutilated by several jagged wounds and the face hacked beyond recognition...*
>
> *"The tissues of the neck were severed all round down to the bone...*
>
> *"The uterus and kidneys [were found, along with] with one breast under the head, the other breast by the right foot, the liver between the feet, the intestines by the right side, and the spleen by the left side of the body...*
>
> *The flaps removed from the abdomen and thighs were on a table...*
>
> *"The face was gashed in all directions, the nose cheeks, eyebrows and ears being partly removed. The lips were blanched and cut...*
>
> *"The right thigh was denuded in front to the bone...*
>
> *"The left thigh was stripped of skin and muscles as far as the knee. The left calf showed a long gash...*

CARROTY NELL

"The lower part of the [right] lung was torn away... the heart [was] absent."

Dr. George Bagster Phillips, the veteran police physician, also examined the body. His report differs from Dr. Bond's in only one respect. Phillips said the body was clad in a chemise, or some other linen undergarment. Most of it, however, had been cut away. Phillips also noted that death was caused by the severance of the carotid artery when the victim's throat was slashed.

When the first investigators looked about Kelly's room, they noticed that a few embers were still glowing amid the ashes in the small fireplace. The heat from the fire had been intense; it melted the spout of a kettle hanging nearby. The killer apparently lit it for illumination, as the only other source of light in the room was a small candle on the mantel.

Much of what we know about Mary Jane Kelly comes from her live-in boyfriend, Joseph Barnett. He told the police that Kelly was born in Limerick, Ireland about 1863. Her family moved to Wales a few years later where her father found a job in an iron works. She married a man named Davies when she was sixteen, and she was widowed three years later when her husband died in a coalmine explosion. Soon afterward she came to London looking work. It didn't take her long to find something—in a brothel in Knightsbridge.

Kelly was a heavy drinker, and her fortunes soon began to falter. She and Barnett had lived together for the last eighteen months. They moved four times during that year and a half. Kelly was polite, quiet, and friendly when sober, but unusually loud and unruly when drunk. The Thames Magistrates' Court had fined her two shillings, sixpence for being drunk and disorderly two months before her death. A few weeks later she broke the window in her room while she was drunk.

"Don't Look in There"

13 Miller's Court (1888)

The door to Mary Jane Kelly's room is on the right. Thomas Bowyer discovered Kelly's body when he peered through the broken upper right pane of glass in the window closest to the downspout.

Courtesy of Stewart P. Evans

CARROTY NELL

Barnett moved out on October 30 after he and Kelly had a violent argument. He told the police he left because she let another prostitute share their small room. He continued to visit, however, and was in Kelly's room only a few hours before her death. Another woman was there at the time, but she wasn't the one he had objected to. Barnett only stayed for few minutes, then returned to his new lodging house where he played whist until twelve thirty.

A man named George Hutchinson, who counted Kelly among his casual acquaintances, met her while he was walking along Commercial Street about two o'clock in the morning on November 9. It had been raining for several hours and Hutchinson, who had just returned to the East End from nearby Romford to find the door to his lodging house locked, faced the prospect of spending the rest of the rainy night outdoors.

"Mr. Hutchinson, can you lend me sixpence?" she asked.

"I can't," he replied, "I spent all my money going down to Romford."

"I must go and find some money," Kelly said.

Hutchinson kept his eye on her as she left, and he was still watching when a man approached her. They chatted for a moment, then turned around and started walking back toward him. The man had his right arm around Kelly's shoulder and, as they drew near, he tilted his head so the brim of his hat partially blocked his face. He gave Hutchinson an angry glance as he passed. Hutchinson let them get a head start, then began to follow them.

For someone who supposedly caught only a brief glimpse of the stranger, George Hutchinson was able to provide the police with a surprisingly detailed description. He said the man had a dark complexion, a large dark moustache, dark eyes, and bushy eyebrows. Hutchinson thought he was Jewish. He wore a soft felt hat pulled down over his eyes, a long dark coat with a fur collar and fur-

"Don't Look in There"

trimmed cuffs, a white shirt with a black necktie and a horseshoe pin, and dark spats. He also had a gold chain with a large seal and a red stone across his vest. He held a pair of kid gloves in his right hand and a small parcel with a strap in his left. He was five ft., six in. tall and about thirty-five years old.

Hutchinson followed them as far as the entrance to Miller's Court where he heard Kelly say, "Come along, my dear. You will be comfortable." The stranger gave Kelly a kiss, and the two headed down the passageway toward her room. Hutchinson told the police he waited outside in the rain for about forty-five minutes before he finally walked away.

Elizabeth Prater, who lived directly above Kelly, had come home around one thirty that morning and gone straight to bed, only to awaken sometime later when her kitten crawled over her. She rolled over and was trying to drift back to sleep when someone nearby cried out, "Oh, murder". She thought it was about four o'clock. Prater wasn't the only one to hear it. Sarah Lewis and her husband had a fight earlier in the evening, and Lewis decided to spend the night with a friend in Miller's Court. She sat in a chair all night, occasionally dozing off. Sometime around four o'clock she too heard someone scream, "Murder". Neither woman was particularly concerned, they later told investigators, because such cries were commonplace in Miller's Court. Mary Ann Cox, a thirty-one-year-old prostitute who lived near Kelly in Miller's Court, told the police she heard someone leaving at quarter of six, but couldn't tell which room they came from. "I didn't hear any door being shut," she explained.

A hurried and controversial inquest into Mary Jane Kelly's death took place on Saturday, November 17. Even though Kelly had died in Whitechapel, which fell under the jurisdiction of Coroner Wynne Baxter, her inquest was assigned to Coroner Roderick MacDonald. The rationale behind this strange move was that Kelly's body had been taken to the Shoreditch mortuary, which fell under MacDonald's jurisdiction. In reality, it was almost certainly orchestrated to minimize any further erosion of the public's already shaky confidence in the police.

MacDonald's inquests were generally quick and to the point. He rarely strayed from a simple course of merely determining the cause of death. Most of them were completed in one sitting. Wynne Baxter, on the other hand, liked to delve deeply into any suspicious death. His inquests sometimes dragged on for weeks. Baxter was certainly within his rights in doing so. A coroner was responsible for investigating all aspects of sudden deaths from unknown causes that occurred within his jurisdiction. Baxter's inquests were also popular with reporters. Police officials were often quite selective with the information they chose to reveal to the press, while a coroner was under no such restriction. His inquest was open to everyone, and reporters could always count on getting more information about a suspicious death by attending Baxter's inquest than by pressing police officials for details.

As expected, Roderick MacDonald concluded his inquest in one day, and he didn't pursue any lines of inquiry that might prove embarrassing to the police. His jury returned a simple verdict, "Willful murder against some person or persons unknown".

Once again, a lack of witnesses hampered the police investigation. Only two people came forward and claimed to have seen a man who may have been the killer. One of them was almost certainly mistaken.

George Hutchinson's unusually detailed description of someone who supposedly passed him rather quickly on a rainy night, coupled with his claim that he waited in the rain outside Kelly's room for three quarters of an hour, obviously raised some eyebrows. Inspector Frederick Abberline interviewed him on November 12, and believed his story.

"Don't Look in There"

Hutchinson, who had known Kelly for three years, apparently was merely waiting for the stranger to leave with the hope of persuading Kelly to let him spend the rest of the night in her room.

One other witness reported seeing Mary Jane Kelly that morning. Caroline Maxwell, a casual acquaintance, claimed they met in Miller's Court at eight thirty.

"What brings you up so early?" Maxwell asked.

"Carrie, I feel so bad," Kelly replied. "I have the horrors of drink upon me."

"Why don't you go over to the Britannia and have half a pint? You'll feel better."

"I already have," Kelly answered. "I brought it up again." She pointed to some vomit on the pavement.

Maxwell walked to a nearby store where she bought some milk. She was on her way home when she spotted Kelly again, this time talking to a man outside the Britannia. He was about thirty years old, heavyset, and five ft., five in. tall. She described the maroon woolen shawl Kelly had on, and told investigators she hadn't seen her wearing it for a while.

The police were certain Maxwell was mistaken. Dr. Phillips had placed the time of Kelly's death at about four o'clock, approximately the same time Elizabeth Prater and Sarah Lewis heard someone cry out. Maxwell continued to insist she was correct, and not only stuck to her story, but repeated it at the coroner's inquest, even after being cautioned that she was under oath. On November 12, *The Times* reported that a clerk confirmed that Maxwell was in the store at the time she claimed. They also said the police found a woolen shawl in Kelly's room that closely matched the one Maxwell described.

Caroline Maxwell was the only person who claimed to have seen Kelly that morning, even though Kelly was well known in the neighborhood, and many people were on the streets. Maxwell's strange story added one more layer to the

CARROTY NELL

mystery surrounding Kelly's death.

Mary Jane Kelly was buried in St. Patrick's Roman Catholic Cemetery in Leydonstone on Monday, November 19. None of her family attended the services.

Chapter 7

Castle Alley

The police continued to put every man they could spare onto the streets of Whitechapel as investigators carried out their search for the killer of Mary Jane Kelly. One inspector, nine sergeants, and one hundred twenty-six constables were still on plainclothes duty a month later. Commissioner James Monro reminded his superiors that those men were working up to fifteen hours a day, and he suggested they should be given an extra allowance to compensate for the wear and tear on their clothing. The Home Office granted his request.

Monro began to cut back on the number of men working the special patrols after several weeks went by without incident. The cost had become significant, and a new problem was developing. The temporary transfer of men to Whitechapel had left many of the other divisions short-handed, and some of them were starting to see an increase in street crime. On March 15, 1889, a little over four months after Mary Jane Kelly's death, Monro told the Home Office the special patrols had come to an end. Four months later, many of the men who worked those patrols were back once again on the streets of Whitechapel.

At ten minutes to one on Wednesday morning, July 17,

CARROTY NELL

1889, Metropolitan Police Constable Walter Andrews was walking through Castle Alley, trying doors to make sure they were locked. A steady rain had been falling for about ten minutes, and the roadway was deserted. Castle Alley could best be described as an extension of Old Castle St., but the two didn't quite line up at the point where they converged. Because of the slight offset, a person looking into it from Whitechapel High Street might easily mistake it for a blind alley. *The Times* described it as "one of the lowest quarters in East London."

Calling it an alley was almost a misnomer since the greater part of it was over twenty ft. wide. Only at the Whitechapel High St. end did it narrow to three ft. Many local businesses left their carts and wagons parked in Castle Alley overnight—so many, in fact, that despite having five gas lamps for illumination, much of the alley remained in shadows.

As Andrews glanced about, he saw a woman lying on the pavement next to two wagons chained together under a gas lamp. Drunks and derelicts often slept in the wagons at night, and he assumed she had fallen asleep. He walked over to investigate.

The woman was on her right side, and the first thing Andrews noticed was the vacant stare in her lifeless eyes. Blood was seeping from a deep cut in her throat and gathering in a puddle under her head. Her skirt was raised above her waist, revealing a long cut in her abdomen. Andrews blew his whistle to summon help, and Sgt. Edward Badham responded a moment later. He told Andrews to stay with the body and make sure no one disturbed it, and rushed off to seek help.

Inspector Reid of the Whitechapel Division arrived at the scene fifteen minutes later. Blood was still seeping from the gash in the victim's throat. Dr. George Bagster Phillips, the Metropolitan Police surgeon, showed up a short time afterward. By then it was raining quite hard. After Dr. Phillips completed his initial examination, he gave permission

Castle Alley

to move the body to the mortuary. When constables lifted it onto a stretcher, they found the ground underneath was dry. That placed the time of death between twelve thirty, when Constable Andrews last walked through Castle Alley, and twelve forty, when it began to rain.

The victim was clad in a brown skirt and paisley shawl, old button boots, and mismatched stockings. She was about forty years old, five ft., five in. tall, and had dark brown hair and a freckled complexion. The tip of her right thumb was missing—apparently severed some years earlier by accident. Investigators soon learned that her name was Alice McKenzie. They were sure she was an occasional prostitute.

Virtually nothing is known about her early years. No one has been able to pinpoint where or when she was born, but her lodging house deputy thought she was thirty-nine. She apparently never married, and she sometimes told people her sons lived abroad. She had lived in the East End for at least fifteen years—for the past six or seven of them with a laborer named John McCormack. At the time of her death they lived in a lodging house on Gun Street in Spitalfields.

McCormack arrived home from work about four o'clock in the afternoon on July 16, after first stopping for what he called "a little drop of drink." He told investigators he and McKenzie "had a few words" when he got home. McCormack decided to lie down and take a nap but, before going to bed, he gave McKenzie one shilling, eight pence to pay the rent. He told her she could do what she liked with the rest. McCormack woke up around eleven o'clock, went downstairs, and asked Elizabeth Ryder, the lodging house deputy, if McKenzie had paid the rent. Mrs. Ryder said she hadn't. McCormack was upset, but he eventually went back to bed and stayed there until quarter of six the next morning.

Mrs. Ryder told the police Alice McKenzie had gone out at about eight thirty that night. She was sober at the time,

CARROTY NELL

Alice McKenzie

Mortuary photo

Courtesy of Stewart P. Evans

Castle Alley

although she had been drinking earlier, and was drunk when McCormack came home from work.

At eleven forty, about three hours after McKenzie left her lodging house, a woman named Margaret Franklin was talking with friends in front of a doss house at the intersection of Flower and Dean Street and Brick Lane. She saw McKenzie approaching, walking down the sidewalk rather quickly. The two had known each other for almost fifteen years, and Franklin asked her how she was.

"All right. I can't stop now," McKenzie replied, and hurried on her way.

Margaret Franklin was the last known person to see Alice McKenzie alive. A little over an hour later Constable Andrews came upon her body in Castle Alley, a quarter of a mile away.

Dr. Phillips conducted his postmortem examination on the afternoon of the murder. He noted that the victim's neck had been cut twice, and that each cut was about four inches long and made in a left-to-right direction. Phillips was certain the killer knew the position of the blood vessels, or at least where to cut to cause speedy death. There was no indication the victim had put up any struggle. Death had resulted from the severance of the left carotid artery. It was probably instantaneous.

The following day Dr. Thomas Bond, one of the men who examined the body of Mary Jane Kelly, also performed a postmortem examination. The two men came away with decidedly different opinions as to whether the murder had been committed by Jack the Ripper. Bond was sure it had. He told Commissioner Robert Anderson he saw "evidence of similar design" to the other Whitechapel murders, and he believed "the same hand" performed it. Dr. Phillips disagreed. He couldn't satisfy himself "on purely anatomical and professional grounds," but he did note, however, that the circumstances and other evidence argued strongly in favor of the one-man theory. There was one point on

CARROTY NELL

which both doctors agreed—the wound to the abdomen wasn't nearly as invasive as those inflicted on the other victims. The killer had made no attempt to remove any internal organs. He hadn't even opened the abdominal cavity.

Metropolitan Police Commissioner James Monro had no doubt as to whom the killer was. In his July 17 report to the Under Secretary of State, Monro wrote:

> *"I need not say that every effort will be made by the Police to discover the murderer, who, I am inclined to believe is identical with the notorious 'Jack the Ripper' of last year. It will be seen that in spite of ample Police precautions and vigilance, the assassin has again succeeded in committing a murder and getting off without leaving the slightest clue to his identity."*

Most newspapers agreed with Monro. The *East London Advertiser's* headline for July 20, 1889 was typical:

ANOTHER WHITECHAPEL MURDER.
"JACK THE RIPPER" AGAIN.

Alice McKenzie was buried at the East London cemetery in Plaistow on Monday afternoon, July 22. Two local businessmen shared the cost—her landlord, and the owner of her favorite pub.

* * *

The fear that gripped the East End following the murder in Castle Alley once again began to ease when several weeks passed without incident. The weeks turned into months, and the dreaded killer still made no reappearance. He seemed to have simply vanished. Slowly but surely, life in Whitechapel returned to normal. By early 1891, a year and a half after Alice McKenzie's death, the streets were once again crowded at night, pubs and music halls did a brisk

Castle Alley

business, and women walked about unafraid. Jack the Ripper was probably the furthest thing from Ernest Thompson's mind when the young constable paused at the entrance to Chamber Street, puzzled by the mysterious footsteps that echoed through the darkness.

CARROTY NELL

Part Two

The Final Victim

CARROTY NELL

Chapter 8

"She's Known As Carroty Nell"

Constable Thompson's thoughts raced back to the instructions he heard time and time again during the course of his training—look around carefully and make a mental note of every detail of a crime scene. Thompson followed those instructions to the letter while he waited for help to arrive. Here's how he later described the passageway while testifying at the coroner's inquest: "The entrance to the arch is opposite the Catholic school. At that time I did not know the place was known by the name of Swallow Gardens, but I have heard so since. The roadway under the arch is partially taken away and boarded up from the crown of the arch to the ground. What remains is a roadway, enabling one cart to pass at a time. I should say the length of the arch is something over forty yards."

His estimate was surprisingly accurate. It was just over thirty-seven yards long. *The Times* and *The Eastern Post & City Chronicle* got it wrong when they told their readers the next day that it was fifty yards long.

When the massive viaduct was constructed in the early 1840s, its arch-shaped passageways for pedestrian and wagon traffic gave it a classic Roman look. Some time afterward the railway decided to reclaim some of the interior space of many of those archways, including Swallow Gar-

CARROTY NELL

dens, and use it for storage. They typically erected a wooden partition that ran from the ceiling of the arch down to the pavement along the entire length of the passageway, and then fenced off both ends. The only way to access the blocked off portion was through a doorway at either end. The side left open to the public was so narrow that a wagon could barely squeeze by. Some of those blocked-off sections were later leased to private businesses. At the time of the murder, a firm called Reuben Cull & Son used the secured part of Swallow Gardens to store building supplies.

There were no lamps inside any of the archways. Even before the alterations, their interiors were dim on all but the sunniest days. Blocking off half of the opening at each end drastically reduced the amount of light that filtered inside. The change was most apparent at night when the only light came from dim, gas-lit streets outside. Reporters used phrases like "totally dark" and "in deep shade" when describing Swallow Gardens. A letter to the editor of *The Times* claimed that at night the interior was "opaquely dark". *The Daily News*, however, told their readers the interior wasn't as dark as had been previously reported, but then, a few paragraphs later, described the middle of the passageway as having practically no light.

* * *

Constable Frederick Hyde was the first policeman to respond to Thompson's whistle, although it took him a minute or two to get there. Hyde walked a beat quite similar to Thompson's, but on the opposite side of the viaduct. That beat took him past the other entrance to Swallow Gardens while he walked along Royal Mint Street. Unlike Thompson, he wasn't required to go inside and check the interior. Hyde was on Royal Mint Street, about eight hundred feet away, when he heard Thompson's whistle. He wasn't sure at first where it had come from, but he started to run in the direction of the whistle, which he was able to trace to Swal-

"She's Known As Carroty Nell"

Swallow Gardens, viewed from Royal Mint Street

The board fence that ran from the dome of the arch to the pavement is clearly visible.

Courtesy Stewart P. Evans

CARROTY NELL

low Gardens. Hyde took one look at the gash in the victim's throat, and told Thompson to stay at the scene while he ran to fetch Dr. Frederick Oxley from his home on nearby Dock Street.

Constable George Elliott arrived a minute or two later. Like Hyde, he came into Swallow Gardens from the Royal Mint Street end but, unlike Hyde, he wasn't in uniform. Elliott was working a special plainclothes detail that night in front of a refinery further down Royal Mint Street. He too had heard Thompson's whistle and came running. Elliott took one look at the victim, then ran to the Leman Street Police Station to report the attack.

Inspector James Flanagan was on duty at the Leman Street Station that night. After sending word to Superintendent Thomas Arnold and Police Surgeon Dr. George Bagster Phillips, he hurried over to Swallow Gardens. By the time he got there, the victim had succumbed. Dr. Oxley was crouched over the body, making his examination.

The victim was five ft. tall, with brown hair, brown eyes, and a pale complexion. Flanagan thought she was about twenty-five years old. Her body was lying on its back in the middle of the roadway, her head about forty-two feet from the Chamber Street entrance, her feet pointing toward Royal Mint Street. It was at a slight angle, not quite parallel with the side of the archway. One arm rested by her side, the other lay across her chest. Her feet were crossed at the ankles. There was a large cut in her throat that extended from just below the left ear to the right side of the neck. At one point it was almost three inches deep. Her head was slightly tilted the left, and resting in a pool of blood.

A quick glance at her clothing showed that she was clearly someone who was down on her luck. She was dressed in a black diagonal jacket, a long black dress with a satin bodice, and buttoned boots. She was also wearing one black earring, and she had a black velvet ribbon around her neck. The jacket was old and shabby; the heels of her boots

"She's Known As Carroty Nell"

were almost completely worn away. A brand-new black crepe bonnet—a small hat secured by a ribbon tied under the chin and very much in style at the time—was on the ground alongside her. The police spotted another bonnet, one that had plainly seen better days, pinned to her skirt. A search of her pockets turned up three pieces of black crepe, an old striped stocking, a comb, and one earring. They were her only possessions aside from the clothes she was wearing. She had no money on her person whatsoever.

Inspector Flanagan saw some scar tissue where part of the lobe of her left ear had been torn away, apparently some time before. It looked like someone had pulled off an earring. The victim's father later told the police the injury had occurred about four years earlier.

Dr. Phillips arrived a few minutes later. After examining the body, he made the necessary pronouncement that "life was extinct" and gave permission to move it. For some reason, perhaps at Phillips's request, the police brought it to the Whitechapel Mortuary even though Swallow Gardens fell within the jurisdictional boundaries of the civil parish of St. George-in-the-East. Their mortuary was on Cable Street.

The constables who carried the body away in a hand drawn ambulance made a stop at the Leman Street Police Station where several men recognized the victim as someone they had often seen loitering in the vicinity of Tower Hill. They were sure she was a prostitute, but none of them knew her real name. People in the neighborhood usually called her "Carroty Nell".

After the police had removed the body, Inspector Flanagan searched the passageway from one end to the other and discovered two shillings hidden behind a drainpipe about fifty-five ft. from where the body was found. They were wrapped in a scrap of newspaper that detectives later determined was torn from *The Daily News*. The discovery of the coins led to speculation that the victim had collected her money in advance and hidden it, intending to return to the desolate passageway later and retrieve it. Such

CARROTY NELL

Swallow Gardens, from
Chamber St. (2008)

The elevated structure that was built two years after the murder drastically altered the exterior appearance, but the outline of the original arched shape is still visible. At the time the photo was taken a local business was using the old passageway for storage.

Photo by the author

"She's Known As Carroty Nell"

Interior of Swallow Gardens, looking toward Chamber St. (October, 2009)

Frances Coles's body was found close to the wall on the left side, just beyond the edge of the picture.

Photo courtesy of Philip Hutchinson

CARROTY NELL

a precaution wouldn't be unusual for a street person to take when they were dealing with a stranger. More than one prostitute found herself in the unhappy position of having kept her part of the bargain only to find that her client refused to pay. A woman in that situation had very few options; going to the police certainly wasn't one of them. Although investigators never found out who stashed the two coins, the location—over fifty ft. from the body but only seventeen ft. in from Royal Mint Street—argues against it being the victim.

At three o'clock the police at Leman Street sent a telegram to every other police station in London. The message was brief: "Another murder in Whitechapel". Five minutes later a second message was transmitted: "Woman found in Swallow Gardens, Whitechapel, with her throat cut." If a story in *Lloyd's Weekly* is correct, it also included the warning: "The supposed work of Jack the Ripper." A third telegram a half-hour later provided more details: "Found dead with her throat cut, a woman, aged twenty-five; height about five feet; hair and eyes brown; left ear torn with earring; enlargement of third knuckle of right hand; black jet earring, black clothes, and crepe hat; light button boots, striped stockings." At six thirty they sent a final telegram that included a comprehensive description of the victim: "A woman aged about twenty-five; length five ft.; hair and eyes, brown; complexion, pale; dressed in black skirt and satin bodice, brown petticoat, grey stays, black diagonal jacket trimmed with braid, white chemise and drawers, striped stockings, buttoned boots. She wore a black ribbon round her neck. In her right ear was a black vulcanite earring, the fellow to which was in her pocket. She wore a black crepe hat and carried another similar hat in the folds of her dress. In the pocket of her dress were found three pieces of black crepe, and old striped stocking, and a comb. The lobe of the left ear has been torn as if by an earring, but not recently. All the clothing is old and dirty."

"She's Known As Carroty Nell"

Crowds flocked to Swallow Gardens as news of the murder spread throughout the city. Several local youngsters "did a roaring trade" on the day of the murder, according to one newspaper, "taking advantage of the intricate and labyrinthine character of the neighborhood" to guide strangers, for a small fee, to "the very spot". The competition among them was "quite severe", the paper added.

Later that night, hours after the last of the curiosity seekers had left, several groups of young people made their way to the desolate archway. *The Daily News* described their behavior in the next day's edition:

> *"Groups of people, young lads and girls especially, were lounging or coarsely sporting about the spot all night. Many a box of matches was spent by half-brutalized larrikins in examining the police mark—a cross ..... The match burners and the creatures round about them laughed, joked, and swore as they searched for traces of the deed. Thrice in less than ten minutes some roughs in the gang amused themselves by seizing hold of their female companions and showing them how 'Jack' must have 'done it'. A loud piano organ struck up a tune, and the roughs and the girls danced, the former bawling improvised choruses about 'Jack'."*

People continued to gather at Swallow Gardens all weekend. On Sunday it was still crowded with spectators, some of whom had come a considerable distance.

* * *

On Saturday a laborer named James Murray left his rundown lodging house on Old Nichol Street in Bethnal Green and, like countless other Londoners, bought a newspaper and began to read of the murder. It was front-page news, the "Shocking Murder in Whitechapel". He only got as far as the words *Carroty Nell* when he froze. The article said the

CARROTY NELL

Swallow Gardens, viewed from Chamber Street

Crowds thronged to the scene when news of the murder reached the streets.

Penny Illustrated Paper
Courtesy Stewart P. Evans

"She's Known As Carroty Nell"

police were still trying to learn her real name. Murray knew what her name was—and he knew what she did for a living. He had been one of her clients a few years back, a rather steady one, in fact.

Murray was in something of a quandary, torn between doing the right thing by going to the police and keeping quiet, thereby protecting his reputation. What if it got in the papers? What if people found out he had paid to have sex? Maybe he should just wait; someone else might come forward and identify her. He must have wrestled with his conscience for some time, for the sun had already set by the time he went to the police and told them he had known a girl named Carroty Nell, and that she was a prostitute.

They had met some time ago—it might have been eight years as far as he could remember—and he had been "intimate" with her several times. He said their relationship lasted for about four years. Since then, he had seen her from time to time walking the streets around Tower Hill. The police asked if he knew her name. It was Frances Coleman, he said, at least that's what she had told him. She lived at Wilmott's Lodging House at 18 Thrawl Street back then, but he couldn't say if she still lived there. When asked if she had any relatives, Murray remembered that her father was in the workhouse over in Bermondsey. "She used to go over there and visit him every week," he added. The police asked him if he would walk over to the mortuary and see if he recognized the body. One glance was all it took for him to confirm what he already feared—it was the same girl, Frances Coleman.

After Murray left the police station, Sergeants Record and Kuhrd set out for Bermondsey. It was Saturday night, and traffic on the crowded streets was heavy and slow moving. They finally reached the workhouse on Tanner Street and spoke to the official on duty. He told them they had no inmates named Coleman at the time, but the description of the victim sounded a lot like the daughter of James Coles, an elderly inmate. She came to visit him al-

CARROTY NELL

most every Friday, and she oftentimes came on Sunday mornings to sit with him at church services. Even though it was getting late, the two policemen decided to speak to Coles. When he told them his daughter hadn't come to visit the day before as she had promised, they asked the frail old man if he would mind taking a ride with them over to the Whitechapel Mortuary. By the time they got there it was after ten o'clock. When he saw the body, Coles struggled to fight back his tears as he told the two policemen it was his youngest daughter Frances. To the best of his recollection, she was twenty-six, he said.

James Coles was mistaken. His daughter was thirty-one. His incorrect guess, coupled with Superintendent Thomas Arnold's estimate that she was about twenty-five, helped perpetuate one of the many inaccuracies about Frances Coles that still linger more than one hundred and twenty years after her death.

"She's Known As Carroty Nell"

Frances Coles

Mortuary photo

Courtesy of Stewart P. Evans

Chapter 9

Rumors, Hearsay, and Misinformation

It wasn't done with any sense of malice, but many nineteenth-century police departments engaged in a practice that newspaper reporters found particularly frustrating—they were selective with the information they chose to share. They could be quite talkative when it might prove beneficial, like helping them apprehend a suspect. Otherwise they could be decidedly closemouthed, leaving a reporter who had been rebuffed when trying to get information about any new developments on a particular case with no alternative but to seek out someone else who might be able to shed some light on the crime, or the victim. All too often the information gained in that manner turned out to be incomplete, exaggerated, or just plain wrong. Some of the mistakes were honest errors made by well-intentioned people who simply repeated something they had heard. Others originated with people who couldn't resist the temptation to enhance their story in order to feel a little more important. Editors could have avoided publishing many of those mistakes by insisting that reporters verify information before writing their copy. Sadly, few of them did so. The sheer number of errors reported by the press in the days following the Frances Coles murder suggests that

Rumors, Hearsay, and Misinformation

late-Victorian newspapers were somewhat less concerned about "getting it right" than their modern day counterparts.

When the first news of the murder in Swallow Gardens broke, no one knew the victim's name, and initial reports described her as "a woman unknown". Soon afterward, as additional details began to filter in, news reports identified her not only as "Carroty Nell", but also *Carroty Annie*, and even *Carroty Hannah*. William Fryday, a railway employee who went to the police with information soon after the murder, was "William Girdley" in some newspapers. The *Liverpool Mercury* called Metropolitan Police Sergeant Wesley Edwards "Constable Westley". James Sadler, a man who would play a major role in the murder investigation, was John Sadler in many newspapers. In *The New York Times* he was simply "a saddler".

An enterprising reporter with *Lloyd's Weekly* stopped by the Midland Railway Storage Depot on Royal Mint Street several hours after the murder with the hope of gleaning some information from the people who worked there. He had no sooner begun his questions when one of the men made a startling revelation. The murder victim wasn't Carroty Annie, as people were saying; it was a woman named Hawkins. She was married, lived on Cadiz Street in the East End, and had recently fallen on hard times. The man told the reporter she was well known in the Tower Hill neighborhood. *Lloyd's Weekly* ran the story in the next edition under the headline THE VICTIM'S IDENTITY without bothering to determine whether or not any of it was true. It wasn't. But that short, one-paragraph account went on to spawn two major myths that have become ingrained in the lore of Frances Coles: that she sometimes used the name *Hawkins*, and that she was married, or had been married at one time.

The *Western Mail* told their readers there were two cuts on the victim's throat—a slight wound, "not even dangerous", and a "wonderfully clean cut, made by a firm hand wielding the strongest and firmest of knives". The two doctors who examined the victim's body completely contradicted those statements when they later testified at the coroner's inquest.

One news agency claimed the victim was drinking with another woman in a pub near Swallow Gardens a short time before the murder. Someone supposedly overheard her telling her companion, "Make haste, because I have to meet someone at the arch at the half-hour."

"What arch?" her friend asked.

"Why the shedway arch, at the school end," she replied.

The incident never happened. The news account was pure fiction.

Almost every newspaper reported that Constable Thompson saw the victim open and close one of her eyes. Some of them, however, enhanced their account by claiming that he also saw her move her lips in a vain attempt to speak. Another error had the police taking her body to the Leman Street Police station "where it awaits an inquest". Bodies were held in a mortuary, not a police station.

A twenty-two-year-old wagon driver for the Great Eastern Railway was one of several people who went to the mortuary after the murder to view the body. William "Jumbo" Fryday (*) thought he had seen the victim on Royal Mint Street a short time before the murder, and he reported the incident to the police. They asked him to take a look at the body and verify that it was the same woman he saw. He told a reporter from *Lloyd's Weekly*:

> *"I was then taken to the mortuary and shown the body. It was a sight, and I don't want to see it any more; the great big gash in her throat makes you feel awful. Well, I never ate any dinner or tea. Yes, it was the same woman I saw speaking to the man; if I hadn't seen her face, I could tell*

(*) Contemporary news reports incorrectly spelled his name "Friday"; authors and writers continue to perpetuate that error.

Rumors, Hearsay, and Misinformation

by her clothes. She was lying on a table, and while I was there one of the big people from Scotland Yard lifted her head up with a stick, and then parted the hair away from the back of her head and he said, 'They can say what they like—that's a clean cut and must have been done with the same knife. It was never done with the fall.' Then he said to someone 'If she fell on the back of her head, how is it the side of her face is all bruises?'

"I was very glad to get out of the place. I can tell you it looks a bit horrible. I don't think her face has changed much; she ain't good-looking, but the cut made her look horrible. The cut starts just under her left ear and goes right round her neck."

The police later dismissed Fryday's story, and his identification, when they found out the woman he mistook for the victim was a resident of Royal Mint Street, and she was standing in her own doorway talking with her boyfriend.

Some local women also reportedly wanted to see the body but were frightened away by superstition. "You know them that goes to see his bodies are always his next victims," a reporter claimed to have overheard one middle aged woman telling another.

The injuries on the victim's head led to more confusion. Some newspapers claimed she had a scar on the back of her head, which they attributed to an accidental fall. They told their readers a local woman, the wife of a coffee shop owner, knew the victim and had seen her stumble and hit her head on the pavement three weeks earlier. That same woman later testified at length at the coroner's inquest. She never mentioned the incident. Other newspapers correctly described the injuries as contusions, but reported that they had been bandaged. They hadn't been—they were the contusions Drs. Oxley and Phillips noticed while examining her body—the ones she received while being attacked in Swallow Gardens.

CARROTY NELL

The two bonnets caused a great deal of speculation. One newspaper claimed they couldn't have both belonged to the victim as they were different sizes, and then went on to rationalize that the killer must therefore have been a woman, or possibly a man disguised as a woman. The newspaper was wrong—both hats were the same size!

The possibility of the killer being a woman seemed to gain some acceptance, at least in the newspapers. The *Western Mail* reprinted an interview that had appeared in the *Pall Mall Gazette* a year and a half earlier in which "the eminent surgeon, Mr. Lawson Tait" argued why the murderer must have been "a big, strong woman engaged at a slaughter house in cleaning up." Some of his reasoning was a bit bizarre, to say the least. The killer would have gotten spattered in blood, he said, and a man with blood on his pants would arouse suspicion. But a woman, by rolling up her skirt and walking through a crowd in her petticoat, could avoid detection. Tait didn't explain how the woman might manage to walk through the streets in her undergarments without attracting anyone's attention. A man would also instinctively use hot water while trying to remove the traces of blood from his clothing, according to Tait, and would only succeed in setting the bloodstains, but a woman, being more accustomed to doing laundry, would use cold water and thus remove all traces of the incriminating evidence.

It didn't take long to discover that the victim's first name was Frances. Once that was revealed, more misinformation followed. *Lloyd's Weekly* claimed that a poorly-dressed woman walked into the Leman Street Police Station twelve hours after the murder and reported that one of her lodgers, a married woman named Frances, was missing. No one had seen her since eight o'clock the previous night when she left the lodging house on Thrawl Street to run some errands. The woman said that Frances was separated from her husband, and went on to describe her as quiet and unobtrusive. She gave the police a detailed description, even

Rumors, Hearsay, and Misinformation

mentioning that one of Frances's ears was torn, as if an earring had been pulled out by force.

It was an interesting story, obviously pieced together from several news reports, but it was untrue. Frances was never married. The poorly-dressed woman apparently was Sarah Fleming, a lodging house deputy. She did go to the police on Friday afternoon, but she never said Frances was married, or that she left the lodging house at eight o'clock. And Fleming's lodging house wasn't on Thrawl Street, it was on White's Row.

Nothing was considered too trivial to mention. One news agency reporter found out where Frances bought the stockings she was wearing when she died—a haberdashery shop on Brushfield Street. The owner claimed he knew her quite well.

The revelation that the victim's left ear had been torn, "as if an earring had been forcefully removed", was followed by more questionable news accounts. Florence Monk, a twenty-eight-year-old resident of a lodging house called Spitalfields Chambers, told a reporter from *Lloyd's Weekly*: "I have known Frances for some time by sight, and as coming to the house, but never made her acquaintance till last week. On Thursday afternoon one of the women—Mrs. King—fell down the stairs, and thought she would have to go to the London Hospital again. Frances said to her, 'Why I was there once for five weeks with my left ear when I had a piece pulled out.' After that she washed herself and went out, and wasn't seen again until half past eleven when she came in much intoxicated. She sat resting her head on the kitchen table, and while I was standing in front of the fire a man came in who looked like a seafaring man. He asked for Frances and then saw her sitting with her head on the table. He said something quietly to her, which I could not hear, and then he walked out. She then got up and, three or four minutes after that, she followed him out, and I did not see her alive again."

CARROTY NELL

Florence Monk's account of what transpired was undoubtedly influenced by the various stories she had read in the newspapers. It fails on several points. Frances wasn't in the lodging house at two o'clock in the afternoon; she had left at eleven o'clock that morning and didn't return until late that night. The "seafaring man" who came into the kitchen wasn't quiet and he didn't walk out shortly afterward; he was drunk, loud, and belligerent, and he stayed in the kitchen for some time until the watchman got fed up and told him to leave. Finally, it seems just a bit too contrived that Frances would happen to mention the injury to her ear—the same injury that newspapers had just reported—on the last day Ms. Monk saw her alive.

The *Pall Mall Gazette* questioned why the police weren't using the bloodhounds they had tried out in the autumn of 1889[sic]. The tests had been a complete success, the paper claimed, and the dogs had even managed to track down a bicyclist who had "merely passed his hand down along the wheel of his bicycle". The report went on to say that the bloodhounds took a dislike to London, and they ran away to their homes in the country. The story was riddled with errors. The police did conduct a few experiments with two bloodhounds after the Double Even. During the most notable one, the dogs successfully tracked Commissioner Charles Warren who had volunteered for the task. No mention was ever made of the dogs being able to track someone who had "merely passed his hand along a bicycle wheel". The dogs didn't "run away"; their owner reclaimed them when he became concerned that they weren't receiving proper care. Some reports indicate he also began to suspect there was a good chance he would never be paid.

The errors continued. The *East London Advertiser* reported that Frances's two sisters, Mary Ann and Selina, were known to be living on Kingsland Rd. The newspaper was mistaken. Mary Ann lived on Kingsland Road; Selina was a patient in a mental hospital.

Rumors, Hearsay, and Misinformation

A reporter with the *Pall Mall Gazette* happened to be on Commercial Road Friday night when he noticed someone walking unusually fast. He recognized the man as Rev. Arthur J. Robinson, the distinguished Rector of St. Mary's Church in Whitechapel, and he hurried over and asked Robinson if he could spare a few minutes to talk about the latest murder. Robinson said no—he was on his way to a ceremony at All Saints Church in Stepney, and he was late. If the reporter wanted to talk, he'd have to keep up with him. Robinson had quite a bit to say during their decidedly brisk walk. Surprisingly, he didn't seem to be too upset by the latest murder, but he was angered by the negative publicity it was generating. Publishing the details of the crimes in newspapers was "the most serious evil," he said. To illustrate his point he told the reporter about two West End ladies who had been helping in his church, but stopped coming after they read lurid newspaper accounts of the Ripper's earlier atrocities. "What nonsense," one girl in his parish supposedly said when she heard of the incident. "We don't mind. We're in bed long before the murderer is on his rounds."

Robinson said that Swallow Gardens had always been a likely spot for a "Ripper-type" murder, and he thought the police had issued special instructions to keep a close eye on it. He was sure that the same man, probably a monomaniac, had committed all the murders, but he wouldn't be a local man. Instead, he would turn out to be a cattle slaughterer, and probably a foreigner. "Foreign refugees throng the streets", Robinson told the reporter, "and every one is a stranger to his neighbor." The rector didn't mention who the foreigners might be, but the East End had recently seen a large influx of Russian Jews who had fled their homeland to escape the pogroms that followed the assassination of Alexander II. So many of them had settled in the area that many native East Enders had begun using the term "foreigner" as a synonym for "Jew".

The *Pall Mall Gazette* also incorrectly reported that Frances had formerly worked as a servant in a private home. Frances never worked as a domestic.

One wire service claimed that several local women, "clearly of the unfortunate class", recognized Frances as someone whom the Salvation Army had unsuccessfully attempted to reclaim.

Several newspapers suggested using "Salvation Army ladies" to try and win the confidence of "unfortunates" with the hope that perhaps one of them might reveal some information that could lead to the killer's identity. None of the newspapers mentioned that the proposal had originated with a news agency.

Newspapers invariably stopped publishing incorrect information once they became aware of it, but only one told their readers that a previous report was incorrect. That was *The Daily News,* when they admitted that the interior of Swallow Gardens wasn't as dark as they had first stated.

The most persistent error can't be blamed on the newspapers. They had no reason to suspect the victim wasn't twenty-six. After all, that information came from her father. But James Coles was off by five years when he guessed his daughter's age. His mistake went unchecked, and for the next one hundred and nineteen years, until the publication of the first edition of *Carroty Nell* in 2010, every book, article, and document—even her death certificate—continued to perpetuate that error.

Chapter 10

Frances Coles

Frances Coles was born at her family's home in Bermondsey on Saturday, September 17, 1859. Her father was a thirty-nine-year-old shoemaker from the small hamlet of Wollard, near the village of Publow in Somerset; her mother, a twenty-nine-year-old native of Armagh, Ireland. James Coles and Mary Ann Carney already had two daughters—seven-year-old Mary Ann, and Selina Adelina, who was almost four. Although they had been living together for eight years and were raising a family, they hadn't taken the trouble to legalize their relationship with a church wedding. In Victorian times, people who lived in better surroundings would have looked upon that type of arrangement as scandalous, but in the poorer neighborhoods it wasn't considered the least bit unusual.

Bermondsey was, and still is, part of Metropolitan London. It is situated on the south side of the River Thames, in the Borough of Southwark. The Coles family lived at 18 Crucifix Lane, almost directly across the river from the Tower of London. Bermondsey had been a fashionable neighborhood at one time, know for its fine gardens and stately suburban homes, but the gardens and country lanes of the wealthy were long gone by the time Frances was born. In their place stood a maze of narrow, twisted streets that linked factories, warehouses, and wharves. Much of the section near the river had deteriorated into slums. Charles Dickens immortalized the blighted area adjacent to Bermondsey's St. Saviour Docks in his novel Oliver Twist:

> "... *crazy wooden galleries common to the backs of half a dozen houses, with holes from which to look upon the slime beneath; windows, broken and patched, with poles thrust out, on which to dry the linen that is never there; rooms so small, so filthy, so confined, that the air would seem to be too tainted even for the dirt and squalor which they shelter; wooden chambers thrusting themselves out above the mud and threatening to fall into it - as some have done; dirt-besmeared walls and decaying foundations, every repulsive lineament of poverty, every loathsome indication of filth, rot, and garbage..."*

Frances's parents had lived on Crucifix Lane for several years—since before their first child was born in 1852. They had met the year before when Coles and his older brother Charles were sharing a rented room that faced a small, dingy courtyard behind 56 Bermondsey Street. It had the colorful name *Pail and Puncheon Court*. Mary Ann was visiting a young couple named Sullivan at the time, and they lived only three blocks away at 25 Melior Street. Her relationship to the Sullivans isn't known but, like Mary Ann, twenty-seven-year-old Daniel Sullivan was from Ireland. His twenty-year-old wife Joanna came from Chiselhurst in Kent. The Sullivans and their infant son had only recently moved to Bermondsey. Before that they lived in Croydon, ten miles away.

James and Mary Ann didn't notify the authorities when their first daughter was born, leaving the exact date of her birth in question. They did register Frances's birth, along with those of their other two children—Selina, born on October 25, 1855, and their last child and only son, James Jr. who was born on August 30, 1862. The family still lived

Frances Coles

Crucifix Lane, Bermondsey (2008)

Although the house where Frances Coles was born no longer stands, this period building a few doors down the street suggests how the neighborhood might have appeared.

Photo by the author

CARROTY NELL

on Crucifix Lane at the time.

James Coles may have enjoyed a brief period of prosperity early on in his career, but by the time Frances was born his finances were already in decline. It wasn't supposed to be like that. Shoe making had always been a secure, well-paying trade. Unfortunately, Coles entered the field a little too late. Shortly after he began his apprenticeship, England reduced the protective tariff on footwear imported from France. From the standpoint of domestic shoemakers, the move was disastrous. The imports were more stylish and less expensive than domestic boots. Not surprisingly, their popularity quickly soared. English manufacturers fought back by drastically cutting their costs. Among the cost-cutting measures was a slash in the piecework rates they paid their shoemakers. Despite the cost savings and the resultant lower prices, consumers still favored the imports. In the nineteenth century a skilled workman's occupational training began with a structured apprentice program. Because of that formalized training, once a man had acquired a work skill he rarely if ever changed trades. So while the demand for domestic boots continued to decline, the number of men who competed with one another for less work at lower rates remained about the same. While the shoemakers continued to suffer, the factory system was becoming more entrenched, and its power-driven machinery changed the process of shoe making forever. To James Coles and his fellow shoemakers that change was devastating, for the machine operators in the factories were almost exclusively unskilled women.

Coles eventually left Crucifix Lane and moved his family to 8 White Lion Court, a squalid little enclosure behind 207 Bermondsey Street. Frances shared that tiny room with her parents, her two sisters, and her brother. It also served as James Coles's workshop when he was lucky enough to find some piecework. Some years earlier the Surrey County

Frances Coles

Coroner had looked into the death of a woman named Ann Galway in almost-adjacent 3 White Lion Court. His report gives a disturbing account of the extreme poverty he encountered in that little courtyard:

> *"She had lived at No. 3 White Lion Court, Bermondsey Street, London, with her husband and a nineteen-year-old son in a little room, in which neither a bedstead nor any other furniture was to be seen. She lay dead beside her son upon a heap of feathers which were scattered over her almost naked body, there being neither sheet nor coverlet. The feathers stuck so fast over the whole body that the physician could not examine the corpse until it was cleansed, and then found it starved and scarred from the bites of vermin. Part of the floor of the room was torn up, and the hole used by the family as a privy."*

With six people crammed into one room, living conditions were almost unbearable by today's standards. James and Mary Ann probably didn't have a bed; the children almost certainly didn't have one and, like Ann Galway, slept on a pile of rags or feathers. The old building had no indoor plumbing, and water had to be brought from a central spigot that served the entire court. Laundry could be hung outside to dry on a rope stretched across the small courtyard during good weather; otherwise it had to dry inside. Without refrigeration, food spoiled quickly, forcing Frances's mother to sometimes buy one meal's worth at a time. Rats posed a constant problem, as did the swarms of insects that came with the warmer months. The cramped quarters were stifling in the summer, and freezing in the winter.

A man Frances worked for some years later said she had "all the educational advantages an ordinary day school could provide." The "ordinary day school" she most likely attended was St. John's Charity School at the nearby corner of Tooley Street and Potters Fields. Her attendance can't be verified, as school records from the nineteenth century haven't survived. St. John's was situated directly across the street from the prestigious St. Olave's Grammar School, an institution for boys that was founded back in 1571. In contrast, the student body at St. John's was made up of poor girls from St. John Horsleydown Parish. Frances's schooling would have only lasted for a few years—just enough to provide her with minimal skills in reading, writing, and arithmetic. Ripper-victim Catherine Eddowes had attended the same school several years earlier.

The family still lived at White Lion Court in 1871 when the national census was taken. That was the last time all of them were known to be living together under the same roof. It was also the last time Frances's mother's name appears on any official British record, and that break with officialdom ended on a mysterious note. Although she was born in what is now Northern Ireland, for some reason she reported her birthplace as Hammerton, Scotland on that year's census. It was a fictitious location. There isn't any community in Scotland named Hammerton. The only place with a similar name is Kirk Hammerton in North Yorkshire, but Mary Ann Carney had no known connection with that region.

Moving to White Lion Court had been a big step down for the Coles family, and the hardships only got worse as money became increasingly scarce. Sometime around 1873 conditions got so bad that James Coles couldn't even provide his family with the basic necessities of life—food and shelter. If he were a single man he could have tried to survive on the streets, but with a family he had no choice. With at least some of his family accompanying him—Selina, Frances, and James Jr. most likely—he made his way over to nearby Russell Street in Bermondsey and knocked on the door of a stark, formidable, red brick building that could easily be mistaken for a prison. It was the St. Mary Magdalen Workhouse, and the similarity to a prison was no coincidence. Everything about a Victorian workhouse was

Frances Coles

carefully orchestrated to make it uninviting. James Coles swallowed any lingering remnants of pride, and begged to be taken in.

At the time of Frances's death several years later, some newspapers described him as crippled. It's possible that he had that affliction in 1873, and was thus unable to work. Regardless of the reasons for his financial ruin, when he crossed the threshold and entered the unknown world of the workhouse that day, he had no way of knowing that he would end up living there for the rest of his life.

Caring for the impoverished had always been the responsibility of individual parishes. An 1834 law transferred that responsibility to groups of parishes, called "Unions", and directed each union to construct a large building resembling a prison to house paupers. A clergyman, writing in 1832, expressed the prevailing attitude toward those forced to seek shelter in workhouses:

> *"The Workhouse should be a place of hardship, of coarse fare, of degradation and humility; it should be administered with strictness, with severity; it should be as repulsive as is consistent with humanity."*

Workhouse conditions were deliberately kept uncomfortable to ensure that only the most needy sought admission. Every day was structured to make sure inmates were never idle. The routine was purposely made tedious, and the work assignments were difficult and boring. The food was cheap, and portions were skimpy, with little variety from one day to another. Discipline was unbending, and even a minor infraction like talking during mealtime could result in solitary confinement on a diet of bread and water. A more serious offense, like breaking a window, was often punished by several months' imprisonment at hard labor. Inmates were given a half-day off once a month and allowed to leave the workhouse for a few hours. Most destitute people saw little difference between entering the workhouse and going to prison, and many chose to take their chances on the streets.

In order to gain admission to the workhouse, Coles would have had to satisfy officials that there was no possibility of anyone else providing for him or his family. That makes it seem almost certain that at least some, and perhaps all, of his family suffered the humiliation and degradation of having to join him. Unfortunately the records for that workhouse haven't survived. If Frances and other members of the family were confined there, they didn't live together as men, women, and children were housed separately. They could have been punished for even speaking to one another.

If Selina Coles entered the workhouse with her father, she didn't stay long. She was unmarried, pregnant, and desperately poor in the spring of 1877 when she sought refuge in the St. Olave's Union Workhouse in Southwark. She was still confined there a few months later when she gave birth to a daughter. Little Selina Adelina Coles only lived for seven weeks. Her death certificate simply identifies her as "daughter of Selina Coles, a factory worker."

A person growing up in a nineteenth century slum had few, if any, opportunities to learn a meaningful trade or job skill. Boys generally ended up joining the army or working as laborers; girls, who didn't have the military as an option, often found their only choice was to become a domestic servant. The plight of *slaveys*—as Victorians facetiously called their overworked household servants—is legendary. Frances must have heard some of those stories first hand since her own sister worked briefly as a domestic servant. Selina Coles had found that position, probably with the help of the matron at the St. Olave's Union Workhouse. Frances made up her mind that being a *slavey* wasn't for her. Instead, she found a job as a trainee in the packing department of a soap and toiletries manufacturer called James

Frances Coles

Sinclair & Son at 65 Southwark Street. About the same time, she moved into a lodging house at 192 Union Street, about a five-minute walk from where she worked. For some reason she told the people at Sinclair's, and at the lodging house, that her name was Coleman. She went on to use that alias for the rest of her life.

If an account in the February 17, 1891 edition of the *Western Mail* (Cardiff, Wales) is correct, she advanced rapidly at Sinclair's, and was soon promoted to the position of forewoman at a weekly wage of fifteen shillings, or about twice what a skilled female laborer earned. That information came from Frances's sister Mary Ann, however, and she appears to have stretched the truth quite a bit in some of her other statements. It should also be noted that she ended the interview by telling the reporter her sister Selina worked as a laundrywoman in Kent, but she couldn't remember exactly where. Selina Coles wasn't in Kent—she was a patient in a mental hospital. In any event, Frances left Sinclair's for some unknown reason, and was apparently out of work for quite a while before she took a job as a day laborer in the packaging department of another firm.

She was still living at 192 Union Street when the 1881 census was taken, and still calling herself Coleman. The occupation she reported, "powder packer", makes it seem apparent that she had already left her job at Sinclair's and moved on to the next one, with a small wholesale druggist company in the East End.

Neither Frances's mother nor her sister Mary Ann appears in that year's national census—an indication they weren't living in England at the time. Her father was still in the St. Mary Magdalen Workhouse on Russell Street in Bermondsey. Selina's domestic servant job hadn't worked out, and she was back in the St. Olave's Union Workhouse on Parish Street. Eighteen-year-old James Coles, Jr. was a Private in the 2nd Surrey Militia, stationed at the Stoughton Barracks in Stoughton Guildford.

Winfield Hora & Co., where Frances worked after she

CARROTY NELL

left Sinclair's, was located at 58 Minories Street. They had been doing business at that location for over forty years. Their flagship product, Macord's Transparent Waterproof Isinglass Plaster, was in widespread use as early as 1844, and it was still a big seller. The company also produced a variety of medicinal drugs and medicated powders for the wholesale and export market, packaging them in square glass bottles that were sealed with snug-fitting cork stoppers. Paper labels were then affixed to the bottles to identify the contents. Frances took turns between inserting the cork stoppers, or "stoppering the bottles" as she called it, and applying the paper labels with glue. The stoppers had to be forcibly twisted into the medicine bottles by hand, and Frances soon developed calluses on her knuckles.

Henry Winfield Hora, the man who owned the company where Frances worked, was in his fifties at the time. For some reason, he preferred to be called Winfield rather than Henry. In addition to running a successful business, he took an active part in church and civic affairs and religious charities. He held the honorary title of Lieutenant of the City of London, and served as a representative of St. Botolph's Church in Aldgate on a charity called *The Churchwardens and Trustees of the Parochial Charities of the City of London* even though he and his family didn't reside in the parish. They lived across the Thames in a large, comfortable house on Peckham Road in Camberwell. He was also a member of the charity's Executive Committee. In later years he claimed to remember Frances quite well, even recalling that she told him she was born on Crucifix Lane.

When Frances started working at Hora's it took her almost forty minutes to walk to work. She could have ridden part of the way in one of the many horse-drawn omnibuses that plied the streets, but her earnings were far too meager to permit a luxury like that. Her sister Mary Ann later said Frances had earned between six shillings, two pence and seven shillings a week, but that was a gross exaggeration. Frances didn't earn anywhere near that amount. In fact,

Frances Coles

Frances Coles

Penny Illustrated Paper, February 28, 1891
Courtesy of Stewart P. Evans

some weeks she didn't earn anything for she wasn't a full-time employee at Hora's; she was a casual, or day laborer. When things were slow she didn't work—or get paid.

Work hours during the 1880s generally ran from eight o'clock in the morning to seven o'clock at night, with an hour off for lunch, plus another five hours on Saturday morning.

Margaret Harkness, in *Toilers in London* (1889), pointed out that factory girls typically earned between four and eight shillings a week, with the average being four shillings, sixpence. Girls who produced butterscotch and other candies were among the lowest paid workers in the city, while those who made cigars and cigarettes were among the highest paid. As an unskilled "powder packer", Frances's earnings were on the low end of the scale—similar to those of the butterscotch and candy makers.

Harkness wasn't impressed by the factory girls she met, saying they had:

> *"no governess to dog their heels, no mammas to talk to them about the laws that govern society, no wish to be fashionable or correct. The chief characteristic of the factory girl is her want of reverence. She has a rough appearance, a hard manner, a saucy tongue, and an impudent laugh."*

According to her foreman at Hora's, Frances didn't fit that description. He remembered her as "an exceptionally quiet, retiring, and well-behaved girl." She was quite skilled at what she did, he said, and he thought she was "thoroughly respectable."

Frances worked for Winfield Hora & Co. as an occasional day laborer for at least a few years. Her last separation might have been as early as 1883. The next time the company had some work for her, they sent a telegram to her last known address, a Christian mission on Commercial Road, but someone at the mission told the delivery boy she no longer lived there. The people at Hora's assumed she

Frances Coles

had left the area and was no longer available for work. They never tried to contact her again.

Only part of their assumption was correct. She wasn't interested in coming back, but she hadn't left the area. Her new residence—Wilmott's Lodging House at 18 Thrawl Street in Spitalfields—was only a few blocks from Hora's. She could have walked there in a few minutes and told them how to reach her, but she never did. Frances had found a new way to earn a living—one that she thought would be more lucrative and a lot steadier than being a "powder packer". Frances Coles had become a prostitute.

She probably began working as a prostitute during her furloughs from work at Hora's. She had to do something to come up with the money she needed for food and shelter. According to Howard J. Goldsmid, in his 1886 book *Dottings of a Dosser*, girls in the slums are taught:

> *"day by day, by precept and example, to see little or no harm in a career which, as often happens when work is slack and food scarce, is frequently adopted without hesitation or compunction, and in many cases without even the knowledge of sin."*

Regardless of whatever reason Frances had not wanting to return to Hora's, she never held a permanent job again and depended on prostitution for her livelihood. The recollection of James Murray, a former client, indicates she was working as a prostitute as early as 1883, but he didn't say whether or not she was also working at Hora's. Inspector Henry Moore's February 15, 1891 report that includes the statements, "she is not known to have had any kind of regular employment for many years, and "she has walked the streets the whole of the past eight years" was based almost exclusively on Murray's comments. Moore's statements may not be completely correct. One newspaper reported that Frances had worked as a packer for nine years, but they didn't say when she started. Also, the infor-

CARROTY NELL

mation was attributed to her father and Frances had done her best to keep him from learning of her slow but steady downward spiral. One thing remains puzzling—when he testified at the coroner's inquest, James Coles said Frances had calluses on the knuckles of her left hand that were caused by her job at Hora's. The doctors who examined her body also spotted them. It's unlikely the calluses would still be noticeable if she hadn't worked there for eight years. Comments made by others who knew her, like Charles Guiver, a doss house watchman, suggest that she may not have become a full-time prostitute until perhaps as late as 1887. Unfortunately neither the police nor the coroner thought it was very important to find out exactly when Frances turned to full-time prostitution.

Wilmott's catered exclusively to women. It was small by East End standards, having only about seventy beds. By one account, it was "remarkably clean". Ripper victim Mary Ann Nichols also lived there for a while, renting a fourpence-a-night bed for most of the month prior to her death.

Moving to Thrawl Street put Frances right in the heart of the East End, on one of the lowest, meanest streets in London. Goldsmid gave an unsettling description of Thrawl Street in *Dottings of a Dosser*:

> *"This thoroughfare, though short and narrow, contains probably as much destitution and depravity as any that are wider and more pretentious. It leads only from Commercial Street into Brick Lane, and in that short distance are concentrated elements of discord and degradation sufficient to shock even the most callous. The dwelling houses are all poor and mean; the gutters in the daytime are full of squalling children; and refuse of all sorts is lying about in every direction. When closing time comes, and the dram shops and gin palaces have sent their contingent to reinforce the representatives of sinning and suffering humanity that*

Frances Coles

crowd the unwholesome street, Thrawl Street is a thing to shudder at, not to see. Women who have reached the lowest depth of degradation to which their sex can sink, are rolling unsteadily along the footpath, or quarrelling in front of the public-houses from which they have just been expelled. Men are fighting, swearing, and hiccoughing out snatches of objectionable songs. Babies, who have been taken in their mothers' arms to the drinking dens, which rob them of their food and clothing, are wailing loudly; and the noise of quarrelling, intoxication, and lamentation, is to be heard on every side. It is needless to say, therefore, that it is the happy hunting-ground of 'doss-'ouse keepers' and that nearly every second house is a common lodging house."

Her decision to become a full-time prostitute turned out to be an incredibly poor one. Frances was quite attractive, something several newspapers pointedly noted. She was also extremely quiet, almost aloof. That's the first thing most people remembered about her. Her landlady, her former supervisor at Hora's, the night watchman at Spitalfields Chambers—they all commented on how quiet she was. She must have realized she wouldn't feel comfortable soliciting strangers on the street.

Thanks to information that has come down from one of her clients, we know she went out of her way to avoid people she considered "rough", and that she "hated" the low-class prostitutes she often encountered. Why she chose an occupation that put her in the midst of them on a day-to-day basis is almost beyond comprehension. But, as subsequent events tragically showed, Frances didn't always exercise good judgment.

Only two of the Whitechapel victims relied on prostitution for their livelihood—Frances and Mary Jane Kelly. The others were what were called "casual prostitutes". It was something they did only when they desperately needed money—perhaps to pay for their bed for the night. If Frances harbored any hopes that prostitution would lead to a

CARROTY NELL

better and more glamorous life, her dreams ended in bitter disappointment. She never earned enough to allow her to escape the noise and dirt and drunkenness of Thrawl Street. Eventually she reached the point where she had no choice but to walk the streets. Her clothes had become so worn and dingy they kept her from being considered for virtually any type of employment. She still crossed the Thames every Friday to visit her father in the Bermondsey Workhouse on Tanner Street. She also went to see him every holiday and on most Sundays as well. Whenever her father commented on her increasingly shabby appearance, she always had a ready excuse—business at Hora's was slow, and her hours had been cut back.

Although the Tower Bridge that now links the East End with Bermondsey was under construction at the time, it didn't open until 1894 and it took Frances over half an hour to get to the workhouse by crossing the London Bridge. She could have gotten there much quicker by using a pedestrian tunnel that ran under the Thames from Tower Hill to Bermondsey. It was originally built for a single-car subway line, but the business soon failed and the tunnel was converted to a pedestrian footpath with a halfpenny toll each way. A person in Frances's position who struggled to come up with four pence every night for a bed would think twice before paying any toll. It's a good bet she usually took the longer London Bridge route.

At some point Frances picked up the street name "Carroty Nell". It wasn't descriptive, and it wasn't original. English humorist William Schwenck Gilbert, who later corroborated with Sir Arthur Sullivan on several well known comic operas including *H.M.S. Pinafore*, *The Pirates of Penzance*, and *The Mikado*, may or may not have coined the catchy phrase, but he brought it into widespread use two decades before someone applied it to Frances. At the time Gilbert was the drama critic for *Fun* magazine, and they paid him a little extra money on the side to write and illustrate some light,

Frances Coles

"Amelia & Carrotty Nell"

Original Sketch by W. S. Gilbert
Fun, March 27, 1869

Courtesy of the Gilbert and Sullivan Archive

nonsensical poems for the magazine. To keep readers from learning that the humorous little rhymes were the product of the dignified drama critic, Gilbert used the pen name *Bab* for his whimsical little poems. His submission for the August 29, 1868 issue, *Sir Barnaby Bampton Boo*, went on to become one of his best known. It told the tale a rich nobleman who was searching for a wife. In a small village he chanced to meet a farmer with two daughters, Amelia and Carrotty Nell. Milly was "good but plain"; Nell was "pert and vain". For some reason Gilbert chose to use the archaic spelling "Carrotty", adding a second 't'.

Later that year, London publisher John Camden Hotten produced a collection of the most popular of Gilbert's illustrated rhymes in a book entitled *The Bab Ballads – Much Sound and Little Sense*. Gilbert continued to tinker with his little poems, and their illustrations, as the collection went through several additional printings over the years. The farmer's daughter was still "Carrotty Nell" [sic] in 1876, but by 1906, when Macmillan Publishing took over, her name had changed to "Volatile Nell". American playwright Thatcher Howland Guild later borrowed "Carrotty Nell" for the title of his 1905 play, which he set in an orphanage, and for the name of its precocious, redheaded heroine.

Why someone chose to call Frances a nickname like that is puzzling for *carroty* had the same meaning in Victorian times as it has today—reddish-orange. It was almost always used to describe a redhead, but Frances didn't have red hair. Her hair was dark brown. The name was probably nothing more than simple Cockney rhyming slang. What it stood for, however, is anyone's guess. While people on the street may have called her Carroty Nell, she was always *Frances* to her close friends.

Her descent didn't go unnoticed. James Sadler, a client who later faced charges in her death, was surprised by how far she had fallen since his last meeting with her some eighteen months earlier. On March 28, 1891, the *East London Observer*

Frances Coles

quoted Sadler as saying:

> *"When I first knew her she was a very reserved kind of girl, keeping to herself, and never mixing with any other women of her class. When I came home last time, though, I found her very much altered so far as her position went. She had come down in the world like they all do in time, but even then, she hated the women with whom she had to associate."*

Frances wasn't the only member of her family for whom things weren't going well. Her brother James had discovered that he wasn't cut out for a military career. When his term of enlistment was up he returned to civilian life, found a job as a laborer, and rented the small room at No. 3 White Lion Court, only a few doors from where he grew up. It was the same room where Ann Galway died in abject poverty several years before. On January 9, 1889 he was suddenly taken ill and brought to Guy's Hospital in Southwark where died shortly after his arrival. The cause of death was attributed to heart failure. His death certificate incorrectly stated that he was twenty-three. He was twenty-six.

Selina Coles continued to reside in the St. Olave's Union Workhouse where she gradually began to show unmistakable signs of mental illness. Around 1886 she was committed to the Leavesden Asylum in Watford.

Frances's other sister Mary Ann reappeared in London during the 1880s, living in a rented room at 32 Ware Street in Shoreditch. When she filled out the 1891 census, she said she was a charwoman, someone who cleaned houses or offices. There is some question as to whether or not that was true. The only clue as to the fate of Frances's mother comes from the 1891 census where James Coles's marital status is listed as *widower*.

Since Wilmott's was a lodging house for women, Frances couldn't bring her clients there even if she wanted to. Instead, she took them to one of the many lower class doss houses in the area. Charles Guiver, the night watchman at a doss house on White's Row, testified at the inquest following her death:

> *"I have known the deceased for the past three years as a casual lodger. She only stayed a night or two a week, and was known as a prostitute. She used to bring different men to the house to sleep with her."*

It was a surprisingly candid remark for someone in his position to make. Most doss houses rented double beds, separated from those on either side by flimsy screens, for eight pence—twice the cost of a single, and few took the trouble to verify whether the couple that wanted the bed were married. Prostitutes often utilized them. While the practice was so widespread that reformers often claimed some doss houses were little more than brothels, most owners and employees routinely denied that such a thing ever took place in their establishment.

Guiver had earlier told a reporter from Lloyd's Weekly:

> *"Frances has lived here for three or four years on and off—when she had any money. She was a quiet, inoffensive sort of woman—of course she was "an unfortunate," but for her class she was tolerably decent. She very rarely got drunk, very rarely went into the kitchen, and in the morning went off quietly."*

Mrs. Sarah Fleming, the fifty-seven-year-old deputy of that lodging house, echoed a similar sentiment:

> *"I don't know her surname for certain. She had rather dark hair, very fair skin, and was rather slender. She was a very quiet kind of woman, though she would take a little beer sometime."*

Frances Coles

Mary Ann Coles said she was surprised to smell alcohol on Frances's breath when they met the day after Christmas, 1890. "I don't think she used to drink", she testified at the coroner's inquest. Apparently that's not what she told the police. Inspector Henry Moore's report dated February 15 states that, according to Mary Ann, her sister "was very poor, and of drunken habits." Later on, in the same report, he added, "[she] has, for several years past, given way to drunken habits."

Four people—four conflicting points of view! "I don't think she used to drink", "she would take a little beer sometime", "she very rarely got drunk", "for several years she has given way to drunken habits"! Regardless of when she started to drink, or how much she had drunk in the past, by late 1890 Frances was drinking heavily. Her descent was starting to accelerate.

Mrs. Hague, the landlady at Wilmott's, always spoke well of Frances, whom she later described as "a young woman of a superior type." She sometimes let Frances spend the night even though she couldn't pay for her bed, trusting her come up with the money the next day. That was a very unusual practice in an East End doss house. By early January 1891 it was happening a little too often, and Frances was falling further and further behind with the money she owed. Mrs. Hague had no choice but to turn her away.

Frances had only a little over one more month to live when she reluctantly left the familiar surrounding she had called home for the past several years. It turned out to be the worst month of her life. With no regular place to sleep, her only option was to seek shelter in the lowest and meanest doss houses. Suddenly they were no longer just places to take an occasional client—now she was reduced to living in them. She must have hated it. Many of the residents were either down-and-out, or they lacked a steady source of income. Some had physical disabilities or mental handicaps that prevented them from holding a regular job. A few simply couldn't find work; others didn't want it. The large

CARROTY NELL

number of thieves, pickpockets, and other criminal types in the low class doss houses was legendary.

Montagu Williams, in his 1891 book *Later Leaves*, provides a vivid description of the lowest East End doss houses:

> *"It is on Saturday nights that the East End lodging house is to be seen at its worst. As soon as the public houses close, the orgie begins. Horrible oaths, disgusting language, and filthy songs become the order of the night. Nor is this condition of things restricted to the houses for men only. So far as downright obscenity is concerned, the houses containing both women and men are the worst.*
>
> *"Many deputies have a sly supply of spirits on the premises—stuff calculated to drive the consumer to madness; and, when all the public houses are shut, they dispose of this deadly refreshment at exorbitant prices...*
>
> *"In some cases the East End lodging houses are receptacles for stolen property, as was shown in a case that came before my colleague, Mr. Bushby, two years ago. A boy admitted to the police that watches were frequently brought to the Three Bells Chambers, Flower and Dean Street, and sold there....*
>
> *"In many cases, before you can enter the doss house proper, you have to pass through another building and traverse a back yard. The house is often of three or four stories, the staircases are narrow and winding, and the rooms are small; thus, should a fire break out, the conditions are all favorable for a holocaust of victims. I doubt very much whether the fires in the coke stoves standing in the center of the room are ever put out. The flooring is like tinder, and the staircases are mere match board."*

And now Frances was living among them in con-

Frances Coles

ditions that were repulsive. Compared to Wilmott's, they were filthy. She may have even had to sometimes settle for sharing a double bed in one of those doss houses with the understanding that she wouldn't receive any payment. A woman without money for a bed could often find a man who was willing to go along with such an arrangement.

Lodging houses were supposed to be regulated and routinely inspected. That rarely happened, as the police often looked the other way. Williams described the inspections:

> *"The doss house is often structurally unfit for the purpose to which it is put, and only passes the inspection of the Scotland Yard authorities by being strong enough to bear the weight of the beds and their inmates, by being sufficiently spacious to admit the regulation number of cubic feet of air, and by possessing a sufficient number of washing places, etc."*

Owners usually had advance warning when an inspection was scheduled, giving them ample time to remove any signs of overcrowding and other violations. Despite license restrictions that placed a cap on the number of occupants, beds were often crammed together until they almost touched. Even worse, bed bugs, fleas, and lice often infested the bedding and the bedclothes that were only changed once a week.

James Coles didn't learn that his daughter had descended into the world of the lowest doss houses until after her death. Frances told him she was renting a room in the home of a respectable older woman at 32 Richard Street. It didn't matter that it was an address she made up (Richard Street didn't have a number 32), for there was no chance he would ever come to visit.

Even as her world continued to crumble around her, Frances clung to the hope of someday returning to Wilmott's. According to a report in the *East London Advertiser*, she returned to her former lodging house five weeks after being put out and asked Mrs. Hague if she could come back. She promised to repay everything she owed. If the information in the article is correct, it could shed some light on Frances's movements and activities at a critical time, for the newspaper claimed that the meeting took place sometime between nine and ten o'clock on Thursday night, February 12. That was only a few hours before her death, and Ripper historians can't pinpoint her exact whereabouts at that particular time. Other statements in the same article, however, indicate that the meeting probably took place the previous night. Regardless of which night she was there, she obviously didn't receive the answer she hoped for since she left right after speaking with Mrs. Hague. Assuming that the meeting took place on Wednesday, her next stop was only a few minutes away—a pub at the corner of Wentworth and Commercial Streets. It was called The Princess Alice.

Chapter 11

Friday, the 13th

Frances didn't have far to go when she left Wilmott's—just to the end of the street, and then a short distance around the corner. Even so, she must have hurried as she walked. The temperature was still in the upper-thirties, but a strong, gusty wind made it feel a lot colder. She was wearing a black diagonal jacket—an unusual style where the front buttons, rather than running in a normal pattern down the front of the chest, instead ran diagonally from the right shoulder down to the left front side of the waist. It didn't offer much protection from the cold, however. It was old and almost threadbare. Like most of her clothes, she had gotten it second-hand—probably from one of the many outdoor used clothes stalls on nearby Petticoat Lane. Her black dress was also second-hand, but in a lot better condition. Her sister Mary Ann had given it to her the day after Christmas. It reached to her ankles, and she tried to dress it up a bit by wearing a black velvet ribbon around her neck. She kept her bare hands thrust deep into the pockets of her jacket to shield them from the cold, biting wind. Gloves were a luxury she couldn't afford. A well-worn black bonnet trimmed with beads rounded out her attire. It would have been unladylike to step outside without a hat of some sort. Even in slum areas most women, and men too

CARROTY NELL

for that matter, would have felt conspicuous and uncomfortable if they appeared on the street bareheaded, especially after dark.

The Princess Alice, or "The Alice" as the locals like to call it, has been serving customers from the same location for over one hundred and twenty-five years. A person can't help but suspect that it still looks pretty much like it did when it first opened in 1884. A dark wooden bar runs almost the full length of the back wall, and a well-worn leather couch, some tables and chairs, and a pool table occupy much of the semicircular space between the bar and the front windows. There are two doorways—one at each end of the bar. One leads to Commercial Street, the other to Wentworth Street.

It must have been crowded that night because Frances didn't notice James Sadler when he came in about fifteen minutes later. Sadler was a big man, fifty-three years old, and only two inches shy of six ft. tall—quite imposing by 1891 standards. He sported a full sandy-colored moustache and a square cut beard about four inches long. Both were beginning to show noticeable streaks of gray. His clothing—a close-fitting, double-breasted cloth jacket, woolen trousers, a black silk neckerchief, a sailor's hat, and lace-up rubber boots—suggested that he was a merchant seaman. He was, in fact, a fireman on the steamship *S.S. Fez*. She had left London on Christmas Eve, and had just tied up at the nearby St. Katherine Docks after arriving from Tenerife in the Canary Islands.

His wife and three daughters were at home in Chatham, almost thirty miles away, but they had no idea he was back in London. He and his wife had separated three years earlier, and she moved in with her mother, taking her three daughters with her. Before going to sea, Sadler had worked as a cab driver, a laborer in a tea warehouse, and a carriage conductor. He had even tried his hand at running a fruit and vegetable store in Lower Kensington, but the business

Friday, the 13th

James Sadler

Reynolds Newspaper, February 21, 1891

© The British Library Board
Used with Permission

soon failed. Scrappy, belligerent, and hard drinking, James Thomas Sadler was the embodiment of many people's image of a wanton, reckless, merchant seaman.

He had already stopped at another pub and had glass of gin before coming to the Princess Alice. Once inside, he looked about the crowded, smoky room and spotted Frances. He recognized her right away. The two had spent a few days together a year and a half earlier. He made his way over to her. "Remember me?" he asked.

"Of course I remember you."

He asked her what she wanted to drink.

"Why don't we go somewhere else, Jim?" she suggested. "These people know me. If they think you're flush, they'll expect me to talk you into buying drinks for everyone."

Most of Sadler's friends called him Tom, short for his middle name. Frances always called him Jim.

They left the Princess Alice, walked along Wentworth Street for a few minutes, and went into a pub on Old Montague Street. Mrs. Hague, the deputy at Wilmott's, happened to come in a short time later and she spotted them sitting together. She turned around and left before Frances had a chance to see her.

Later that evening they went to another pub—The Swan on Whitechapel Road. Sadler bought a half-pint bottle of whisky when they were leaving, and took it with him. Their next stop was a dingy little doss house on White's Row that bore the imposing name *Spitalfields Chambers*. Before they stepped inside Sadler gave Frances the bottle of whisky and told her to hide it in her pocket. He took an eight-penny double bed for one night.

At nine o'clock the next morning they were still in bed, hours after most of the other lodgers had left. Around eleven thirty they came downstairs and slipped out the door. Outside, the streets were still dotted with puddles from a brief but heavy shower that had passed by a few hours earlier, and a blanket of lingering low, gray clouds

Friday, the 13th

seemed to foreshadow the likelihood that more rain might begin again at any moment. Not surprisingly, they didn't stay outdoors very long. Instead, they sought refuge in a pub, the first of a few they visited that afternoon.

Around four o'clock they went into a pub on Middlesex Street called The Bell. Sadler ordered two glasses of gin, spiced with cloves, and gave one to Frances. While they were having their drinks she apparently mentioned something about needing a new bonnet. The barman couldn't make out what she said, but he heard Sadler's reply: "A new bonnet? You need new underwear more than you need a new bonnet." They had a few more words, and Sadler finally told her she could look for a bonnet later, and he'd pay for it.

They were there for about an hour. When they left, each one headed off in a different direction. Frances walked around the corner to Shuttleworth's Coffee House on Wentworth Street and ordered a cup of tea. She told Anne Shuttleworth, the owner's wife, that a gentleman would be joining her shortly. After a while she began to grow fidgety.

"He said he wouldn't be a quarter of an hour, and it's already been more than twenty minutes," she complained to Mrs. Shuttleworth just as Sadler was walking in through the front door. He joined Frances for a quick bite to eat, which they finished about quarter to six.

"We might be back later," Frances said as they were leaving.

Anne Shuttleworth later testified at the coroner's inquest that both were perfectly sober.

Their next stop was a pub called the Marlborough Head on Brick Lane. Sadler was still in a generous mood. He bought drinks for some of the customers, and spent two shillings for eight lottery tickets. There is some question as to exactly what he and Frances had to drink. Sarah Treadway, the landlady, told the coroner's jury that Sadler had two quarterns of gin and peppermint, and Frances had one. A quartern was five ounces—one quarter of an imperial

CARROTY NELL

pint. Her husband Charles didn't agree with her. He followed her to the witness stand and said Sadler was drinking whisky and beer. The Treadways did agree on one point—whatever Sadler drank, he drank it quickly as he was only in the pub for about a half-hour. Regardless of what he had been drinking, Sadler was, by his own account, becoming quite drunk. He later told the police the landlady was unhappy with his presence and wanted him to leave. Once again, Mrs. Treadway remembered it differently. She told the coroner's jury it was apparent that he had been drinking before he came in but, despite having two large gin and peppermints in the space of thirty minutes, she didn't think he was "tight" when he left.

Sadler's binge wouldn't have surprised most merchant seaman. Firemen, trimmers, and other members of the "black gang" had a reputation for getting drunk as soon as they came ashore. To many of them it was a well-earned reward after a week or more of backbreaking toil under extremely disagreeable conditions. When at sea, they labored far below the main deck in the hot, smoky environment of the boiler room where temperatures often reached one hundred and twenty degrees. Stripped to the waist, marine firemen not only shoveled coal into the roaring furnaces; they also had to constantly rake the burning coals to keep the fire at the right temperature. It was a physically demanding and exhausting job. Heavy seas made it even more difficult as they had to struggle to keep their balance while working in front of open furnace doors while the ship pitched and rolled.

Around seven o'clock Frances walked into a ladies' hat shop on Nottingham Street. Peter Hawkes, the owner's son, later told the police she was "three sheets to the wind". She looked at several hats before deciding on a black crepe bonnet. When Hawkes told her the price, just under two shillings, she stepped outside and spoke to Sadler. The two walked away only to return a few moments later. Frances

Friday, the 13th

handed Hawkes two shillings, and bought the hat. She could have gotten almost six nights lodging in a doss house with that much money. When she left the shop, she took her old hat with her. Sadler told her to throw it away but she wanted to keep it, and she pinned it under her long skirt. The bonnet wasn't Sadler's only gift. He had given her a penny to buy a pair of cheap earrings made from vulcanite, a hard, ebony-colored rubber, as they passed a peddler's shop in Brick Lane earlier in the day.

Sometime afterward Sadler told Frances he was going to meet a friend on Spital Street. He gave her a shilling and told her to pick up another half-pint bottle of whisky, and then go back to Spitalfields Chambers and get a double bed.

Frances walked with him part of the way. When he turned to start walking down Thrall Street, she tugged on his arm. She knew quite well how dangerous it was for a stranger, especially someone who had been drinking, to walk down that particular street. After all, she had lived there for almost eight years.

"Don't go that way," she said. "The street is full of thieves. They wouldn't think anything about robbing a sailor."

"I've traveled all over the world, and in all kinds of company, and I've never yet turned back on anything. I ain't going to fence this street," he replied, and kept on walking.

He should have listened to her. Thrawl Street's reputation was well known. A few years earlier *The Daily Telegraph* printed a description of that infamous street:

> *"...the population is of such a class that robberies and scenes of violence are of common occurrence. It is a risk for any respectable person to venture down the turning even in the open day. Thieves, loose women, and bad characters abound..."*

He hadn't gone fifty yards before woman in a red shawl

CARROTY NELL

Frances Coles

Like other contemporary sketches, it probably bears little resemblance to her actual appearance. The mortuary photo is the only known picture of her, and it wasn't made public until long after the newspaper sketches were drawn.

Reynolds Newspaper, February 21, 1891

© The British Library Board
Used with Permission

Friday, the 13th

came up behind him and hit him over the head with a folded umbrella. He stumbled forward and tumbled to the ground. Two men rushed out from the shadows and began to kick him in the ribs. One of them ran off with his wallet; the other took his watch. Sadler managed to get back up onto his feet. His judgment was obviously impaired by alcohol, for he suddenly became extremely angry because Frances hadn't come to his assistance.

"You're a pretty pal," he said, "to see me knocked about like this and not do anything for me."

Frances was stunned. "How could I, Jim?" she answered. "You know if I'd lifted a finger for you I would have been marked by those people, and they'd pay me out when they got the opportunity."

But Sadler wasn't in any condition to listen to reason, and he staggered away. Frances was livid. It was bad enough that he ignored her pleas not to go down Thrawl Street, but to imply that she was callous and unconcerned because she hadn't tried to fight off the two thugs was going just a bit too far. Exactly what either one did immediately after that remains something of a mystery. If the *East London Advertiser's* account is correct, Frances took the shilling he had given her for a bottle of whisky and a bed at Spitalfields Chambers, and walked a short distance down Thrawl Street to her former lodging house where she tried to talk the deputy into letting her return. It's more likely, however, that she simply headed straight to the nearest pub.

It was ten o'clock when she returned to the lodging house on White's Row. Charles Guiver, the thirty-four-year-old night watchman, saw right away that she was drunk. She walked into the kitchen and sat down on a bench behind a long table without saying a word to anyone. A few moments later she put her head down onto the table and fell asleep.

The room Frances walked into was a typical doss house kitchen. A greasy accumulation of several years' worth of

CARROTY NELL

grime and soot from the coke fireplace clung to its walls and ceiling. The stale, smoky atmosphere reeked of the pungent odor of cooked bloaters—large fat herring that were impaled on a metal rod and toasted over an open flame. They were a doss house favorite as they could often be gotten from fish markets for little or no money at closing time. Without modern-day refrigeration, they wouldn't keep overnight. A large basin of dirty, soapy water served anyone who wanted to wash his or her clothes. There were several tables and benches in the kitchen where lodgers could linger before turning in for the night. Some might read a newspaper while others played cards. Some just sat and talked or, like Frances, fell asleep.

Sadler came in around eleven thirty and found Frances sitting at the table. Her head was still resting on her arms, and she was sound asleep. He sat down beside her and gave her a gentle nudge.

"Did you get a bed for us?" he asked.

Frances didn't look up. "No," she mumbled.

"Do you still have the money I gave you?"

"No". She still didn't look up.

"I haven't even got a farthing," Sadler said. "Do you think they would trust you for one night?"

Frances looked up at him, then put her head back down onto the table without answering.

What Sadler said was true. The two men on Thrawl Street had emptied his pockets. Although he was technically broke, he was also owed four pounds, fifteen shillings for the seven weeks he worked since the *Fez* sailed on December 24, and he planned on collecting it in the morning. Charles Guiver overheard their conversation, and knew he would eventually have to put them out. He'd take care of that later. Doss houses often let their regular customers linger in the kitchen even though they didn't have the price of a bed. At some time however, usually about two o'clock, they had to leave. No one was ever allowed to spend the entire night at Spitalfields Chambers without paying.

Friday, the 13th

James Sadler and Frances Coles

Contemporary sketch shows Sadler and Coles in the kitchen of Spitalfields Chambers a few hours before her death.

Courtesy of Stewart P. Evans

CARROTY NELL

Sadler rambled on about having been robbed, and what he would do to the people who robbed him if he could only find out who they were. In the meantime Frances had drifted back to sleep. After a while Sadler realized no one in the room was listening to him, and he started to become belligerent. It seemed to Guiver that he was deliberately trying to provoke a fight. Guiver decided there was no point in waiting any longer—he told Sadler to leave. Frances stayed in the kitchen a little while longer, and then got up and walked out without saying anything. Sarah Fleming, the lodging house deputy, watched her leave. It was just after midnight.

Where she went after she left Spitalfields Chambers remains a mystery, but about twenty-five minutes past one she came into Shuttleworth's, where she and Sadler had had their supper about eight hours earlier. After fumbling about inside her pocket, she took out all the money she had—two pence. One penny and two halfpennies. She ordered some mutton and bread, handed over the three coins, and then took her food to a table where she sat by herself. When she finished, she put her head down and once again began to doze off.

About twenty minutes to two the part-time night manager, Joseph Haswell, began his regular ritual of coaxing the last lingering patrons to leave. Only a few customers were still there—women like Frances with no place to sleep. None were very anxious to move, for once outside, they faced the prospect of spending the rest of the chilly night outdoors. The temperature was thirty-eight degrees, and it was windy.

Haswell finally managed to get everyone out but one. The little brunette was still sitting there with her head resting on her arms. It didn't matter to Haswell that she was something of a regular customer; it was past closing time and he wasn't in the mood for diplomacy. He walked over to Frances's table.

"And what about you," he asked. "When are you going

Friday, the 13th

to leave? I want to shut the door."

She didn't look up. Her voice was barely audible. "Mind your own business," she said.

That was the last thing Haswell wanted to hear. He probably said something like, "Out you go, m'lady!" as he reached down, grabbed her arm, and pulled her to her feet. Still holding her by the arm, he pushed her toward the door a lot faster than she expected, and then gave her a gentle shove out onto the sidewalk. He watched her hesitate for a few moments as though she were trying to get her bearings. She finally turned and started slowly walking up Wentworth Street. Haswell glanced at the clock—it was quarter of two.

A few minutes later Frances reached the corner of Commercial Street and saw a woman she knew standing outside The Princess Alice. Ellen Calana's recollection of the events that took place during the next few minutes helped prevent an innocent man from having to suffer the terrifying ordeal of standing trial for a murder he didn't commit.

Her real name almost certainly wasn't Calana. No one has ever been able to establish her true identity. Inspector Henry Moore of the Metropolitan Police thought her last name was Colanna, but he wasn't sure of the correct spelling. *The Times* provided its readers with two different versions of her name: Callaran (Feb. 14) and, two weeks later, Callana (Feb. 28). Other sources have identified her as Callaron, Callagher and Callaghan. Research by the author suggests that her real name may have been Ellen O'Connor. None of the names she's been called match any records in the 1891 national census. All of them, however, have one thing in common—her first name is always Ellen. She was living in a doss house at 3 North East Passage, a small alley than ran off Cable Street, when she testified at the inquest into Frances's death in late February. The 1891 census, taken a few weeks later, shows only one Ellen at 3 North East Passage—fifty-two-year-old Ellen O'Connor. She was a native Londoner and single. When asked for her occupa-

CARROTY NELL

tion for the census, she replied, "None."

Calana couldn't help but notice Frances's new hat, and she must have made a comment about it. Frances was more concerned about something else; she told her friend how she had just been put out of Shuttleworth's. The two women began to walk down Commercial Street while they tried to decide what they should do next. Calana already had a place to sleep that night; Frances didn't. They were almost at the intersection of Whitechapel High Street when a short man with a dark moustache crossed the street and came over to them. Calana noticed that he was wearing a pea jacket, a cheese cutter hat (a flat cap known today by many names, including "scally cap"), dark blue trousers, and "shiny boots". He looked like he might be a sailor. He took her to one side, made a proposition, and told her he'd give her a half crown—a silver coin worth two shillings, sixpence. To a streetwalker in Whitechapel, it was quite an enticement. It was also a lot more than the going rate. Perhaps that's what made Calana suspicious. Maybe he looked like he had no intention of paying. But her instinct told her there was something about him that wasn't right. She said she wasn't interested.

He didn't say a word. Instead, he reached out and grabbed her jacket, tearing it as he did so, and punched her in the face. When he let go, he walked over to Frances who was standing about ten or twelve ft. away.

"Frances, don't go with that man. I don't like his looks," Calana said.

"Yes, I will."

Calana was somewhat miffed that Frances chose to ignore her advice. "Well, if you are going with that man, then I'll bid you goodnight," she said, with a hint of sarcasm in her voice.

Frances didn't answer. Instead, she and the short little man with the quick temper began to walk away. Ellen Calana kept her eye on them until they turned the corner onto Whitechapel High Street. Once they were out of sight, she

Friday, the 13th

headed back to Theobald's, a doss house on Brick Lane where she was staying at the time.

Frances Coles had just made the biggest mistake of her life! She and her companion spent the next ten minutes walking to Swallow Gardens, a half-mile away. One minute later she was lying on the ground deep inside, bleeding to death from a mortal wound in her throat.

Chapter 12

"You Are Hereby Charged ..."

Ellen Calana didn't sleep well that night. Her face throbbed where the angry little man on Commercial Street had punched it. After tossing and turning for some time, she got up around five o'clock and walked into the kitchen, sporting a noticeable black eye. Several of the other lodgers had already risen, and the kitchen was abuzz with the latest news—another woman had been found with her throat cut. This time it was in Swallow Gardens. Calana began to get an uneasy premonition as she listened to the sketchy details. The more she thought about it, the more worried she became that her friend Frances might be the woman who had been killed.

She told the others about her encounter with the stranger, and how he had punched her in the face, and how Frances had ignored her warning and gone away with him. Did they think she should go and tell the police? The consensus in the kitchen was that she should. Fifteen minutes later Ellen Calana walked into the Metropolitan Police Station on Leman Street and told her story. A policeman took her to the Whitechapel Mortuary where she looked down upon the body of the girl who had failed to heed her advice only a few hours earlier. She told the policeman the victim's name was Frances. Even though she had known her for

"You Are Hereby Charged ..."

five years, she didn't know her friend's last name. The constable took Calana back to Leman Street to speak to the detectives. The record of the interview is among the many documents that have gone missing, but it's probably safe to assume that Inspector Flanagan handled the questioning. Calana related everything in detail, from meeting Frances outside the Princess Alice to watching her and the stranger walk away together. She also mentioned that she and Frances had both been drinking earlier that evening. "Just getting over drunkenness," was the way she later described their condition at the coroner's inquest. When asked what time they met the stranger, Calana didn't hesitate. "Three o'clock," she said, putting the time about three quarters of an hour after Frances's body was found.

"Are you sure about the time?"

"Yes. I heard the bell in the Tower strike."

Whoever was questioning her thanked her for taking the time to come in.

She returned to Theobald's where everyone wanted to know what had happened. While she was telling her story the deputy interrupted her. "It couldn't have been three o'clock. You came in a little after two last night."

"Are you sure?"

The deputy assured her it was only a few minutes past two when she came in.

"What do you think I should do?"

"I think you should go back to the police and tell them you made a mistake. It might be important."

Calana retraced her steps back to Leman Street and said some of the information she had given earlier was wrong. It was two o'clock when she saw Frances walking away, not three o'clock.

The police apparently never put much faith in any of the statements she made. The *Morning Post* more or less confirmed that when they reported that the body was identified as that of a woman named Frances by someone who was "in a maudlin condition from drink", and that the police

CARROTY NELL

weren't completely satisfied. Although the newspaper had the incident taking place in the afternoon, they were almost certainly referring to Calana. Three other people did go to the mortuary that afternoon to identify the body, but none of them had been drinking.

If Ellen Calana was, in fact Ellen O'Connor, she was typical of the women the Ripper chose as his victims—more so than Frances. All of the victims except Elizabeth Stride and Mary Jane Kelly were either drunk or had been drinking shortly before their deaths. Stride's whereabouts in the last few hours of her life have never been determined. All of them were poor; some desperately so. Kelly told George Hutchinson she had to get sixpence when they met at two o'clock in the morning. Catherine Eddowes's friend had to pawn his boots so they could have breakfast. Nichols and Chapman didn't have the money to pay for a bed. Neither did Frances. But Ellen Calana might well have been the only woman who was approached by the killer and lived to tell about it. The failure to follow up on the information she provided was unfortunate, for her description of the stranger with the violent temper bears an uncanny resemblance to a local man who came to the attention of the police some time later. His name was Severin Klosowski. Today many people consider him to be a prime suspect in the Whitechapel murders.

At the time there was little doubt in the public's mind that the dreaded killer had resurfaced and struck again. The day after Frances's body was discovered, the *East London Advertiser's* headline: proclaimed:

ANOTHER WHITECHAPEL HORROR.
"JACK THE RIPPER" AGAIN.

It was almost identical to the headline they ran on July 20, 1889 following the death of Alice McKenzie. Several police officials shared the same view. On the day of the

"You Are Hereby Charged ..."

murder Sir Robert Anderson, the head of the Metropolitan Police Criminal Investigation Division, sent a memo to the Home Office that included the statement:

> *"The officers engaged in investigating the former Whitechapel murders were early on the spot, and every effort is making [sic] to trace the criminal. But as in former cases he left nothing, and carried away nothing, to afford a clue."*

Some people at the Home Office were a little more cautious. Godfrey Lushington, the Under Secretary, scribbled a note on Anderson's memo that he had shown it to Henry Matthews, the Home Secretary, but cautioned him that it would be premature to venture an opinion as to the killer's identity as this particular case "may not be connected with any previous cases."

Sir Robert wasn't alone in thinking that Jack the Ripper was responsible. Detective Inspector Edmund Reid, who was in charge of the Whitechapel Division during the time of the Whitechapel murders, was quoted in the *Morning Post* on the day after Frances's death as saying: "In my opinion, the crime has been done by the same hand that has perpetrated the other murders. We have as yet no definite clue, but hope soon to lay our hands on the fiend."

Newspaper coverage tended to reaffirm the widespread belief that Jack the Ripper had struck again, although one newspaper had a unique reason for questioning Frances's candidacy as a Ripper-victim. She was too young and too attractive, they thought, "quite different from the Ripper's former attentions". In the end they concluded that she most likely was a Ripper-victim.

Mary Ann Coles learned of her sister's death the following day when she answered a knock on her door. The woman standing outside told Mary Ann her name was Miss Pitt. She said she was with the Christ Church Mission House on

CARROTY NELL

Dorset Street, and she was afraid she had brought bad news. Mary Ann immediately thought of her father in the workhouse, and she steeled herself for the news that he had died. She was stunned when she found out it was her youngest sister who was dead, and not her elderly father. Learning the cause of her sister's death made it even harder to bear.

The next day she went to the mortuary to identify the body. She said Frances looked "wax like, and peaceful." She recognized the dress as one she had given Frances several weeks earlier. She told one reporter she occasionally gave her sister some of her old clothes, and she had a bundle of them all wrapped, ready to give to Frances the next time she called.

Ellen Calana wasn't the only person to go to the police after hearing of the murder. Charles Harris, a longtime resident of Spitalfields Chambers, had been in the kitchen Thursday evening and overheard the conversation between Frances and Tom Sadler. When he learned of the murder the next morning, he ran back to the lodging house. Sarah Fleming, the lodging house deputy, and Florence Monk, one of the lodgers, were the only ones there. Harris asked them if they had seen Frances. They hadn't, and Harris told them he was afraid she might be the victim. The three decided to go over to the Leman Street Police Station. During the subsequent questioning, they described what had taken place in the kitchen, and gave the police a detailed description of Frances's companion. Fleming told detectives his name was Tom Sadler.

On Saturday morning, February 14, Sergeant John Don and Constable Gill of the Metropolitan Police asked Harris if he could help them find Sadler. The trio visited several common lodging houses and pubs without finding any sign of their prey. Around noon Harris walked into a pub called The Phoenix at 24 Upper East Smithfield and spotted Sadler. He stepped back outside and told the two police-

"You Are Hereby Charged ..."

men. The men went inside and asked Sadler to accompany them to Leman Street. He didn't offer any resistance. Both men noticed that he had bloodstains on his clothes, a cut on his face, and scratches on his hands.

On the way to the police station he mentioned that he was married, and told the two men he was sure his wife would leave him once it became known that he had spent some time with a prostitute. He also said he had expected to be questioned. "I admit I was with her but I have a clean bill of health and can account for my time. I haven't disguised myself in any way, and if you couldn't find me then the detectives in London are no damned good," he added. He also told them, "I had a row with her because she saw me knocked about and I think it was through her."

When they reached Leman Street, Chief Inspector Donald Swanson of Scotland Yard, the detective branch of the Metropolitan Police, personally took charge of the questioning—an indication the police seriously suspected Sadler might be Jack the Ripper. Swanson cautioned Sadler that he was under no obligation to answer any questions, and then began his interrogation. It lasted all afternoon. Sadler continued to maintain his innocence while he gave Swanson a blurred and confused account of his whereabouts since his ship docked late Wednesday afternoon. "I don't remember exactly what the time was," and "I'm not sure of the name of the street," were typical of his answers. He placed several events in the wrong time sequence. He had been drinking heavily since he arrived in London, and his recollection of specific times and events suffered accordingly. Sadler's complete statement is too long to be included here. It is reproduced in its entirety in the Appendix.

At one point detectives brought a man named Joseph Lawende to the police station and had him take a look at Sadler. Lawende had seen a woman resembling Catherine Eddowes talking to a man shortly before the murder in Mitre Square. Even though he told the police he probably wouldn't recognize the man if he saw him again, detectives

CARROTY NELL

thought seeing Sadler might spark some recognition. It didn't. Lawende told investigators Sadler didn't look anything like the man he had seen. Surprisingly, his description of that man: "aged thirty to thirty five, height five ft. seven, with brown hair and moustache. Wore pea jacket, muffler, and a cloth cap with a peak of the same material. Had the appearance of a sailor," is strikingly similar to the man Ellen Calana encountered on the night of the murder.

Swanson didn't buy Sadler's story. He couldn't ignore Sadler's inability to give an accurate account of his whereabouts at critical times, or the blood stains on his clothes and the cuts and scratches on his face and hands. On Monday afternoon, February 16, the police brought Sadler to the Thames Police Court where Inspector Henry Moore formally charged him with "the willful causing of the death of Frances Coles by cutting her throat with a knife or other sharp instrument at Swallow Gardens on 13 February."

The police continued to press their investigation, and some of them apparently suspected they might have finally apprehended the long-sought Jack the Ripper. Their efforts to link Sadler with the other Whitechapel murders ultimately led them nowhere for Tom Sadler had an airtight alibi. He was on the high seas between August 17 and October 2, 1888, when four of the first five killings took place.

Nonetheless, the case against Sadler in connection with Frances Coles's death seemed to be getting stronger. A man named Duncan Campbell came to the Leman Street Police Station on Sunday evening and said he had been in the Sailor's Home on Well Street at ten thirty on the morning of the murder when a stranger walked in and offered to sell him a clasp knife for one shilling. He thought the man might be Sadler. A clasp knife is similar to an ordinary jack knife, but the blade locks in place when it's opened, and it can't be retracted until a catch is released. Campbell told the police he bought the knife only to sell it shortly afterward.

Two police sergeants accompanied him to the home of Thomas Robinson, the man who bought the knife, and

"You Are Hereby Charged ..."

James Sadler at the Thames Police Court

Penny Illustrated Paper, February 28, 1891
Courtesy of Stewart P. Evans

seized it as evidence. The three men returned to the police station and soon afterward Campbell was taken downstairs where he saw a line of fifteen or sixteen men arranged in a semicircle. Most of them were sailors. The police asked him to pick out the man who sold him the knife. Campbell slowly passed by the entire line without recognizing anyone. He passed along the line a second time with the same result. To learn what happened next, we have to turn to Tom Sadler, who later told a reporter:

"One of the police came and stationed himself right opposite where I was standing and looked straight at me with his eyes.

" 'Can't you recognize him?' says the policeman—and he was looking as hard as he could at me all the time.

"Then Campbell, of course, looked toward where I was standing; but even then he didn't seem quite sure. So he goes all along the line of men again and lifts off their hats one by one. At last, when he comes to mine, and sees the blood on the cap and the wound on the head, he says

'That's the man.' "

Sadler swore Campbell was lying and gave investigators the names of two men who could verify he never carried a knife. Sergeant Kuhrt of the Metropolitan Police later spoke to two of Sadler's shipmates, Mathew Curley and Frederick Bowen, but his report doesn't give any indication if the conversation with the two men concerned Sadler's carrying a knife. He did say that he wasn't able to obtain any additional information.

When the newspapers learned that the police had taken a suspect into custody, and had charged him with murder, they immediately turned their attention to James Sadler. Many of their initial reports were tainted by what today would be considered inexcusable, unprofessional bias. To most editors, being arrested was apparently tantamount to being guilty.

Newspapers carried interviews with his wife, his mother,

"You Are Hereby Charged ..."

and his former neighbors. Those accounts almost unfailingly painted Sadler in the most unflattering light. "A man of ungovernable temper," and "capable of any act of violence," were typical of the phrases used to describe him. In *The Standard*, his mother was quoted as saying he behaved like a madman when he had been drinking. One wire service had his wife "admitting" that on several occasions he had stood over her for a quarter of an hour or more, "with a long knife in his hand." Mrs. Sadler and her husband weren't on the best of terms, but she was furious with the way newspapers were twisting her statements, and she refused to speak to any more reporters. Those alleged incidents with a knife never came up for discussion during any of her numerous interviews with the police.

Not surprisingly, the knife that Sadler supposedly sold to Duncan Campbell became big news. It was almost always "large and sharp", and usually had been "traced to Sadler". "A formidable blade with a razor-like edge," was how the *Aberdeen Weekly Journal* described it. Some newspapers even told their readers it was "stained with human blood". None of those statements were true. The police never uncovered any evidence that Sadler carried a knife. Far from being large and razor-sharp, it was small enough to easily fit inside someone's pocket, and the blade was so dull that it's next owner had to sharpen it before he could cut a slice of meat. The "human blood" proved to be nothing more than just plain rust.

The embellished stories didn't stop there. The *New York Times* cited a February 16 dispatch from London as the basis for their report that a large crowd surrounded the Arbour Square Police Station after learning that Sadler was being held, and that "threats of lynching and tearing the prisoner to pieces" were made. To protect Sadler, the police decided to move him to the relative safety of the police court under the cover of darkness, but the word got out and angry crowds once again surrounded the police station, "howling for his blood". London newspapers simply said that a crowd had gathered. The people apparently just wanted to catch a glimpse of Sadler.

Some London newspapers, perhaps unwittingly, tried to implicate him with the murder even before he was arrested. Any suggestion that the police were setting him up would have been met with disbelief, but a disturbing news item that appeared in a few local newspapers on Saturday morning, February 14, several hours before Sadler was located and taken in for questioning, raises the possibility that someone associated with either the police or a news agency deliberately misled the press in order to build a case against Sadler. For example, under the headline "SHOCKING MURDER IN WHITECHAPEL", *The Times* reported that a railway employee saw a woman talking with a man inside Swallow Gardens at one thirty on the morning of the murder, and that the police were confident the woman was the victim. The man was described as "being above the middle height, and having the appearance of a foreigner, after the style of a ship's fireman".

London's *Morning Post* ran essentially the same story, and identified the informant as "a laborer named Friday[sic]". They claimed that he saw the murdered woman talking to a man, "apparently a fireman", on Royal Mint Street at half-past one. The reports were completely untrue! *The Scotsman*, a leading Edinburgh daily, was far more accurate when they stated:

> *"The description given of the man is, however, vague, and amounts to little more than that he wore a brown overcoat and a black felt hat. The woman wore a crape hat. Her companion was about five feet seven inches, and looked like a working man."*

Neither Frances Coles, nor James Sadler, nor anyone else was observed inside Swallow Gardens prior to the murder, and no one reported seeing anyone "having the appearance of a foreigner" or dressed "after the style of a

"You Are Hereby Charged ..."

ship's fireman". The laborer whom the *Morning Post* spoke about did tell the police what the man he saw on Royal Mint Street was wearing, but that description, "a brown overcoat and a black felt hat", would never lead anyone to suspect the man was ship's fireman. Marine firemen didn't wear any particular type of uniform. In fact, they usually wore only trousers and clogs while working. The clogs were to protect their feet from the hot ashes on the boiler room floor. There was nothing about a marine fireman's attire that revealed his occupation.

Placing someone "having the appearance of a foreigner" at the murder scene was just an attempt to cover all bets. Many people were certain that the killer had to be a foreigner. No Englishman, they reasoned, could be capable of committing such atrocities.

The actual incident bore little resemblance to the newspaper accounts. At quarter past one on Friday morning, February 13, an eighteen-year-old girl named Kate McCarthy arrived at her home at 42 Royal Mint Street, not far from the entrance to Swallow Gardens. She was accompanied by her fiancé, Thomas Fowles. McCarthy was wearing a black bonnet that was quite similar to the one Frances Coles had just bought. While she and Fowles were standing in her doorway, a wagon driver from the Great Northern Railway's Royal Mint Street freight depot happened to walk down the other side of the street and noticed them. McCarthy and Fowles both recognized the man. His name was William Fryday, but most people just called him "Jumbo". Neither McCarthy nor Fowles spoke to him as he passed. Fowles suspected he had been drinking.

Later that day Fryday heard about the murder and mistook McCarthy and Fowles for the victim and her killer. He went to the police and reported his sighting. Metropolitan Police Superintendent Thomas Arnold, in a February 13, 1891 report, wrote that Fryday: "could not discern their faces distinctly but noticed that the woman wore a black hat. He has seen the hat worn by the deceased and identified it as that worn by the woman he saw talking in Royal Mint Street. He has also given a slight description of the man she was with but says he could not recognize him as he did not see his face." Two weeks later, at the inquest into Frances's death, Fryday's memory showed a significant improvement. He testified that the man in the doorway wore a dark brown overcoat with a velvet collar—hardly the attire one would expect to find on a marine fireman!

Fryday hadn't been able to identify the victim's body when he saw it in the mortuary, but that didn't stop him from telling reporters it was the same woman. He was sure because her black bonnet looked just like the one the woman in the doorway on Royal Mint Street was wearing.

In their February 14 edition, *The Daily News* reported that a man (presumably William Fryday, although the newspaper said that he worked at the St. Katherine's Dock where Sadler's ship was tied up) was walking with a friend on Royal Mint Street at one-thirty in the morning when they came across a man and woman who were standing, not in Kate McCarthy's doorway, but right outside the entrance to Swallow Gardens. The couple had to step to one side to allow the man and his friend to get by. The article went on to say that the man went to the mortuary at eleven o'clock Friday night and identified the deceased as the woman he saw on Royal Mint Street. Every one of those statements was untrue!

While *The Daily News* didn't try to place Sadler at the murder scene, they did try to implicate him. After writing that a police search of the crews of some cattle boats in the river failed to turn up any clue, they added: "One of the old theories as to the Ripper's personality is that he must be a fireman, or sailor, or something of the sort."

Some newspapers weren't satisfied with having a passerby spot someone who just happened to look like a ship's fireman at the murder scene. *Lloyd's Weekly*, in their February 22 edition for example, printed Fryday's description of the man he saw on Royal Mint Street that included a

"You Are Hereby Charged ..."

strange observation—the man's ears. "What made me notice him more was his ears—they came out, like," Fryday allegedly said.

A few paragraphs later, they told their readers what Sadler looked like:

> *"His hair is grizzled and unkempt, and his grayish goatee and straggling thick moustache alike are untidy. His features are strongly marked; the nose is large and prominent; the peculiar eyes are bleared, and with a habit of half-closing as he listens."*

Whoever wrote the description then added this peculiar comment:

> *"The man's [Sadler's] ears stick out noticeably from the side of his head."*

If they did, the *Lloyd's* reporter seems to be the only person who noticed them, and *Lloyd's* was the only newspaper that was aware of Fryday's alleged observation. He hadn't mentioned it to the police.

No one could blame James Sadler for believing he was being set up. He was so upset that on February 18 he sent a letter to the Stokers' and Firemen's Union and asked for their help. It was addressed to a Mr. Wildgoose, and read:

> *"From T. Sadler, a stoker and member of your Union, Burntisland Branch, No. 311 (my last payment was made at Tower Hill last Friday, the 13th).*
>
> *Wishing prosperity to the Union I must apply to you to act as my friend, as I have no claim on anyone else in particular. My wife was always a doubtful friend. My mother is too old, and I have no brothers or sisters or public house pals worth a damn. I should like a reporter connected with seafaring and The Star to watch over me. The police will*

CARROTY NELL

hurry my case to suit their own ends. Anything turning up in my favour will be squashed. All the money and sense of Scotland Yard will be used to hurry me to a finish. What a godsend my case will be to them if they can only conduct me, innocent as I am, to the bitter end. The whole detective system of Scotland Yard will be whitewashed in the sight of the whole world, and money presents will roll in to them. But on the other hand, if I have a true friend in a reporter to see that I am not talked down or sat on entirely by the police and court, I hope to walk out as I deserve to. The knife business is false. I have neither bought nor sold any knife. I had one knife and fork only—a pair given me by my old mother a few months ago.

J.T. Sadler"

Two days later, on February 20, a wire service reported the incident, but had Sadler appealing directly to *The Star*. They continued: "*The Star* has engaged counsel to defend Sadler, who is without means to defend himself, and proposes to see that no injustice is done him. The belief in Sadler's innocence is growing."

Fortunately for James Sadler, the Metropolitan Police weren't the only ones investigating the death of Frances Coles. Northeast Middlesex County Coroner Wynne Baxter, whose district included Whitechapel, conducted a lengthy, drawn-out inquest into her death.

The term coroner generally calls to mind the image of some grim, humorless individual. Wynne Edwin Baxter was anything but the typical coroner. Blunt, outspoken, and quick to get to the point, Baxter was an attorney and the author of a well-known and respected legal treatise, *The Law and Practice of the Supreme Court of Judicature*. He also wrote several religious articles using the pen name "Llewellyn Acton". Before moving to London, he had served as the mayor of his hometown, Lewes in Sussex. He was an avid

"You Are Hereby Charged ..."

plant collector, a Fellow of the Royal Geological Society of London, and a member of several archeological societies. He owned an extensive collection of antique books, and was considered an expert on the seventeenth-century English poet John Milton. He was fluent in French, and translated several technical books from French into English.

Baxter also had one habit the police found annoying—he seemed to take a particular delight in pointing out every mistake they made. He uncovered a few more during his inquest into Frances Coles's death, and his summation to the jury at the conclusion of that inquest completely demolished the case the police had built against Sadler.

Chapter 13

Mr. Baxter's Inquest

When Wynne Baxter accepted the post of coroner he joined a select group that could trace the history of their position back to Medieval England. The first coroners acted as representatives of the Crown, and they monitored court proceedings that concerned the king or queen. They also made sure that any property owned by an executed convict found its way back to the royal treasury. They had one additional duty—they looked into suspicious deaths, but only if the deceased belonged to the Norman ruling class. Other groups eventually took over most of those responsibilities until coroners were left with only one—investigating the causes and circumstances of all sudden, suspicious, or violent deaths that resulted from other than natural causes.

Nineteenth-century coroners conducted their probes at public inquests where a panel of male jurors reviewed all pertinent evidence and returned a verdict stating when, where, and how the death had occurred. If the jurors determined that it was caused by murder or manslaughter, they could name a suspect. A coroner's jury resembled a grand jury in that it could bring accusations but, unlike a grand jury, it could not hand down indictments. English coroners can still convene juries today, but they rarely do.

Mr. Baxter's Inquest

The only time a jury is required is when a death takes place in prison or in police custody, or if it might impact public health and safety.

Wynne Baxter decided to conduct his inquest into the death in Swallow Gardens at the Working Lads Institute at 137 Whitechapel Road, a location he had used several times before. Founded by a private citizen thirteen years earlier to provide working boys with an alternative to spending their free time in pubs and dance halls, it had a library, classrooms, a gymnasium, and a swimming pool. Fourteen prospective jurors had received summonses ordering them to appear at the opening session at four thirty in the afternoon on Saturday, February 14. Baxter could have impaneled as many as twenty-three jurors to ensure that he would have the necessary twelve votes to reach a verdict, but he knew jurors didn't receive any compensation for their time off from work, and an inquest such this would be adjourned and reconvened several times. As the victim's body had not yet been identified, the summonses to prospective jurors described her as "a woman unknown".

The proceedings had no sooner gotten under way than a minor furor erupted. Only eight of the men who had been summoned showed up, and the coroner had to fill the vacant slots with substitutes. A man named Albert Bachert stepped forward and volunteered to serve in place of one of the no-shows. Bachert was the chairman of the Whitechapel Vigilance Committee, and a spirited social activist. Somehow, his name seemed to have a way of cropping up quite often in connection with the Whitechapel murders.

Soon after the "Double Event" he wrote a letter to the *Pall Mall Gazette* and said he had met a suspicious-looking man in the Three Nuns Hotel in Aldgate a short time before the two victims were slain. The man had a black bag, and asked several questions about the habits of the loose women who frequented the bar. The following July Bachert was back in the news, right after the murder of Alice McKenzie. *The Scotsman* reported that someone attacked another prostitute a few nights after the assault on McKenzie but Bachert and several other men subdued the assailant and held him until the police arrived. Bachert took pen in hand once again right after the attack in Swallow Gardens and fired off a letter to *The Daily Chronicle*. This time he outdid himself. He not only claimed to have seen the murdered woman shortly before her death—he said he saw her twice! The first time she was in front of the Leman Street Railway Station. A short time later he saw her again, right outside his home—"only a few yards from the scene of the murder". It was during the second sighting that he heard her male companion threaten, "If you don't, you will never go home with another man." The couple then walked away in the direction of Swallow Gardens. He ended his letter by saying he had been called to serve on the coroner's jury that was going to look into the death. His letter appeared in the following morning's edition, the same day Wynne Baxter began to impanel the jury.

None of Bachert's statements were true. He didn't live "a few yards" from the murder scene—he lived several blocks away. Frances Coles was still in the doss house kitchen when he said he saw her outside the Leman Street Railway Station. And he hadn't received a summons to appear on the jury.

The coroner listened politely while Bachert offered to serve, and then turned him down. Bachert demanded to know why.

"Because I decline."

"You decline simply because I happen to be chairman of the Vigilance Committee, and you think I shall fully investigate this matter. I'm a ratepayer (a person who paid a regular utility bill and thus wasn't a transient) and I have a right to be on the jury."

The two men had a few more words before Bachert walked away. When he reached the back of the room, he shouted, "You will hear more about this."

The coroner ignored him and began to swear in the jury.

Mr. Baxter's Inquest

When he finished, he sent them to the mortuary to view the body. Bachert waited until they returned, then shouted, "It was only after you heard who I was that you wouldn't allow me to serve."

Baxter had had enough. "You be quiet, sir. If you don't, I will have you ejected."

Although he didn't let on, the coroner already knew about Bachert. He had received a letter just before the inquest was due to get underway. It read:

"Honored Sir,
The enclosed is Mr. Bachert's letter to the Daily Chronicle. You can see what he says, and what he intends to do. He is to the front again in this case. May I suggest that he be a little more truthful than he was in the last 'Ripper scare', I being the woman he so cruelly belied, and set the whole neighborhood in alarm."

It was signed *"The Woman He So Cruelly Belied"*. These was no enclosure.

The coroner began by calling Constable Ernest Thompson, the man who found Frances Coles lying in Swallow Gardens. Thompson described his beat in detail, and said there were three passageways under the railway tracks, or "arches" as he called them, linking Chamber Street with Royal Mint Street. He was supposed to check each one. It took him between fifteen and twenty minutes to walk the complete beat.

He continued, "I had not seen anyone about that night except the railway men. They are going about all night, and through this arch. The horses that are engaged in shunting have to go backwards and forwards through it. Just before 2 a.m. I went from Chamber Street through the arch to Royal Mint Street and back again ... I did not see anyone....

"The archway is much used by carts and horses belonging to the Great Northern Railway Company. Their stables, which are about thirty yards away from the arch, are in Chamber Street....

"When I turned into the passage I could see the woman lying under the arch on the roadway, about midway under the arch. I turned my lamp on as soon as I got there. I could not see it was a woman until I turned my lamp on. I noticed some blood. I saw her open and shut one eye. I blew my whistle three times. Constables 161 H and 275 H came to me in three or four minutes."

Baxter asked him about the footsteps he reported hearing when he turned into Chamber Street. Thompson said he hadn't seen anyone, but the footsteps "sounded like a person walking at an ordinary rate."

"How far were you from the arch when you heard them?"

"As near as I can tell about eighty yards. I heard no one going through the arch in the direction of Royal Mint Street."

"Can you say whether these footsteps had come out of the arch?"

"No, Sir."

"Then they may have been going right down Chamber Street?"

Thompson didn't think so. If someone had entered Chamber Street from Leman Street he would have seen them, or at least heard their footsteps, while he was patrolling Leman Street. He told Baxter he hadn't.

"Were there any railway people near the spot at the time?" Baxter asked.

"No. Some men were working in the stables, and that was the nearest spot where there was anyone about."

"Did anyone besides the constables come after you blew your whistle?"

"Some railway men arrived with horses after the officers were there."

Thompson's testimony left little doubt that someone had emerged from one of the three passageways and turned

Mr. Baxter's Inquest

left onto Chamber Street, and that he missed seeing whoever it was by only a moment or two.

The coroner called two more witnesses that night. Constable Frederick Hyde described the beat that took him along part of Royal Mint Street, Cartwright Street, Upper East Smithfield, and Trinity Square.

"Did anything happen to arouse your suspicion?" the coroner asked.

"Not until quarter past two. I was then in Royal Mint Street, and heard a whistle. I was then about two hundred and fifty yards from the arch. I went in the direction of the sound, which turned out to be in Swallow Gardens. There I found Constable 240 H, and alongside [him] was the body of a woman."

"When you first turned out of Royal Mint Street, could you see the constable?"

"I could see him immediately I turned down that street by his lamp, but I could also see him without it. At the Royal Mint Street end of the arch there is an ordinary street lamp. The place is lighter at night than in the daytime in the center of the arch."

"Within half an hour of this occurrence had you seen any man or woman there?"

"No."

"Is the place pretty well deserted at this time?"

"It is after one o'clock."

"If you were standing at the end of the arch do you think you could see a body lying in the center of the arch?"

"I do not think I could from the Royal Mint Street end of Swallow Gardens."

"I presume you heard no cry for assistance during the previous half hour?"

"No, Sir."

Constable George Elliott was the last man called. He said he was on plainclothes duty in front of Baron Rothschild's refinery on Royal Mint Street when he heard Thompson's whistle at quarter past two. Baxter asked him

CARROTY NELL

if he saw or heard anything unusual.

"Nothing unusual attracted my attention. Plenty of men and women passed through Swallow Gardens up to 12:30 a.m. I don't recollect seeing anyone pass after that time."

"If there had been any cry for help from the archway would you have heard it?" Baxter asked.

"I would have heard it; it was so quiet."

At that point the coroner decided to adjourn the proceedings for a few days. One of the jurors objected: "The inquest has been opened on the body of a woman unknown. Ought we not, before adjourning, have some evidence of identification?"

Baxter said no. "We made a mistake once. At the first hearing the victim was identified as being a certain person; but she was afterwards found to be someone else." He was referring to the embarrassing mistake made during the inquest into the death of Elizabeth Stride.

Coroner Baxter was back at work two days later, presiding over another inquest. That one concerned a death at a Spitalfields lodging house. As Baxter looked out at the prospective jurors, he couldn't have helped but notice a familiar face. Albert Bachert, the man who had been so anxious to serve on the Frances Coles inquest jury, was among those who had been summoned. This time he was successful, and Baxter swore him in as a juror—something he soon came to regret.

At one point during the proceedings Bachert made a comment that Baxter considered inappropriate, and he told him he didn't want to hear anything like that again.

"You were very nasty to me on Saturday, and I've got a nasty name now because of it," Bachert replied.

Baxter said, "I don't know you. I never heard your name before last Saturday."

"Why wouldn't you let me serve on Saturday?"

"Simply because you weren't summoned. I don't have any feeling against you."

Mr. Baxter's Inquest

"Thank you. I'm much obliged."

The two clashed again before the inquest ended. While the other jurors were going over the evidence they had heard, the coroner noticed that Bachert wasn't paying attention. Instead, he was scribbling on a piece of paper.

"I don't know what you're doing, Mr. Bachert."

"I do. We're getting the verdict ready."

Baxter continued, "If you can't agree, I'll adjourn the case to the Central Criminal Court and take the judge's opinion."

A short time later, Baxter asked for a show of hands. Eight members of the jury thought the death was from natural causes; six disagreed.

"Unless twelve of you agree, I'll adjourn the inquest, but I want you to remain here for the rest of the day and try to come to a decision."

Bachert said, "But we'll be able to go out?"

"Certainly not."

The Corner told two constables to make sure the jurors stayed in the room and didn't get anything to eat or drink, and then got up and left. Two-and-a half hours later the jury reached a verdict. The death was from natural causes.

The inquest into Frances Coles's death was reconvened on Tuesday morning, February 17. Baxter made a few announcements before the proceedings got underway. The police had taken a suspect named James Sadler into custody, he declared, and they had formally charged him with the murder of Frances Coles. As a result, the jurors would have to look into his movements as well as those of the deceased. There was another change. A man named Charles Mathews would be taking part in the proceedings. Mathews was the public prosecutor who would present the evidence against Sadler when his case came to trial in criminal court. While permissible under law, the arrangement was so unusual that it was almost unheard of. The first-hand knowledge gained during the inquest would give Mathews a tremendous advantage with his prosecution.

It didn't take Mathews long to get involved. He took charge of questioning the first witness, James Coles, the father of the deceased. Coles confirmed that the body in the Whitechapel Mortuary was his youngest daughter Frances, and added, "and near as I can say she was twenty-six years of age." He continued, "I last saw her alive on Friday, the sixth of February, when she came to see me. She was in the habit of coming to the workhouse every Friday."

"Where was she living?" Mathews asked.

"She deceived me about that," Coles replied.

"Well, we won't go into that right now. Where did she tell you she was living?"

"At 42 Richard Street, off Commercial Road."

Coles said his daughter had developed calluses on the knuckles of her left hand while working at Hora's, and had a peculiar mark on one ear where an earring had apparently been torn away. That had happened about three or four years earlier. He concluded his testimony by stating, "On Friday, when I saw her, she promised to come again on Sunday, but she did not, and I never saw her alive again. She generally used to come on Sundays and go to church with me."

Baxter told him a charity called The Common Lodging House Mission had offered to pay for his daughter's funeral, and asked if he was willing to accept their offer.

"I would be only too pleased to do so, sir," Coles replied.

James Coles was off by five years when he guessed that his daughter was twenty-six. That guess was never challenged, and as a result every document and publication, from her death certificate, to contemporary newspaper accounts, to the numerous books and articles written about Jack the Ripper, continued to perpetuate that error.

Mary Ann Coles followed her father to the witness stand. Frances's oldest sister was thirty-eight and lived in a rooming house at 32 Ware Street in Shoreditch. Mary Ann

Mr. Baxter's Inquest

testified that she too had identified the body and told jurors, "I haven't seen her since Boxing Day. She was in good health then, but very poor. At her request I gave her some bread and butter and tea. She told me she was living with a widow at Richard Street. I noticed the mark on her ear. Before she left I gave her a dress, the same dress I saw on Sunday when I went to the mortuary. The hat trimmed with crepe and the long black jacket I know she bought."

The coroner asked if she knew Frances had left Mr. Hora.

"No, I did not. She said they were short of work in the winter, and she could only earn from six shillings, tu'pence to seven shillings a week."

One of the jurors was curious whether she had ever visited Frances at Richard Street.

"No. I never called at Richard Street and I didn't know she didn't live there. I never saw any of her friends. She always came to me alone."

She ended her testimony by telling the jurors "I don't think she used to drink."

The following day a few newspapers had Mary Ann making another statement that morning—a rather startling one. They said she testified that Frances told her, apparently during their last meeting on Boxing Day, that she buried a child three years before, and that the little girl was responsible for the tear in her ear. That information appears to be incorrect. Newspapers whose reporters attended the inquest, like *The Times*, the *East London Advertiser*, and the *East London Observer*, made no mention of Frances having a child. Nor do any of the surviving police reports. James Coles had just completed his testimony only a few minutes earlier, and he was almost certainly still in the room. During that testimony he described the injury to Frances's ear, and told the jurors he wasn't sure what had caused it, but he thought an earring had been torn off. He never said anything about Frances having a child. A great many newspapers in Great Britain used the Press Associa-

CARROTY NELL

tion report as the source of their next day's coverage of the inquest, and many of them copied that report practically verbatim, but only a handful of them mentioned the little girl. Either most editors suspected it was wrong and chose not to print it or, more than likely, the wire service realized they had made a mistake and sent out a corrected version. Without knowing the child's name along with her birth date and location, it is impossible to prove or disprove her existence. In any event, several of the statements Mary Ann Coles made on the witness stand that day appear to be untrue. They will be taken up in another chapter.

Peter Hawkes, who waited on Frances in his mother's hat shop, described the events that took place. When a juror asked if she was sober, Hawkes said, "She was what I should call 'three sheets to the wind' ". A burst of laughter rippled through the crowded room.

In response to a question by Baxter, Hawkes said he had gone to the mortuary and could confirm that the hat he was shown was the same one he had sold the deceased.

"I went to the police station on Leman Street on Saturday," he added, "and there saw a number of men."

Mathews asked, "From among those men did you identify the man who looked through your shop window on the 12th?"

"Yes."

"And that man was Sadler?"

"I believe so. I read in the newspaper that it was he."

Baxter stepped in, "Have you not seen Sadler and had Sadler pointed out to you since?"

"No."

"Then I am afraid your evidence will not connect the two."

Mathews assured Baxter that he would prove later on that Sadler was the man Hawkes had identified.

Two more witnesses were called that day—both had connections with the doss house called Spitalfields Chambers. Charles Guiver was the night watchman. When Baxter

Mr. Baxter's Inquest

learned that he hadn't seen the body, he sent him over to the mortuary, and then called a man named Samuel Harris.

Harris testified that he lived at Spitalfields Chambers and spoke of seeing Frances and Sadler in the kitchen Thursday night. He also said he helped the police locate Sadler on Saturday morning.

"What condition was he [Sadler] in when you saw him in the kitchen?" Baxter asked.

"He was intoxicated."

"And on Saturday?"

"He looked half and half."

Guiver had returned while Harris was testifying, and Baxter recalled him when the latter had finished. He confirmed that the body was the woman he knew as Frances, and continued,

"I remember her coming in on Wednesday night about ten or ten thirty. She was with Sadler. I first saw her standing by the office door. Sadler was standing at the bottom of the staircase. I showed them upstairs to their room. They remained in bed until after nine o'clock on Thursday morning. I did not see them go out. About ten o'clock at night I saw Frances come into the kitchen drunk. She went and sat on a form near the fireplace, and rested her head on the table. Sadler came in and said two men on Thrawl Street had robbed him. They took his watch and three shillings, sixpence. His face was bleeding, and I advised him to go out into the yard and wash the blood off. He went, and when he came back he looked as if he had been thrown down and got the gravel rash. I did not notice any blood on his clothes. He began wrangling with the lodgers in the kitchen and creating a disturbance. He said he had given Frances a shilling previously to pay for the bed."

Mathews asked what time he turned Sadler out.

"A little before midnight."

"How long did Frances remain there?"

"Till one thirty or one forty five. She was in the kitchen all the time."

CARROTY NELL

"Are you sure of the interval of an hour or so between Sadler going out and Frances going out?" Baxter asked.

"Quite sure. I saw her go through the passage towards the street door."

There were two points on which Harris and Gyver disagreed—the time Frances arrived in the kitchen and the time she left. Harris said she was already in the kitchen when he arrived at eight o'clock. Gyver said she came in at ten. Harris testified that she left shortly after twelve thirty while Gyver said it was between one thirty and one forty five when she left. Testimony in the days to come showed that Gyver came closer to giving the correct time of Frances's arrival while Harris was more accurate in noting the time she left. Discrepancies like this surfaced time and time again as the inquest plodded on. They annoyed Baxter; Mathews didn't seem to care. "You can't expect the times to be exact. It's near enough for our purpose. If we are to go so minutely into the times, there will be no end to the inquiry," he later told Baxter.

Mathews had a few more questions for Guiver. "Did you see Sadler come back that morning?" he inquired.

"Yes, just after three o'clock. I know the time, as I was going to call a man up to go to his work and had just looked at the clock."

"Did Sadler knock at the door?"

"The door was open. I was sweeping up, and he asked me to let him come into the kitchen. I said, 'I have no power, you must ask the deputy,' Blood was running down his face, and he said he felt faint."

"What did he say then?"

"He said, 'I have been knocked about and robbed in the Highway.' I said, 'What, have you been at it again? I thought you were robbed of three shillings, sixpence in Thrawl Street, and that was all you had.' He said, 'Well, they thought I had some money about me, but I had none.' The deputy then opened the office window and asked what he wanted, and he said, 'Let me go into the kitchen; I feel so

Mr. Baxter's Inquest

faint.' The deputy refused to allow him to go, and he then asked me again. I told him I could not, and advised him to go to the London Hospital and get his head seen to. I did not notice any blood on his clothes. His clothes were dirty, as though he had been on the ground again. I went down into the kitchen, and Mrs. Fleming called me shortly afterwards and told me to put Sadler out. I went towards him, but he walked out of his own accord. That was about half past three."

When Guiver stepped down, Baxter told the jurors that Mr. Mathews thought they should adjourn.

Another name was added to the growing list of participants when the inquest reconvened at ten o'clock Friday morning, February 20. It was the longest session of the five, lasting over seven hours. Fifteen witnesses testified that day. A man named H. H. Lawless, of the law firm Wilson and Wallace, sat in on the proceedings as legal counsel to James Sadler. Many reports claim that Sadler's union, the Stokers' and Firemen's' Union retained the firm after Sadler complained that the police were withholding evidence that could clear him. In reality, the popular evening newspaper *The Star* bore most, if not all of the cost.

Once again there was disagreement as to the time something took place. Anne Shuttleworth was the first witness called that morning. She said Frances came into her husband's restaurant at five o'clock. The next witness was William Steer, the head barman of The Bell, a pub on Middlesex Street. He was positive that Frances and Sadler didn't leave his establishment until five thirty.

Mrs. Shuttleworth also stated that Frances and Sadler were perfectly sober when they had their dinner, while Sarah Treadway, the landlady of the Marlborough Head pub on Brick Lane said Frances was sober when the couple came in a short time later, but she thought Sadler had been drinking.

Sadler's attorney asked her, "If either of the parties had

been drunk you wouldn't have served them?"

"No, we should not."

Sarah Fleming, the deputy of Spitalfields Chambers, testified that it was ten thirty on the night of February 12 when Frances came in. She said Sadler arrived a half hour later. She was also sure Frances left around midnight. Mathews asked if Sadler had come back later that night. She said he had, at 3 a.m., and wanted to know if Frances was still there. She told him Frances had left hours earlier.

"Was my client sober at the time?" Sadler's attorney asked.

"No. He was very drunk," she replied.

Much of the day's testimony concerned Sadler's activities during the crucial period between 11:30 p.m., when he left Spitalfields Chambers, and 3 a.m., when he returned. What he did right after he left the lodging house is unknown, but he eventually made his way to the St. Katherine Docks and tried to board his ship. The guard at the gate thought he was too drunk and refused to let him pass. Shortly afterward he collapsed on the pavement. A Metropolitan Police constable named William Bogan found him on the ground and told him to get up and move on. A few workmen were leaving the docks at the time, and they walked over to see what was going on. One of them offered to give Sadler the four pence he needed for a night's lodging.

"I don't want your money, you dock rats," he shouted.

Sadler struggled to get to his feet while he continued to insult the workmen standing nearby. As soon as he was able to stand up, Constable Bogan turned and walked away even though it was apparent that a fight would break out. His superiors later criticized him for not taking Sadler into protective custody. A few moments after Bogan left, Sadler took a swing at one of the dockworkers. The man easily dodged the blow but one of his companions, a man named John Dooley, retaliated by punching Sadler hard enough to knock him down. Sadler hit his head on the gate as he fell

Mr. Baxter's Inquest

Anne Shuttleworth (l), Sarah Fleming

Lloyd's Illustrated Newspaper, March 1, 1891

© The British Library Board
Used with Permission

CARROTY NELL

and began to bleed. Dooley kicked him in the ribs a few times before the other men stepped in and broke up the fight.

Dooley and his friend then left and headed to a doss house called the Melbourne Chambers. They went into the kitchen as soon as they arrived. About ten minutes later Sadler staggered in and asked if could have a bed. He was so drunk he didn't recognize either man. The landlord took one look at him and he told him to get out. That was about quarter of two.

Fifteen minutes later Constable Bogan came upon Sadler once again. This time he was across the street from the Mint, talking with Metropolitan Police Sergeant Wesley Edwards. Bogan approached them and heard Sadler saying he had been beaten at the St. Katherine Docks.

Edwards told the jury, "I walked with him [Sadler] about thirty yards in the direction of the Minories. I parted from him soon after the clock struck two, and it would take him about three minutes to walk from there to the scene of the murder."

Constable Frederick Hyde, one of the men who responded to Thompson's whistle in Swallow Gardens, also saw Edwards talking with Sadler, and be confirmed Edwards's statement that it was just after two when Sadler walked away.

When Constable Bogan took the stand, he painted an entirely different picture. He said it was at least ten minutes past two, maybe even twelve minutes past, when Sadler left. He also testified, "Sergeant Edwards only walked about seven yards with the man and then came back to me."

Mathews asked him, "When you left the man [Sadler] outside the Mint, could he have got to Swallow Gardens without passing you?"

"The only way would be if he went up Sparrow Court to Royal Mint Street. If he had gone along the Minories he would have passed me."

"How long would it take for a man to walk there from

Mr. Baxter's Inquest

where you left him?"

"It is about a five minute walk."

"For a sober man?" one of the jurors asked.

"Yes,"

Bogan's estimate of the time it would take to reach Swallow Garden was a little too generous. Sergeant Edwards was closer with his three-minute estimate—if the person were sober. However all three men testified that Sadler headed toward the Minories (i.e. not toward Swallow Gardens) when he left. If Hyde and Edwards were correct as to when Sadler walked away, he still might have had enough time to reach the murder scene by taking a short cut through Sparrow Court. If Bogan's account was correct, he couldn't have done so, even if he were sober.

Once again, Baxter was concerned about the discrepancy in the time. Mathews didn't seem to care. While he listened to the three policemen testifying about their encounter with Sadler, it must have dawned on him that if he were to go forward with Sadler's prosecution, he would have to overcome a major obstacle. Regardless of the discrepancy as to when he walked away, three Metropolitan Police officers had placed an extremely drunken James Sadler in front of the Mint less than fifteen minutes before Frances Coles was killed. Admittedly, that put Sadler near the murder scene, but it also raised a serious problem. There were only two ways to enter Swallow Gardens— from Royal Mint Street or from Chamber Street. The Royal Mint Street entrance was the closer of the two—about five hundred yards from where the policemen encountered Sadler. Even though he was so drunk that a half hour earlier he could barely stand, Sadler could have reached the Royal Mint Street entrance by going through Sparrow Court, at least if the timeline given by Edwards and Hyde was accurate. That drunken condition, however, would make it far less likely that he could have gotten all the way around to the entrance on Chamber Street. The obstacle Mathews would face was that Constables Hyde and Elliott

CARROTY NELL

had already made it clear in their testimony that they hadn't seen anyone on Royal Mint Street near Swallow Gardens for some time prior to the murder. What were the chances that someone in Sadler's condition would be able to stagger along the practically-deserted street without being spotted by either of the two policemen, especially Elliott, who was on plainclothes duty on Royal Mint Street the whole time, in clear view of the entrance to Swallow Gardens? The killer must have entered Swallow Gardens from Chamber Street, but Sadler, in his drunken condition, almost certainly didn't have enough time to get to Chamber Street. The thought must have occurred to Mathews that maybe, just maybe, the police had arrested the wrong man!

It was probably just a coincidence, but it's worth noting that Sergeant Edwards received a coveted promotion shortly afterward, while Bogan's reaction to being criticized for not taking Sadler into protective custody resulted in his being transferred to another division for using abusive and threatening language toward a superior officer. The target of his abuse was none other than Sergeant Edwards! Several months later Bogan was dismissed from the force for assaulting a shopkeeper after refusing to pay for food he had ordered while on duty.

The coroner called a few more witnesses that afternoon. Constable Arthur Sharp said he spotted Sadler on Whitechapel Road about three thirty—a half-hour after he heard of the murder. Sadler was still drunk. Sharp patted him down looking for a weapon but didn't find one.

William Fewell was the last witness to testify that day. Fewell worked in the London Hospital Receiving Room and treated the wounds on Sadler's face and scalp when he came in about quarter of five in the morning on February 13. Sadler apparently didn't remember being knocked down and hitting his head on the gate at the St. Katherine Docks. When Fewell asked him how he got hurt, he replied, "I have been with a woman. She is a very decent woman, but she did me. I wouldn't have minded that, but they knocked

Mr. Baxter's Inquest

me about."

Fewell asked how much he lost.

"Seven or eight shillings and my watch."

Fewell's testimony was significant for two reasons. It showed that Sadler was so drunk he couldn't remember being kicked in the ribs at the St. Katherine Docks. It also confirmed what until then had only been a suspicion—Sadler might have had a motive. He apparently thought Frances had set him up to be mugged, or at least he thought so until he sobered up.

It was quarter past five when Fewell stepped down, and Baxter decided to call an end to the day's proceedings. They would be taken up again on Monday at eleven o'clock.

The fourth session of the inquest began with the testimony of two men—the manager of a coffee house on Whitechapel Road, and one of his waiters. Both thought Sadler was still drunk when he came in at six thirty on the morning of the murder.

A man named Frederick Smith testified next. Smith was a waiter on Tower Hill, and he happened to look out the window about five minutes to two and saw Sadler talking with two constables. He continued to watch until Sadler walked away with one of the men.

"Did they walk about twenty yards?" Sadler's attorney asked.

"Not that I know of," Smith replied.

His answer supported Constable Bogan's claim that Sergeant Edwards had not, as he testified, accompanied Sadler for some thirty yards. It did, however, confirm Edward's estimate of the time. "I cannot fix the time of his leaving, but I am certain he was not there more than five minutes," Smith testified.

Joseph Haswell was called next. He spoke of the events at Shuttleworth's that led to his putting Frances out, and he told the jurors she was a regular customer. Baxter asked if she was sober.

CARROTY NELL

"She was tipsy, but she knew what she was about. She was a very wide woman."

That caused a wave of laughter to ripple through the room, for *wide* could be taken two ways—a sarcastic implication that she had big hips or, as Haswell undoubtedly intended, short for "wide awake". The latter implied that a person was crafty or clever. Today we'd be more likely to say "street smart".

Sadler's attorney asked him if he was sure the clock was correct.

"The clock is set right once a week," Haswell said. "Mr. Shuttleworth put it right last Tuesday when it had lost a quarter of an hour."

One of the jurors said, "If the clock was a quarter of an hour slow it would be two o'clock when the woman left."

"I am sure it was right, as it was timed by a public house clock the night before, at eleven."

Two key topics were covered that day. Duncan Campbell described the events surrounding his alleged purchase of a clasp knife from James Sadler on the morning on the murder, and Drs. Oxley and Phillips described the results of their examinations of the victim's body. Campbell testified first.

He said Sadler came into the Sailor's Home on Well Street sometime between ten fifteen and ten thirty on the morning of the murder, and spotted Campbell near the fireplace. He said, "Mate, I am nearly dead. I have been out all night and I got robbed. I am dying for a drink." He asked Campbell if he wanted to buy a clasp knife for a shilling. Campbell looked at the knife and noticed it wasn't English. Sadler told him he bought it in America. Campbell decided to buy the knife, and he gave Sadler one shilling and some tobacco for it. According to Campbell, Sadler was inside the Sailor's Home for about five or six minutes.

Campbell heard about the murder a short time later. He took another look at the knife, opened the blade, and then washed it in a basin of water. By the time he finished, the

Mr. Baxter's Inquest

water had a reddish-brown tint to it. He dried the knife, put it in his pocket, and went back to bed. The following afternoon he was short of money and sold the knife for six pence—one half of what he paid for it the day before.

On Sunday evening he decided to tell the police about the knife, and he walked over to the Leman Street Police Station. Two sergeants listened to his story, and then accompanied him to the home of Thomas Robinson, the man who bought the knife. Despite Robinson's loud protests, the two policemen seized the knife as evidence. The three men returned to Leman Street. Soon afterward, the police brought Campbell to the basement where about fifteen or sixteen men stood in a semicircle. They asked him to pick out the man who had sold him the knife. Campbell told the jurors he recognized the man by his hat and by the scar over his eye. It was James Sadler.

Sadler's attorney had a few questions for him before he sat down. He reminded Campbell that, contrary to what he had just said, he couldn't recognize anyone in the lineup, and he asked him for an explanation. Campbell said the man who sold him the knife had a scar over his eye and he didn't see anyone in the lineup with a matching scar until Sadler took off his cap. He also said he had poor eyesight, and the light in the basement was dim.

Baxter asked him if he thought the reddish-brown tint to the water might have come from dried blood on the knife. Campbell said no, he never thought the discoloration was caused by blood. "The blade was rusty," he explained.

Thomas Robinson was called next. He confirmed the fact that he had given Campbell six pence for the knife, and told the jurors he used the knife the next day to cut up his dinner. Mr. Lawless asked him if the blade was sharp.

"No. I had to sharpen it on our whetstone. I couldn't cut the bread and meat with it before I sharpened it."

A man named Edward Delaforce testified that Sadler came into his office on Tower Hill at ten thirty on the morning of February 13 and gave him paperwork showing he was owed four pounds, fifteen shillings, one penny for his last voyage. Delaforce said it took him about twenty minutes to process the payment. Sadler remained in the office the entire time.

Once again, the timing was critical. Campbell claimed that Sadler came into the Sailor's Home between ten fifteen and ten thirty, and stayed for five to six minutes. If he came in at ten fifteen, he would have had enough time to reach Delaforce's office by ten thirty. Had he come in much later, he wouldn't have been able to do so.

Dr. Frederick Oxley, who made the first examination of the body, said that someone who was incapably drunk could not have made the cuts on the throat. He was also certain that the little clasp knife that Sadler had supposedly sold couldn't have made those large, clean cuts.

Dr. George Bagster Phillips, the divisional surgeon, gave a more detailed description of the victim's wounds. He and Oxley disagreed on one critical point. Phillips thought the knife in question might have been able to inflict the wounds on the neck.

Dr. Phillips stated, "On Saturday morning I made a minute examination of the incision in the throat. There was an external wound, the edges of the skin being not exactly cut through, there being a portion of about an inch long undivided. In my opinion, there were three distinct passings of the knife across the throat—one from left to right, one from right to left, and the third from left to right. Below the wound there was an abrasion, as if caused by a fingernail. Above the wound there were four abrasions, possibly caused by fingernails. From the position of these marks I opine that the left hand was used.

"There were some contused wounds on the back of the head, which I am of the opinion were caused by the head coming into violent contact with paving stones. I came to the conclusion that death had been almost instantaneous, occasioned by the severance of the carotid arteries and other vessels on the left side. In my opinion, the deceased

Mr. Baxter's Inquest

was on the ground when her throat was cut. I think that her assailant used his right hand in making the incisions in the throat, and that he had used his left hand to hold her head back by the chin; that he was on the right side of the body when he made the cuts. The tilting of the body to the left was to prevent the perpetrator from being stained with blood.

"There was a complete absence of any struggle or even any movement from pain, but it may have arisen from the fact that the woman was insensible from concussion.

"The knife produced would be capable of inflicting all the wounds found on the neck. It was not a very sharp knife that caused the wounds."

He added that he didn't think that the woman was drunk at the time of her death.

Baxter didn't ask Phillips to reconcile his guess that death had been almost instantaneous with Constable Thompson's sworn testimony that he saw the victim open and close one of her eyes, and that he detected a slight pulse several minutes after the attack. The coroner knew that estimating time of death wasn't Phillips's strong point. This wasn't the first time he had been mistaken in placing the time of death of a Whitechapel murder victim. When he examined the body of Annie Chapman he was sure she had been dead for two or three hours. She had, in fact, died only forty-five minutes earlier. Dr. Phillips also disagreed with another doctor by several hours as to when Mary Jane Kelly met her death.

As the afternoon wore on, Charles Mathews read the lengthy statement Sadler had given at the Leman Street Police Station on February 14. It contained a rambling and often disoriented account of his drunken wanderings from the time his ship docked on February 11 until he was brought in for questioning three days later. The document is too long to be included here. It is reproduced in full in the appendix.

When Mathews finished, the coroner called for an ad-

CARROTY NELL

journment and told the jurors they would only need to meet one more time.

The final session of the inquest took place on Friday, February 27. Like the others, it was held at The Working Lads Institute.

Thomas Johnson, a merchant seaman, testified that he was at the Sailors' Home about ten thirty on the morning of the murder when he noticed a man walk down the hall and leave. A few minutes later Duncan Campbell told him he had just bought a clasp knife from the man for a shilling. If Johnson's estimate of the time was correct, it might eliminate Sadler as he was in the shipping office at ten thirty. But Johnson said "about", and no one asked if he could narrow it down.

After Inspector Henry Moore and Detective Inspector Edmund Reid recounted their roles in the investigation, Mathews told the coroner he didn't intend to call any more witnesses. Mr. Lawless, Sadler's attorney, said he had a few he wished to call.

Ellen Calana, the last person to have seen Frances Coles alive, was the first witness Lawless called. Her testimony completely exonerated James Sadler.

Calana told the jurors how she met Frances and how Frances complained about having been thrown out of Shuttleworth's. As the two women walked along Commercial Street, a man approached them. Calana continued, "He was a very short man, with a dark moustache, shiny boots, and blue trousers, and had the appearance of a sailor. Because I wouldn't go with him, he punched me and tore my jacket. Frances was about three or four yards away at the time. We were both just getting over drunkenness. He went and spoke to Frances then, and I said, 'Frances, don't go with that man, I don't like his looks.' She replied, 'I will,' and I then said, 'If you are going with that man I will bid you goodnight.' "

She said she watched them walk down Commercial

Mr. Baxter's Inquest

Street until they reached Whitechapel High Street where they turned the corner, and then she went home to Theobald's lodging house on Brick Lane. Three hours later she heard of the murder and went to the Leman Street Police Station and reported what had happened.

Mr. Lawless asked her if she had ever seen James Sadler. She told him she had.

"Was he the man who accosted you?"

"No, it was not Sadler," she told Lawless.

Baxter asked her why she first told the police that it was shortly after three o'clock when she watched Frances walk away.

"I never told anyone that it was three in the morning when I saw Frances with a man."

Mathews reminded her that she had made that statement at the Leman Street Police Station.

"I made a second statement to the police, and I then said it was a mistake. It was not three o'clock."

She also admitted that she had been drinking on and off all day.

One of the jurors wanted to know how she knew it was two o'clock.

"The deputy at Theobald's Lodging House could tell the time I arrived there."

"Have you asked?" Baxter inquired.

"Yes. It was about two o'clock."

Lawless called three more witnesses. William "Jumbo" Fryday, the Great Northern Railway employee who had mistaken Royal Mint Street resident Kate McCarthy for the murder victim, reiterated his story and insisted the woman he saw about five minutes to two was not McCarthy, although he did admit that the couple were in her doorway. He said the woman was somewhat taller than McCarthy. Since Frances Coles stood only five ft. tall, that alone ruled her out as being the woman he saw.

Fryday admitted that he wasn't able to recognize the victim's body when he saw it in the mortuary, but he said her hat looked like the one he saw on the woman in the doorway. He also said the woman's companion was wearing a felt hat with a broad rim, and a dark brown overcoat with a velvet collar. For some reason he felt compelled to reassure the jurors, "I was perfectly sober."

Kate McCarthy and her fiancé, Thomas Fowles, followed Fryday to the stand. Their testimony left little doubt that they were the couple he had seen. They were in McCarthy's doorway for almost an hour, from one fifteen to two ten, and both saw Fryday when he passed by on the other side of the street. Fowles neglected to mention that he had told the police he thought Fryday had been drinking. He did say he was wearing a short jacket at the time, not an overcoat, and a black felt hat.

The timeline of the events McCarthy and Fowles gave during their testimony was somewhat different from the one they gave the police. McCarthy first told investigators she went upstairs at quarter of two. At the inquest she stated that it was almost quarter past two when she and Fowles parted. Mr. Lawless mentioned the discrepancy and asked her to explain.

"I made a statement to the police that I stood talking for half an hour and that it was a quarter to two when I got upstairs. The clock was striking so it must have been a quarter past two."

Baxter asked, "How do you know it was quarter past two?"

"Because Fowles says so. He looked at his watch."

Fowles had told Inspector Moore he arrived home about 2 a.m. On the witness stand, he stated he didn't get home until quarter past two. He was sure of the time because he had checked his watch.

Lawless reminded him that his testimony didn't agree with the statement he had made to the police. Fowles replied, "I told Inspector Moore it was about two o'clock when I got home. I did not tell him I looked at my watch. I have never mentioned the watch until today."

Mr. Baxter's Inquest

The discrepancy between the police reports and the inquest testimony, along with Fryday's insistence that the woman he saw was not McCarthy, and that her companion was wearing an overcoat, might seem to add to the mystery surrounding Frances Coles's death. It's almost certain, however, that McCarthy and Fowles were the couple Fryday saw in the doorway. At least Inspector Moore felt comfortable with that. In a report written on February 25, 1891, two days before their inquest testimony, Moore noted that the statements of McCarthy and Fowles "are most interesting and entirely clear up the mystery of the man with the billy cock hat who was alleged to have been seen talking to Frances Coles near the archway."

Thomas Fowles was the last of the fifty-five witnesses who testified over the course of two weeks. When he returned to his seat, the coroner suggested they take a short break for lunch. After lunch, Baxter rose and addressed the jury. He briefly reviewed the major points of evidence that had been presented over the course of the five sessions, and then gave his summation. There was no hint of impartiality when Baxter spoke. He obviously thought the police had made a mistake when they charged James Sadler, and he didn't hesitate to make his feelings known.

He began by pointing out that Sadler might have had a motive—he may have thought the victim had set him up to be mugged—but Baxter reminded the jurors that Sadler provided that information voluntarily. For some reason he didn't mention the fact that Sadler didn't show any sign of anger when he sat next to Coles in the kitchen of Spitalfields Chambers for almost thirty minutes only an hour or two after he was mugged on Thrawl Street.

Baxter admitted that the blood on Sadler's face and hands might lead some to the conclusion he had committed the murder, but he reminded the jurors that the sworn statements of several witnesses proved beyond doubt that the blood had come from the injuries Sadler received on Thrawl Street and at the St. Katherine Docks.

CARROTY NELL

He conceded that the knife Sadler allegedly sold to Duncan Campbell several hours after the murder was the most damaging piece of evidence that had been presented. The sale of the knife was critical, he said, since it supposedly took place only a few minutes before Sadler collected his wages for his last voyage. If he had indeed sold the knife, he might well have had some motive other than merely raising a shilling by selling it. Baxter told the jurors however that he thought Campbell "appeared to have been rather imaginative", and he reminded them that no evidence had been introduced to show there were blood stains on the knife. He also reminded them that Sadler wasn't carrying a knife when Constable Sharp searched him an hour after the murder.

One question Baxter didn't raise, but which must have occurred to the jurors, was whether Sadler would be so foolish as to stop and sell a piece of evidence to a total stranger—evidence so damning it could send him to the gallows—for only a pittance while on his way to collect almost one hundred times that much in wages. Wouldn't he be more likely to dispose of the incriminating evidence someplace where it could never be found?

"It's up to you," Baxter told the jurors, "to decide if his actions immediately following the murder were those of a guilty man." He reminded them that Sadler had inquired about Frances as soon as he entered the lodging house in White's Row at 3 a.m. When he discovered she wasn't there, he didn't pursue the subject further. His only concern was finding a place to sleep for the night.

"Is likely that a drunken man who had just killed a woman companion would immediately go to a place where she was well known and where she was recently seen in his company?" he asked. "Would he be artful enough as to casually inquire as to whether she was there? Would a drunken man be composed enough to skillfully avoid pretending ignorance by not making further inquiries, or expressing surprise, or asking for further information?"

Mr. Baxter's Inquest

Baxter reminded the jurors that Sadler was extremely drunk during the hours immediately preceding the murder, and told them they would have to decide if he could have gotten to Swallow Gardens in the four or five minutes unaccounted for. By choosing to use that estimate of the time, the coroner showed he apparently put more faith in the testimony of Constable Bogan than that of Sergeant Edwards and Constable Hyde.

"He would have had to do more than merely get to Swallow Gardens," Baxter continued. "He would have had to find the deceased, and all of his movements after leaving her in White's Row excluded the probability of his having made any appointment with her, for he had been struggling to get a night's rest at the docks, and at a lodging house close by."

"If Dr. Oxley's opinion was sound," Baxter reminded the jurors, "Sadler at the time of the murder was physically incapable of committing the crime even if he had desired to do so."

Like many other people, Baxter apparently suspected Jack the Ripper had struck again, for he told the jurors, "Whatever amount of anatomical skill might have been displayed in this case, the death of the deceased appears to have been carried out very similarly to those which preceded it. The deceased was in this, as in former cases, the worse for drink and of loose morals. The deed was done under such circumstances that any cry for help would have caused detection, and yet nothing was heard. The murder was committed while the woman was on the ground, and in such a manner that it was unlikely that the assailant would get soiled with blood. There was no apparent motive for the crime, no appearance of any struggle, and every reason to believe that death was instantaneous."

He left it up to the jurors to decide for themselves if a merchant seaman, so drunk he could barely walk, would have the knowledge and presence of mind to first tilt the victim's head to one side so the blood that was sure to spurt when he severed a major artery wouldn't spatter him.

It was ten minutes to three when the coroner wrapped up his summation, and the fourteen jurors withdrew to begin their deliberation. Thirteen minutes later they arrived at a verdict. The evidence they heard during the five sessions didn't link James Sadler to the death of Frances Coles. Instead, they agreed her death was caused by "willful murder against some person or persons unknown." They did add, however, that they felt "the police had done their duty" in detaining Sadler.

On Tuesday, March 3, the police brought James Sadler back to the Thames Police Court. This time he heard Charles Mathews tell Frederick Mead, the presiding magistrate, that he had decided not to go forward with the prosecution. It didn't come as any surprise. It would have been pure folly for Mathews to press on after the coroner's jury exonerated Sadler. Mr. Lawless, Sadler's attorney, understandably had no objection to the charge being dropped. The magistrate then told Sadler he was discharged. There must have been some confusion for Sergeant Baker, the jailer, had to tell Sadler, "Go away."

He left the prisoner's dock and followed his attorney into a small anteroom where they waited for some time, hoping in vain for the large crowd that had gathered outside to disperse. Sadler and Lawless eventually left the courthouse in a cab accompanied by a representative of *The Star*. As the cab pulled away, the spectators waiting outside gave Sadler a rousing, enthusiastic cheer.

Wynne Baxter and his deputy, George Collier, had conducted the inquests into the deaths of six of the Whitechapel murder victims, and they held five of them in the Alexandra Room of the Working Lads Institute. After a while the officials at the Institute began to get fed up with the crowds and the disruption that invariably accompanied

Mr. Baxter's Inquest

every one of the numerous sessions. When the inquest into Frances Coles's death came to a close, they told Baxter he'd have to find somewhere else to hold his proceedings in the future.

Chapter 14

Rest In Peace

The funeral service for Frances Coles was held at three o'clock in the afternoon on Wednesday, February 25 at the East London Cemetery in Plaistow. A local charity, The London Evangelization Society and Common Lodging House Mission, or *The Common Lodging House Mission* as most people called it, had volunteered to pay for the funeral, and they solicited donations to help defray the cost. Among those who contributed were a political discussion group known as the Bartholomew Club, the Freemasons Lodge of Instruction 781, and Lady Louisa Ashburton, a wealthy philanthropist.

It was chilly and foggy all morning, but the sun came out shortly after noon, and a brisk southerly wind helped push the afternoon temperatures into the low forties.

The procession got off to a late start. Officials weren't prepared for the large crowd that gathered outside the gates of the Whitechapel Mortuary, and it took the police almost fifteen minutes to clear a path so the open hearse could leave. A few minutes later three coaches pulled up behind the hearse. Frances's father and her sister Mary Ann rode in the first one while officials of the Common Lodging House Mission occupied the other two. A few policemen took up position in front of the hearse, and then the procession be-

Rest In Peace

gan a slow trek toward the cemetery four miles away. A large crowd of mourners—several hundred by some estimates—followed behind on foot. Most of them were women. Thousands of other people, some gathered in small groups, others standing alone, lined both sides of the route to the cemetery waiting to catch a glimpse of the coffin as it passed.

At East India Dock Road the policemen who were leading the way on foot turned around and headed back to the Leman Street Police Station. The drivers then picked up speed, forcing the mourners following behind to almost have to run to keep up.

The procession was still some distance away when cemetery officials began to grow concerned about the size of the crowd that was gathering. Some newspaper estimates placed it at several thousand; the *Bristol Mercury & Daily Post* went so far as to report that twenty thousand people were on hand. Many of those milling around were standing on railings or headstones to get a better view. Officials decided to close the cemetery gates as soon as the last coach passed. As a result, only a few of the hundreds of mourners who had followed the procession all the way from Whitechapel were able to enter. After a few tense moments, police officers stationed outside the cemetery managed to calm the angry crowd and prevent the situation from escalating.

The brief service was dignified and moving despite the distraction that a few hawkers caused as they walked among the spectators, trying to sell one-penny, souvenir memorial cards.

The cemetery chaplain, Rev. William Thomas of Victoria Park, was the principal speaker. He asked God to "bring to the bar of justice the cruel hand that smote the death blow so that right might be done" and "that which cried from the very ground for vengeance might be heard and answered." Rev. Thomas said that every heart there was in a deep sense of sympathy and pity, and he knew that everyone present felt, as he himself did, "the most righteous indignation toward the assassin whose hand committed the deed." Whether it was the man who stood charged on not, he prayed with all his heart that the murderer might be found and "visited with just condemnation." Shouts of "Amen" punctuated his homily several times.

Frances's father wept openly during the service, and he kept staring at the polished-elm coffin with its distinct white studded nails and brass plaque inscribed "Frances Coles, Died 13th February, 1891. Aged 26 years". At the conclusion, a Mr. Harvey from the Common Lodging House Mission told the gathering that Mr. Coles wanted everyone to know that his daughter Frances had never given him a single day's trouble in her life. When he finished speaking, the workmen who had remained discreetly out of view returned to the gravesite and slowly lowered Frances's coffin into a common, or public grave. It was still laden with several bouquets of white flowers even though many of the people in attendance had reached out and taken a flower or two as a memento. Several newspapers reported that Frances's father and her sister were both "visibly affected" as the coffin was lowered into its final resting place. Mr. Harvey then helped James Coles walk back to his carriage; a few of the women from the mission walked with Mary Ann.

No type of headstone or marker was ever erected to identify square 21, grave 19270, the site where Frances's mortal remains lie at rest. Contemporary newspapers described the locale as being "on rising ground, close to a young poplar tree". They didn't mention that the ground was unconsecrated.

As the years went by, the East London Cemetery began to face a problem that was also confronting many other older cemeteries—they were running out of space for burials. That shortage eventually became critical. Soon after the end of the First World War, cemetery officials came up with a

Rest In Peace

Frances Coles

Penny Illustrated Paper
February 21, 1891

CARROTY NELL

solution to help ease the shortage. They decided to cover the section where Frances was interred with a four ft. layer of soil and then bury additional remains on top of the existing ones. They didn't move or disturb any of the original remains during the process, but the resultant change in topography makes it impossible for a visitor today to pinpoint the exact location of Frances Coles's grave.

With her death, the victim count had risen to eight. It climbed no higher. Jack the Ripper never struck again. Frances Coles, the quiet little girl from Bermondsey who had tried so hard to keep her father from learning of her tragic fall, was his final victim.

Chapter 15

Upon Closer Examination

What really happened inside Swallow Gardens? A day or two after the murder almost everyone knew—or at least they thought they knew. Frances had led the way into the dark passageway; her companion followed close behind. When they were far enough inside so anyone who might happen to walk down Chamber Street wouldn't see them, he quietly took a knife from his coat pocket, reached out and clasped his left hand over her mouth to muffle any screams, and pulled his knife across her throat twice. The pathetic little creature slumped to the ground without making a sound. That's what many of the newspapers told their readers. The newspapers were wrong.

Drs. Oxley and Phillips knew right away when they examined the body that Frances was lying on her back when the killer cut her throat. They could tell from the way the blood spattered when his knife cut the carotid artery. Dr. Phillips was sure she was unconscious when that happened. "Insensible from concussion," was how he put it. He formed his opinion from the contusions he saw on the back of her head. He told the coroner's jury he thought they were caused by "violent contact with paving stones". When his remarks were made public, a new theory was born—the killer threw Frances to the ground before he cut her throat.

CARROTY NELL

That one has had a lot more staying power. People still repeat it today. But, just like the earlier one, it's incorrect. Despite what Dr. Phillips may have concluded, Frances's head didn't come into violent contact with paving stones.

For that to have happened one of two conditions had to be true—she was already lying on the ground when she was attacked, or she fell to the ground from a standing position. The first one can be dismissed right away. A quick encounter between a prostitute and client in an open or public area almost always took place in a standing position in a doorway or against a wall or fence, and gave rise to the slang term for the lowest class prostitute, *two-penny upright*. While no one would want to get their clothes dirty by lying down in dirt or mud, the main reason for standing was the need to be able to separate quickly in case a policeman came along.

The absence of any scrapes or bruises on her hands argues against the second condition—that she fell from a standing position. A person who loses their balance instinctively reaches out to try and break their fall, but Frances didn't do that. Other than the gash in her throat and the contusions on the back of her head, the only injuries doctors noted were a small scrape on her elbow, and some fingernail marks on her throat.

There's another valid reason to dismiss the idea that her killer threw her to the ground—Frances didn't make a sound. None of the victims did, with the possible exception of Mary Jane Kelly, and even in Kelly's case, the cry of "Murder" may not have emanated from her room. The two women who heard it weren't very concerned—they said it happened all the time. And some people suspect that Mary Jane Kelly was already dead when that muffled cry rang out about four o'clock.

Two people slept undisturbed while Martha Tabram died just outside their door. No one heard anything on Buck's Row the night Polly Nichols died even though an elderly woman and her three grown children were asleep in

Upon Closer Examination

a house almost right next door. The killer didn't know someone was in the adjoining back yard when he slashed Annie Chapman's throat, but that man didn't hear anything to arouse his suspicion. There were at least a dozen people in the International Workingmen's Club on Berner Street when the killer attacked Elizabeth Stride just outside. No one heard anything unusual. Any sound, even the slightest one, would have echoed across the empty reaches of Mitre Square the night the killer attacked Catherine Eddowes, but nothing disturbed the calm, still silence. The deputy of the Whitechapel Baths was still awake and reading a book in her room when Alice McKenzie was attacked and killed almost right below her window. She didn't hear a sound. Constable Elliott was sure he would have heard any cry coming from Swallow Gardens, but nothing emanated from that dark passageway—no cry for help, no scuffling, no sound of any struggle.

In every instance, the killer's first objective was to silence his victim. Throwing someone to the ground would have only caused that person to scream or shout. It wasn't violent contact with paving stones that caused Frances's injuries; it was violent contact with bricks—the bricks that lined the insides of Swallow Gardens.

She was almost certainly standing with her back against the wall, perhaps holding up her skirt, when the killer attacked. As Ripper historian Philip Sugden pointed out in *The Complete History of Jack the Ripper*, a woman in that position with her hands occupied was especially vulnerable. Ripper victims Tabram, Nichols, and Chapman all showed signs of having been choked into unconsciousness before suffering their fatal wounds, and officials suspected they were standing facing their killer when he reached out and seized their throats.

The killer obviously took Frances by complete surprise. She wouldn't have even seen his hand until it was almost right in front of her face. He shoved her head back against the brick wall as hard as he could, perhaps more than once—Dr Philips spoke of "contused wounds" indicating there were more than one—then caught hold of her, turned her around, and let her fall toward the center of the roadway. Because of the concave shape of the interior of the passageway, the back of her head was the only part of her body to make contact with the wall. The odd position in which she was found—lying on her back with one ankle crossed over the other—indicates she was already unconscious when she hit the ground.

* * *

Dr. Phillips observed three separate cuts on Frances Coles's throat. His exact words at the coroner's inquest were, "There were three distinct passings of the knife across the throat—one from left to right, one from right to left, and the third from left to right." Frances was the only Whitechapel victim to suffer that many injuries. Mary Ann Nichols, Annie Chapman, and Alice McKenzie had two left-to-right cuts across their throats. Elizabeth Stride and Catherine Eddowes had but a single left-to-right cut; Mary Jane Kelly, because her bed was against the wall, had a right-to-left cut. Martha Tabram's throat wasn't cut. Those who argue against Frances being a Ripper victim often use the third cut to support their position. But that additional cut, the right-to-left one, wasn't quite what many people think.

Dr. Phillips was supposed to note every injury, no matter how slight, when performing a postmortem examination. Superintendent Thomas Arnold, who headed the Whitechapel Division, was also expected to be accurate, yet he stated in his February 13 report that Dr. Phillips found two cuts. His exact words were "two cuts in the throat sufficient to account for death". Presumably, they were the left-to-right cuts, made as the killer pulled the knife forward. The cut made while pushing the knife away appears to have been superficial. The Central News Agency described it as "a slight cut, not even dangerous." Crouched

Upon Closer Examination

beside his victim in the darkness, the killer didn't see, and certainly didn't care, that while he was repositioning his knife to make a second cut, the blade penetrated the victim's skin.

* * *

Only two Whitechapel victims escaped mutilation, Elizabeth Stride and Frances Coles. Some people have suggested that the sound of Constable Thompson's footsteps interrupted Frances's killer. That didn't happen. The killer had no idea Thompson was nearby. In order to understand his moves after the murder, it is necessary to look into what he did prior to the killing. Ellen Calana watched Frances and the stranger walk down Commercial Street heading toward Swallow Gardens. Frances probably suggested the location. In order to survive, prostitutes had to be familiar with places where they were unlikely to be observed.

The police had long suspected that Jack the Ripper didn't need to posses extensive knowledge of the East End. He simply let his victims lead him to a spot of their choosing. An article in the *East London Observer* on Saturday, February 21, 1891, a week after Frances Coles's death, best sums up the situation:

> *"The class of women from whom the victims of the murderer, or murderers, have hitherto been recruited, are compelled by the exigencies of the degrading trade to know every secluded lot, and every unfrequented court, alley and bye-way in the district or part of in the district, where they ply that trade. They are as well acquainted - perhaps even better acquainted - with the extent and duration of the police "beats" in their neighbourhood as the local sergeant or inspector. When the measured tread of the police constable on night duty has died away on their ears, they can tell to a minute, almost to a second, at what time to expect it again. Secrecy is essential to their calling, and in securing*

CARROTY NELL

secrecy they are rendering comparatively easy the task of their would-be murderer. In other words, they are accessories to their own murders."

The easiest way to reach Swallow Gardens was to cross Whitechapel High Street and continue on Leman Street for a few minutes. A right turn onto Chamber Street, a two-minute walk, and they would be at their destination. That quick and direct way would also take them past the Leman Street Police Station—an unwise move for a prostitute and her client at that time of night. Instead, when they came to Whitechapel High Street, they turned right and then left onto Mansell, or perhaps Minories Street. By doing so, they passed behind the police station. That detour also brought them into Chamber Street from the other end.

After attacking Frances, the killer retraced his steps back out of the archway, turned left onto Chamber Street and right onto Mansell Street. A few minutes later he was back on the main streets of Whitechapel. He never heard Thompson approaching. If he had, he would have fled in the opposite direction toward Royal Mint Street. Thompson said the footsteps he heard were proceeding at "a normal rate", an indication that the killer wasn't in a hurry. He had no idea how close he had come to being detected. Once again, he was just plain lucky.

Frances may have escaped mutilation for the same reason Elizabeth Stride might have—the murder scene was too dark. It seems more likely, however, that her killer had no intention of mutilating her body, for if that was what he planned he wouldn't have let her lead him some forty ft. into the passageway, each step taking them deeper and deeper into the gloomy darkness, when he could have attacked her closer to the entrance where the illumination from the overhead gas lamp was much brighter.

Frances obviously wasn't the killer's first choice. Whether or not that played a part in his subsequent actions—slamming her head into the brick wall, walking away

Upon Closer Examination

from the body without making any attempt to mutilate it—is a question that hasn't received much attention.

* * *

Jack the Ripper historians generally take Mary Ann Coles's statements at face value. Close examination reveals that she didn't always tell the exact truth.

She is almost invariably described as a "charwoman", someone who cleaned houses or offices. That's the occupation she put down when she filled out the 1891 census. Specifically, she said she did "house cleaning". She may have been cleaning houses the first week of April when the census was taken, but she wasn't cleaning them in mid-February, when her sister was killed. Inspector Henry Moore spoke to her two days after the murder. He described her as "a woman of no occupation". Mary Ann also said she was twenty-eight years old when she filled out the census questionnaire. She was actually thirty-eight.

Many of her statements were obviously intended to protect members of her family. She told one reporter that her sister Selina was in Kent, working as a laundress, but she couldn't remember the name of the village. Selina Coles wasn't washing clothes or linens in Kent. Doctors had diagnosed her increasingly erratic and disturbing behavior as lunacy, and committed her to a mental asylum in Watford.

While testifying at the coroner's inquest, Mary Ann said the last time she saw Frances was the day after Christmas. She told the jurors that during that meeting she noticed the scar on her sister's ear. She didn't come right out and say it was the first time she saw it, and no one questioned her about it. But since the injury had occurred three or four years earlier, the implication was that she and Frances hadn't seen each other for some time before that meeting.

She also said that Frances told her she was living on Richard Street. James Coles never revealed when Frances told him. It could have been several years earlier when she moved to the East End. More likely however, it was in early January when her landlady at Wilmott's told her she had to leave. On December 26, when Mary Ann said she learned of the move, Frances was still living at Wilmott's. She didn't leave there for another two weeks.

The coroner asked her if she knew that Frances had left Mr. Hora's employment.

"No I did not," she replied.

That wasn't true. During the course of an interview with the Central News Agency, she said that Frances had been coming to visit twice a week since she quit her job at Hora's. She also told the reporter she had no idea how her sister earned a living.

Mary Ann made one mistake on the witness stand that day. Her testimony was carefully crafted to imply that the December 26 meeting was the only time she and Frances had seen one another for quite some time, but she also added, "I never saw any of her friends. She always came to me alone." It was a slip of the tongue, but it showed that she and her sister had been in more frequent contact than her other testimony implied.

Wynne Baxter was an astute individual, and he had little patience for witnesses who were being evasive. He listened as Mary Ann gave her testimony—and he said nothing! James Coles was still in the room when his daughter testified, and all Baxter had to do was take one look at his face and see the range of emotions it reflected—anguish over his youngest daughter's sudden, violent death; disappointment and sadness at the revelation of her sordid life; perhaps even a twinge of embarrassment at having been duped—and he would have known why Mary Ann was being less than honest. Who could blame him if he chose not to cause the frail, bewildered old man even more pain by openly suggesting that his oldest daughter was not only aware of Frances's deception, but had probably helped play a part in it?

Part Three

The Aftermath

CARROTY NELL

Chapter 16

Total Disagreement

The public prosecutor may have felt that the evidence against James Sadler was just too flimsy and circumstantial, but some people within the Metropolitan Police weren't convinced that he was blameless. They kept a watchful eye on his activities and whereabouts for almost two more years. He must have been aware of their lingering suspicions, and perhaps the fear of being re-arrested prompted him to go into virtual hiding for the next several weeks. A reporter from the *East London Observer* found him in a cheap, run-down lodging house in Shadwell. The fact that the newspaper took the precaution of hiring a former prizefighter to accompany their reporter when he went to interview Sadler shows how dangerous the area was. Sadler was bedridden with severe bronchitis and a high fever. The lengthy interview appeared in the March 28, 1891 edition. Like Sadler's statement to the police, it is too long to reproduce here. The entire article is included in the appendix.

Sadler continued to maintain his innocence, and insisted that Duncan Campbell lied on the witness stand. He also admitted that *The Star* had provided and paid for his legal counsel. That same legal team happened to be busy at the time preparing libel litigations on his behalf against two of *The Star's* competitors, *The Telegraph* and *The Standard*.

CARROTY NELL

Sadler must have made a quick recovery for he left Shadwell and moved into the Victoria Home, a doss house for men right across the street from the Princess Alice, only a few days after the interview was published. It was large by doss house standards, with about two hundred and sixty beds. Montagu Williams, in *Later Leaves*, had nothing but praise for the Victoria Home, telling his readers:

> *"In the building, there is a large, cozy reading room which is supplied with the daily papers and other journals. Adjoining the house is a lecture hall containing chairs, a raised platform, and a small organ. This is used for temperance meetings, and lectures on domestic and other subjects."*

The house rules specified that admission would be denied to anyone who was intoxicated, and that swearing and obscene language were strictly forbidden. Williams was delighted that at least one doss house took steps to exclude bad characters. One can't help but wonder why Sadler selected it. Whatever his reason, he probably didn't stay very long.

The lawsuits against *The Telegraph* and *The Standard* never came to trial. The parties reached an out-of-court settlement, and Sadler used the money to buy a chandler's shop at 121 Danbrook Rd. in Lower Streatham, a suburb five and a half miles south of the City. To many people's surprise, he prospered—at least for a while.

On December 10, 1891 Sarah Sadler stopped in to see Chief Inspector Donald Swanson. She told him her husband was being "verbally abusive" and had threatened her life several times. The only reason she could think of was that she had refused to work in the store. Swanson suggested she seek a restraining order, and told her she should give serious thought about whether it was wise to continue living with Sadler. After she left, he contacted the Superin-

Total Disagreement

tendent of the Streatham Police Station and asked him to have his men keep an eye on Sadler's house while walking their beat. A few weeks later Sergeant Francis Boswell filed a report that said Sadler rarely left his house and devoted all of his time to running the store. He did a good business, with daily receipts averaging £2.10.

Five months later Sarah Sadler went to the Lambeth Police Court and complained that her husband had threatened to cut her throat. The magistrate issued a summons directing him to appear in court the following week. At that session Sadler was ordered to post a £10 bond and released on his own recognizance with instructions to keep the peace with his wife for the next six months or forfeit his bond money.

Sergeant Boswell made the last entry in the police files on James Sadler on January 2, 1893. He said Sarah Sadler had called upon him the previous day and told him her husband was moving to Walworth Road in Camberwell. She wanted the police to continue keeping him under surveillance. From that point on Sadler's trail grows cold. Efforts to track his whereabouts after that have been unsuccessful.

* * *

James Sadler and Jack the Ripper may both have disappeared but, unlike Sadler, Jack the Ripper wasn't forgotten. In fact he was already well on his way to becoming a legend, for he had managed to accomplish the seemingly impossible—he had gotten away with it! That was a sore spot with many officials, and within a few years some of the men who had dealt with the case in one way or another began to speak out. Several appeared to be embarrassed or angry because of their presumed failure to apprehend the killer. Some attempted to diminish the enormity of the Ripper's crimes by lowering the number of victims. Others engaged in little more than self-aggrandizement—trying to convince the public that they hadn't been fooled and knew the identity of Jack the Ripper all along. As one official after another came forward however, many of them did little but contradict one another.

The first person to speak out was one of the most respected and, with eighty-four commendations and awards to his credit, one of the most decorated members of the Metropolitan Police. In May 1892, only fifteen months after the murder in Swallow Gardens, recently-retired Frederick Abberline said he believed that Mary Jane Kelly was the last of the victims to be killed by Jack the Ripper. While Chief Inspector Donald Swanson had overall administrative responsibility for investigating the Whitechapel murders, Abberline was the senior investigator on the street from the time of the Mary Ann Nichols murder until he was reassigned the following year. Abberline was undoubtedly sincere in his belief, and it's apparently just a coincidence that he had the Ripper murders coming to an end while he was still involved with the investigation.

Less than a year later, on February 3, 1893, the *Eastern Post & City Chronicle* ran a lengthy article about Metropolitan Police Superintendent Thomas Arnold who had just retired after thirty-eight years of service. Arnold said, "I still hold to the opinion that not more than four of those murders were committed by the same hand. They were the murders of Annie Chapman in Hanbury Street, Mrs. Nichols in Buck's Row, Elizabeth Stride in Berner Street, and Mary Kelly in Mitre Square." Arnold was clearly referring to Catherine Eddowes when he named "Mary Kelly in Mitre Square". Eddowes had given that name when she was released from the Bishopsgate Street Police Station a short time before her death. Arnold was the Superintendent of the Whitechapel Division when the murders took place, and it's significant that he didn't include the Mary Jane Kelly who was murdered in Miller's Court as a Ripper victim. He was the only senior police official to place the victim count at four.

Total Disagreement

The following year a high-ranking police official named Melville Macnaughten expressed his views in a confidential report that has since become decidedly controversial. In order to properly evaluate it, a person needs to understand the reason why Macnaughten penned that report.

Melville Leslie Macnaughten was thirty-six years old and had no background in law enforcement when he was named Assistant Chief Constable of the Metropolitan Police Department's Criminal Investigation Division in June 1889. His close personal friend James Monro, the Department's Chief Commissioner, made the appointment. The two had known each other for eight years, having first met in India when Monro, a district judge in Bombay, was presiding over the trial of some local men who were charged with rioting. Macnaughten, whose father was the Chairman of the British East India Company, managed his family's tea plantation, and had been injured during the uprising.

It didn't take Macnaughten long to gain a reputation as a "hands on" administrator, and he was often spotted at the scene of a crime. He had come aboard too late to involve himself with most of the Whitechapel murders, but he did visit the murder site in Swallow Gardens a few hours after the first investigators arrived and, according to some news accounts, he stopped by the Leman Street Police Station while Chief Inspector Swanson was questioning James Sadler. Other than that, the only significant action he appears to have taken in regards to the Whitechapel murders prior to writing his report was issuing a directive in 1892 that officially closed the files on the police investigation.

On February 13, 1894, exactly three years after the death of Frances Coles, a newspaper called the *Sun* began printing a series of articles on the Whitechapel murders that promised to offer "the solution of the greatest murder mystery of the nineteenth century." Police officials soon realized that the *Sun's* suspect was a man named Thomas Cutbush.

Cutbush was a paranoid schizophrenic. On March 5, 1891, when he was twenty-seven years old, he managed to escape from the Lambeth Infirmary where he had been taken after suffering hallucinations. A few hours later he stole up behind sixteen-year-old Florence Johnson as she walked along Kennington Park Road. Miss Johnson felt something hit her back, and turned around to see a man running away. When she got home she was surprised to find that her skirt been cut and that she had also suffered a slight wound. Two days later Cutbush struck again. On March 7, eighteen-year-old Isabel Anderson was walking with a friend on Kennington Park Road when she felt someone pull the back of her dress. At the same time she heard a tearing sound. She turned to see a man running across the street.

Cutbush was recaptured on March 9 and Florence Johnson had no trouble identifying him as her assailant. He was subsequently charged with wounding Miss Johnson and attempting to wound Miss Anderson. At his arraignment, the medical officer of the Holloway Prison testified that Cutbush wasn't able to understand the charges against him, and couldn't enter a plea. Cutbush was sent to the Broadmoor Criminal Lunatic Asylum where he remained until his death twelve years later. His records were opened to the public in November 2008.

Few people today consider Cutbush a serious suspect despite the fact that the murder string ended shortly before he was committed. That appears to be nothing more than sheer coincidence. He remains on the suspect list simply because no one has any idea of his whereabouts during the murder spree.

The *Sun* never named Cutbush as their suspect, but the articles left little doubt that he was the person whom they had in mind. Cutbush happened to have the same last name as Charles H. Cutbush, the retired Executive Superintendent of Scotland Yard, and Macnaughten mistakenly believed that he was the former Superintendent's nephew. He was so certain that he wrote: "Cutbush was the nephew of the late Supt. Executive." His use of the word late has

Total Disagreement

caused some confusion as the former Superintendent was very much alive at the time. In the nineteenth century, however, *late* was often used as a synonym for former.

Macnaughten must have been concerned that some people would think he was covering up for a high level official when he closed the case files, and he responded to the articles by preparing a confidential report dated February 23, 1894 in which he refuted the *Sun's* claims point-by-point. It was significant for two reasons. The first was his statement, "...the Whitechapel murderer had five victims—and five victims only." He went on to name them:

> Mary Ann Nichols
> Annie Chapman
> Elizabeth Stride
> Catherine Eddowes
> Mary Jane Kelly

The second was his conclusion, "the murder's brain gave way altogether after his awful glut in Miller's Court and he immediately committed suicide or, as a possible alternative, was found to be so hopelessly mad by his relations that he was confined in some asylum." He continued:

> *"No one ever saw the Whitechapel murderer; many homicidal maniacs were suspected, but no shadow of proof could be thrown on any one. I may mention the cases of three men, any one of whom would have been more likely than Cutbush to have committed this series of murders:*
>
> *(1) A Mr. M. J. Druitt, said to be a doctor and of good family -- who disappeared at the time of the Miller's Court murder, and whose body (which was said to have been upwards of a month in the water) was found in the Thames on 31st December -- or about seven weeks after that murder. He was sexually insane and from private information I have little doubt but that his own family believed him to*

have been the murderer.

(2) Kosminski, a Polish Jew and resident in Whitechapel. This man became insane owing to many years indulgence in solitary vices. He had a great hatred of women, especially of the prostitute class, and had strong homicidal tendencies: he was removed to a lunatic asylum about March 1889. There were many circumstances connected with this man which made him a strong 'suspect'.

(3) Michael Ostrog, a Russian doctor, and a convict, who was subsequently detained in a lunatic asylum as a homicidal maniac. This man's antecedents were of the worst possible type, and his whereabouts at the time of the murders could never be ascertained."

It was the first time that a police official publicly named someone as being a suspect in the Whitechapel murders. In time, two more names were added to the list. Those suspects will be identified a bit later on.

Even though several other police officials, including men like Frederick Abberline who actually worked on the case, later scoffed at Macnaughten's views, they have had a profound influence on the saga of Jack the Ripper, and his insistence that there were only five victims has become generally, although not universally, accepted. Those five victims are now commonly referred to as "the canonical victims".

Its important to remember that Macnaughten prepared his report for one reason, and one reason only—to discredit any suggestion that the man he thought was the nephew of a former high-ranking police official was also Jack the Ripper. The strongest argument in favor of Thomas Cutbush being the killer was the odd coincidence that the Whitechapel murders came to an end only a short time before his March 1891 committal to an asylum. Macnaughten obviously wanted to use every bit of persua-

Total Disagreement

sion he could muster, and that fact should be taken into consideration when contemplating his assertion that the Ripper's string of murders ended in November 1888, almost two and a half years before Cutbush was sent to Broadmoor.

* * *

On October 14, 1896, a letter arrived at the Commercial Street Police Station. It was written in red ink and stated:

Dear Boss,

You will be surprised to find that this comes from yours as of old Jack the Ripper. Ha Ha. If my old friend Mr. Warren is dead you can read it. you might remember me if you try and think a little Ha Ha. The last job was a bad one and no mistake nearly buckled, and meant it to be best of the lot and what curse it. Ha Ha I'm alive yet and you'll soon find it out. I mean to go on again when I get the chance won't it be nice dear old Boss to have the good old times once again. you never caught me and you never will. Ha Ha

You police are a smart lot, the lot of you couldn't catch one man. Where have I been Dear Boss you'd like to know. abroad if you would like to know, and just come back. ready to go on with my work and stop when you catch me. Well good bye boss wish me luck. Winters coming "The Jewes are people that are blamed for nothing" Ha Ha have you heard this before

Yours truly
Jack the Ripper

Inspector Henry Moore thought the handwriting looked suspiciously similar to the original Dear Boss letter and the Saucy Jacky card, and he noticed several instances where the same words also appeared in the earlier pieces of correspondence. He was puzzled and concerned about the "Jewes" phrase. The words were almost the same as the ones written in chalk on Goulston Street. Moore finally decided that, despite the strange similarities, the letter was probably just a hoax. His reasoning was that the person who sent the original letter and card had addressed them to the Central News Agency, while the latest letter was sent directly to the Metropolitan Police.

No one in the Metropolitan Police knew at the time that a man who later became one of the prime suspects in the case had returned to London after sailing to America soon after the murder of Frances Coles. His name was Severin Klosowski.

* * *

"We find the defendant guilty!." When these five words echoed through a courtroom on March 20, 1903, they brought an end to one of the most sensational murder trials in the early part of the twentieth century. A jury at London's Central Criminal Court had just found thirty-six-year-old George Chapman guilty of murdering his common law wife. When the police arrested Chapman they charged him with three counts of murder, but he was brought to trial on only one of them—the killing of Maud Marsh. Despite strong objections from the defense, the trial judge allowed the introduction of evidence that showed the other two female victims had died in a similar manner. His rationale was to discourage the defense from claiming that Marsh's death was accidental.

Four days later the *Pall Mall Gazette* quoted former Metropolitan Police Inspector Frederick Abberline as saying:

> *"I have been so struck with the remarkable coincidences in the two series of murders that I have not been able to think of anything else for several days past—not, in fact,*

Total Disagreement

since the Attorney General made his opening statement at the recent trial, and traced the antecedents of Chapman before he came to this country in 1888. Since then the idea has taken full possession of me, and everything fits in and dovetails so well that I cannot help feeling that this is the man we struggled so hard to capture fifteen years ago."

The name George Chapman was an alias. The convicted killer's real name was Severin Klosowski, and he was the fourth man to be named a suspect by an official of the Metropolitan Police.

Abberline also challenged Melville Macnaughten's credibility: "There are a score of things which make one believe that Chapman is the man; and you must understand that we never believed all those stories about Jack the Ripper being dead, or that he was a lunatic, or anything of the sort," he told the reporter.

Almost four years later Henry Cox, a Detective Inspector with the City Police, went public with his thoughts. They too cast doubts on Macnaughten's reliability. According to Cox, the prime suspect was a man five ft. six in. tall with curly black hair who had been confined at one time to a mental asylum. He owned his own shop in the East End. For some reason, he relocated that business several times. He also had the habit of taking long, solitary walks late at night. Cox's comments left little doubt that he thought the man was Jewish. Cox claimed he and his colleagues began to suspect the man after the murder of Mary Jane Kelly, and kept him under constant surveillance. The nightly strolls came to an abrupt halt when he realized he was being followed. The man was never arrested, Cox added, because the police couldn't come up with any evidence to conclusively link him with the murders.

Take away the part about having spent some time in a mental asylum, and Cox might well be describing Severin Klosowski, the suspect favored by Frederick Abberline.

CARROTY NELL

Their descriptions seem to match, Klosowski spoke Yiddish, he took long solitary walks late at night, and he operated a barbershop in at least two East End locations. No evidence has been uncovered, however, that shows he was ever confined to a mental hospital.

In 1910, *Blackwood's Edinburgh Magazine* published a series of articles written by Sir Robert Anderson, the retired Assistant Commissioner of the Criminal Investigation Division. They were subsequently released in book form as Anderson's autobiography entitled *The Lighter Side of My Official Life*. One of the *Blackwood's* articles contained a rather startling revelation—the former Assistant Commissioner knew the name of the elusive killer.

Anderson described the victims as "wretched" and "degraded", and he said the Jack the Ripper correspondence was the creation of a London journalist. The article's most sensational disclosure was Anderson's claim that Jack the Ripper was a Jew who was committed to an insane asylum. As proof, he claimed the only witness who ever got a good look at the man readily identified him as the killer. Anderson suggested that he had toyed with the idea of revealing the names of Jack the Ripper and the journalist who penned the hoax letters, but decided against doing so.

He was almost certainly thinking of Aaron Kosminski, one of the three men Melville Macnaughten had named, but while Macnaughten said no one ever saw Jack the Ripper, Anderson not only had someone getting a good look at the murderer, but also identifying him.

Anderson was one of the highest-ranking officials involved in the hunt for Jack the Ripper, and while his views may have gained some acceptance at the time, they have now been all but dismissed.

Sir Robert was nearly seventy when he wrote the article, and his memory of events that took place twenty-two years earlier had likely begun to fade. He might also have been merely trying to boost his own image. Valid arguments exist

Total Disagreement

to support both possibilities.

Stewart Evans and Donald Rumbelow, in *Jack the Ripper, Scotland Yard Investigates*, note that respected crime writer Hargrave Adam was surprised to find Anderson confusing the details of cases they were discussing during an interview. When he wrote the article for *Blackwood's*, Anderson apparently forgot he had written to the Home Office right after Frances Coles's murder, implying that he felt the Ripper was responsible for her death.

Anderson also apparently forgot that he had told a visiting American publisher in November 1889, almost a year after Mary Jane Kelly's murder in Mitre Square, that the rough character of the neighborhood would give a stranger "a much more lenient view of our failure to find Jack the Ripper, as they call him, than he did before."

Researcher Philip Sugden pointed out in *The Complete History of Jack the Ripper* that Winston Churchill, the Home Secretary at the time, reviewed Anderson's articles to determine if the former Assistant Commissioner had revealed any confidential information. Churchill reported back to the House of Commons that they "seemed to be written in a spirit of gross boastfulness," and added that the writer was "anxious to show how important he was."

In his autobiography, Anderson gives the impression of being somewhat arrogant—a man more comfortable giving orders rather than offering explanations. If he intended to mislead his readers, it wouldn't be the first time he practiced such deception. An incident at the height of the Ripper scare illustrates how he could be rather selective in what he chose to believe.

Less that six weeks after the brutal murder of Mary Jane Kelly in Miller's Court, the police came upon the body of a twenty-six-year-old woman in Clarke's Yard in Poplar. They soon discovered that the victim was Rose Mylett, a known prostitute. At first the police had no reason to suspect foul play. There were neither visible injuries nor signs of a struggle, and the victim's clothing hadn't been disturbed. It appeared to be simply a case of death from natural causes.

When Dr. Matthew Brownfield, the police surgeon, conducted his postmortem examination, he discovered a distinct mark where a cord had been tightly drawn around the victim's neck. Someone had choked her to death. Dr. Brownfield thought the killer stood behind her, slipped the cord over her neck, and pulled it tight to throttle her.

The site where the body was found was almost three miles from Whitechapel, and that distance, coupled with the fact that the victim hadn't been mutilated nor had her throat been cut, should have ruled out any possibility of her being a Ripper victim. But Mylett's occupation might lead people to think the dreaded killer had struck again. The Assistant Commissioner didn't want to take that chance.

Anderson didn't agree with Dr. Brownfield's conclusions, and he asked Dr. Thomas Bond, one of the men who examined the body of Mary Jane Kelly, to conduct his own postmortem examination. Bond happened to be out of town that day but his assistant, Dr. Charles Hebbert, undertook the task in his place along with Dr. Alexander McKellar, another police surgeon. Dr. Bond made his own examination of the body the next day. All three men concurred with Dr. Brownfield's finding. The victim had been strangled. Anderson summoned the three doctors to a meeting and, even though he had no medical training, told them why he felt their conclusions were incorrect. All three stood their ground. Later that day Dr. Bond decided to reexamine the body. After making his second postmortem examination, he changed his mind and said the death had been accidental. Rose Mylett had fallen and somehow choked to death on her stiff, velvet collar.

Two weeks later the coroner's jury returned their verdict on Rose Mylett's death. There was no doubt in their minds as to the cause—she was murdered by a person unknown. Anderson was furious when he learned of the verdict and refused to assign anyone to investigate the death, saying it would be a waste of time. He never changed his opinion.

Total Disagreement

Years later, when writing his autobiography, he still claimed Mylett had died from natural causes. If it hadn't been for the Jack the Ripper scare, he wrote, no one would have thought of suggesting she was a homicide victim.

A month after Anderson's article appeared in *Blackwood's*, retired Metropolitan Police Inspector Edmund Reid questioned Anderson's positions, and he challenged the former Assistant Commissioner to prove that Jack the Ripper was a Jew. He said it was never suggested at the time of the murders. He also took issue with a *New York Herald* report that suggested Alice McKenzie was the last victim. Frances Coles was Jack the Ripper's last victim, according to Reid.

Later that year another former police official disputed Anderson's claims. Retired London City Police Commissioner Sir Henry Smith, in his autobiography *From Constable to Commissioner*, took strong exception to Anderson's claim that the murderer was a Jew, and implied that it was little more than blatant anti-Semitism. He also ridiculed the title of Anderson's autobiography. saying there was nothing "light" about indicting a whole class of people (Jews). Smith even went so far as to suggest two books for Anderson's perusal: *Bleak House* and *The Bible*. Both of them, he claimed, provided examples of officials being duped by false messages—an indication that he thought Anderson had put too much faith in the chalked message about Jews that was found on Goulston Street.

Smith wasn't known for his humility. "There is no man living who knows as much of those murders as I do," he wrote, without mentioning that only one of them fell under his jurisdiction. On the other hand he could be refreshingly honest, readily admitting that the Ripper "completely beat me and every police officer in London ... I have no more idea now where he lived than I had twenty years ago."

On May 14, 1910, the *East London Observer* published an interview with Dr. Percy Clark. He was the assistant to Dr.

CARROTY NELL

George Bagster Phillips, and he had examined the remains of several of the victims. Clark's most surprising revelation was his opinion that only three of the murders were committed by the same person. Furthermore, he didn't believe the injuries inflicted on any of the victims indicated that their killer had any medical knowledge or training. When asked about the theory that the killer had committed suicide, he said it was mere supposition and he told the reporter he was sure the police never had the slightest clue as to the killer's identity. Clark was the only official to place the victim count that low.

In September 1913 former Chief Inspector John Littlechild added a new name to the list of suspects while corresponding with writer George Sims. The now-famous letter was unearthed by Ripper writer and researcher Stewart Evans and made public in 1993. In that letter, Littlechild points an accusing finger at an American, Dr. Francis Tumblety. He said Tumblety had been arrested on another charge and was free on bail when he fled to America. The murders ended when Tumblety left England, he claimed. Tumblety was the last suspect to be named by anyone who took an active part in the investigation.

Other names came up as the century progressed—some of them well known—but those names didn't originate with anyone who had a hand in the investigation. No less a personage than Prince Albert Victor, Queen Victoria's own grandson, briefly came under suspicion in 1962 even though he was known to be mild-mannered and well behaved. Any thought that he was the notorious killer was put to rest when official records revealed that he was nowhere near London when many of the murders occurred.

Somehow Queen Victoria's name continued to be linked to the murders. A 1973 BBC program implicated her personal physician, Sir William Gull, in a bizarre, concocted, Masonic/Royal Family plot. The producers ne-

Total Disagreement

glected to inform their viewers that Sir William was seventy-one years old at the time of the murders and in poor health—partially paralyzed after suffering a stroke the year before.

A 1988 television program that featured Michael Caine in the role of Inspector Abberline advanced a variation of the same plot, but with a different suspect—the prominent American actor Richard Mansfield who was appearing on the London stage in *The Strange Case of Dr. Jekyll and Mr. Hyde* when the Whitechapel murders began. The police never considered Mansfield a suspect although they did receive a letter naming him as the killer. The writer claimed that no ordinary actor could make the realistic transformation from respected doctor to cold-blooded killer that Mansfield did on stage. Only a true homicidal maniac would be capable of doing so, he wrote.

As the century drew to a close, a new suspect surfaced with the 1992 discovery of a diary kept by wealthy Liverpool businessman James Maybrick. From the faded pages of the diary a startling revelation unfolded—the unassuming cotton merchant was the infamous Jack the Ripper! Until that time the only notoriety associated with Maybrick was his untimely death in 1889 at the hands of his wife, Florence. According to the diary, Maybrick killed the five canonical victims along with two other unidentified women after being driven nearly mad by the chance discovery that his wife was having an affair with one of his closest friends. He vented his rage against women by attacking prostitutes, the most vulnerable targets he could find.

Maybrick's diary seemed just too good to be true. It was too good. Today it has been all but dismissed as a cleverly crafted hoax.

Chapter 17

The Suspects

To try and cover every person who at one time or another has been named a suspect in the Whitechapel murders would truly be a Herculean task. Christopher Morley, in his 1995 e-book *Jack the Ripper: A Suspect Guide*, gives thumbnail sketches of over two hundred of them. Seventeen were doctors; nine were women. Morley's list includes policemen and clergymen; even a king and a prime minister. The suspects range from the prominent to the obscure, from those who dwelled in palaces to those who slept in hovels. Some rubbed elbows with the most respected and prominent citizens of their time. Others were immigrants who spoke little or no English. Regardless of their place in society, be they rich man, poor man, beggar man, or thief, they share one thing in common—no shred of concrete evidence has ever been found that links any of them to the murders. At best, the evidence is circumstantial; at worst, it's often highly selective. Their names are on the list simply because at one time or another someone argued that they *might* be the Whitechapel killer.

Victorian police not only had more to gain by identifying the dreaded killer than today's arm chair detective does, they had a lot more to lose by not identifying him. The professionals who tried to track him down named five men,

The Suspects

and only five men, as suspects. Those men are the subject of this chapter.

Melville Macnaughten, as was noted, was the first official to publicly name a suspect. He did more than that—he named three of them. The first was simply "a Mr. M. J. Druitt". Macnaughten said he was forty-one, "a doctor, and of good family", and that he "disappeared at the time of the Miller's Court murder." He said Druitt's body was found in the Thames seven weeks later. "He was sexually insane," Macnaughten claimed, "and from private information I have little doubt but that his own family believed him to have been the murderer." Macnaughten was mistaken on several key points, and placing Montague John Druitt on the list of suspects might have been his most serious blunder.

Druitt wasn't a forty-one-year-old doctor; he was a thirty-one-year-old barrister who, for some reason, suspended his law practice and took a position as an instructor at a private boys' school in Blackheath. Macnaughten was also wrong in stating that he disappeared about November 9, 1888, the time of the murder in Miller's Court. Druitt made no attempt to hide in the days and weeks after the murder, and was seen by many people as late as early December. Furthermore, he doesn't come close to matching any of the descriptions of the man suspected to be the Ripper, and he played in a cricket match at Blackheath only six hours after the murder and mutilation of Annie Chapman in the backyard of 29 Hanbury Street.

Druitt took his life in early December, a few days after he was fired from his teaching position for what was termed "a serious offense". Investigators learned that he wrote to the school's headmaster soon after his termination, telling him he intended to take his life. The contents of that note have never been made public. He also left a note for his brother in which he wrote, "Since Friday (November 30, the day he was let go) I felt I was going to be

CARROTY NELL

Montague John Druitt

Named as a suspect in the Whitechapel murders by Chief Constable Melville Macnaughten in an 1894 report.

The Suspects

like mother, and the best thing for me was to die." Ann Druitt, his mother, had been committed to an insane asylum a few months earlier.

No one knows what drove Montague John Druitt to fill the pockets of his jacket and overcoat with rocks, and then leap into the frigid waters of the Thames, but the letter to his brother leaves little doubt that it was related to the incident at school and his subsequent dismissal. Whatever his reason, it almost certainly had nothing to do with the death of Mary Jane Kelly three and a half weeks earlier. Druitt may have hoped that by taking his own life he might keep an explosive scandal from being made public and thereby shield his family from embarrassment. Little did he know that a senior police official would misinterpret his actions, and tarnish the reputation he hoped to protect beyond belief by insinuating that he was a fiendish serial killer.

Macnaughten's second suspect was "Kosminski, a Polish Jew". Macnaughten wasn't the only man to consider him a suspect; two other police officials, Sir Robert Anderson, the former Assistant Commissioner of the Criminal Investigation Division, and former Metropolitan Police Superintendent Donald Swanson shared his view.

In his autobiography, Anderson wrote:

"One did not need to be a Sherlock Holmes to discover that the criminal was a sexual maniac of a virulent type, that he was living in the immediate vicinity of the scenes of the murders, and that, if he was not living absolutely alone, his people knew of his guilt, and refused to give him up to justice. During my absence abroad the Police had made a house-to-house search for him, investigating the case of every man in the district whose circumstances were such that he could go and come and get rid of his bloodstains in secret. And the conclusion we came to was that he and his people were certain low-class Polish Jews; for it is a remarkable fact that people of that class in the East

CARROTY NELL

End will not give up one of their number to Gentile justice.... I will merely add that the only person who had ever had a good view of the murderer unhesitatingly identified the suspect the instant he was confronted with him ; but he refused to give evidence against him."

Retired Superintendent Donald Swanson agreed with Anderson's sentiments. A relative who was looking through Swanson's belongings after his death spotted some handwritten notes in the margin of his copy of Anderson's autobiography. Among them was Swanson's notation that the suspect was identified "at The Seaside Home", and that he was soon afterward sent to the Stepney Workhouse, and then to the Colney Hatch Asylum, and that he died shortly afterward. Someone also added: "Kosminski was the suspect," but they used a different pencil, thereby raising the possibility that the accusation wasn't made by Swanson.

Macnaughten provided a bit more information on the suspect in the draft version of his report: "This man in appearance strongly resembled the individual seen by the City PC (Police Constable) near Mitre Square." For some reason, he chose not to include that statement in the finalized version.

The man they were writing about was Aaron Kosminski. He lived in Whitechapel and worked sporadically as a hairdresser. At the time of the Whitechapel murders he was in his mid-twenties. The main problem with his candidacy as a viable suspect lies in the fact that the statements made by Macnaughten and Anderson contain glaring errors.

Macnaughten relied solely on his memory when he prepared his report. In his 1914 autobiography he claimed that during his entire police career he never used a notebook or kept a diary. It's not surprising, therefore, that his report is laced with factual errors, and the section on Kosminski is no exception. His opinion that the occasional hairdresser "became insane owing to many years indulgence in solitary vices" is certainly questionable, as is his claim that Kos-

The Suspects

minski "had a great hatred of women, specially of the prostitute class, and had strong homicidal tendencies". The statement that "he was removed to a lunatic asylum about March 1889" is incorrect. Aaron Kosminski was committed to the Colney Hatch Asylum on February 7, 1891, almost two years later. Furthermore, none of his surviving medical evaluations, either from Colney Hatch or from the Leavesden Asylum to which he was transferred in April 1894, indicate that doctors felt he might pose any danger to others. He was apparently a schizophrenic—mild-mannered and completely harmless. That's not to say that he didn't have his peculiarities. He thought he heard voices in his head, and he refused to eat anything that someone else had touched. He also stubbornly refused to perform any type of work. The statement from the draft version of Macnaughten's report that Kosminski strongly resembled the individual seen by the City Police near Mitre Square is untrue. No member of the City Police, or the Metropolitan Police for that matter, saw any suspect near Mitre Square on the night of the murder.

Anderson was an administrator, more concerned with preventing terrorist-like attacks from Irish separatists than with the deaths of a few "wretched" and "degraded" women, as he called the victims. Swanson, although a seasoned investigator, relied primarily on reports sent to him by men in the field. He was also a personal and loyal friend of Anderson. Researcher Philip Sugden suggests that Anderson's expressed views may have originated with Swanson.

Anderson's articles for *Blackwood's*, and his subsequent autobiography, were penned in 1910, twenty-two years after the first of the Whitechapel murders, and much of what he wrote was also based on memory—memory that had begun to fade after twenty-two years. There appears to be no evidence that "the only person who had ever had a good view of the murderer unhesitatingly identified the suspect the instant he was confronted with him." Sir Robert's Jewish witness could be one of only two people: Joseph Lawende or Israel Schwartz. Both men claimed to have caught at least a glimpse of someone they thought might be Jack the Ripper on September 30, 1888, the night of the "Double Event". Lawende thought he saw Catherine Eddowes with a man a short time before her death. He didn't get a good look at Eddowes's companion, and he told investigators he probably wouldn't be able to recognize him if he saw him again. It's highly unlikely that his memory improved to the point where he unhesitatingly recognized the man over two years later. Israel Schwartz claimed that saw someone push a woman to the ground on Berner Street about fifteen minutes before Elizabeth Stride was murdered. According to Schwartz, the man was heavy-set and broad-shouldered. The only surviving information about Kosminski's build comes from his medical records at the Leavesden Asylum. He weighed one hundred and seven pounds!

While retired Chief Inspector Frederick Abberline, the man who arguably knew more about the Whitechapel murders than anyone else, more or less dismissed Kosminski's candidacy when he said: "We never believed all those stories about Jack the Ripper being dead, or that he was a lunatic, or anything of the sort," it's important to remember that his immediate superior during the murder investigations, Superintendent Donald Swanson, didn't share those views.

The last suspect on Macnaughten's list was a man named Michael Ostrog. Macnaughten penned two descriptions of Ostrog. In the draft version of his report, he wrote:

> *"Michael Ostrog, a mad Russian doctor and a convict and unquestionably a homicidal maniac. This man was said to have been habitually cruel to women, and for a long time was known to have carried about with him surgical knives and other instruments; his antecedents were of the very worst and his whereabouts at the time of the Whitechapel*

The Suspects

murders could never be satisfactorily accounted for. He is still alive."

He toned that description down for the final version of his report:

"Michael Ostrog, a Russian doctor and a convict, who was subsequently detained in a lunatic asylum. The man's antecedents were of the worst possible type, and his whereabouts at the time of the murders could never be ascertained."

Ostrog was fifty-five when the murders began, some twenty to twenty-five years older than the Ripper's generally assumed age. A review of his police records fails to uncover any evidence of his being a homicidal maniac, or being "habitually cruel to women", or even being known to carry surgical knives and other instruments. Instead, they depict a petty thief and conman who seemed to have a knack for getting into habitual trouble with the law. Thanks to research by noted Ripper-historian Philip Sugden, Macnaughten's claim that Ostrog's whereabouts at the time of the murders could never be ascertained can now be addressed, and any thought of Ostrog being Jack the Ripper readily dismissed. During the late summer and early fall of 1888, when Jack the Ripper was casting a web of fear over London's East End, Michael Ostrog was under lock and key in Paris, awaiting trial for theft. The police had arrested him on July 26, almost two weeks before the murder of Martha Tabram. He was convicted on November 18, and spent the next two years in a French prison.

* * *

"You've got Jack the Ripper at last." Retired Chief Inspector Frederick Abberline supposedly made that remark in March 1903 shortly after a London Central Criminal

CARROTY NELL

Court jury found thirty-six-year-old George Chapman guilty of poisoning his common law wife. "George Chapman" was an alias. The defendant's real name was Severin Klosowski, and he became the fourth suspect to be named by a police official—in this case a retired one. Since nothing mentioned during the trial would link the defendant in any way to the Whitechapel murders, Abberline must have already had some suspicions about Klosowski. It's easy to see why. In many ways Klosowski proves to be an almost identical match with the unnamed suspect favored by retired Detective Inspector Henry Cox of the City Police. The two departments routinely shared information while attempting to track down the infamous killer.

Klosowski was born on December 14, 1865 in the small village of Nargonik in the eastern Poland province of Mazovia. Although raised as a Roman Catholic, he spoke fluent Yiddish, a language he picked up from the many Jews who lived close by. After finishing primary school in Nargonik, he spent the next five years in the nearby town of Zwolen working as an apprentice under a feldscher—a barber who also performed minor surgery such as removing moles. He later moved to Warsaw and took at least one course in practical surgery.

He moved to London in the early part of 1887 and soon found work as a hairdresser's assistant in a shop on West India Dock Road. A year later he was operating his own shop on Cable Street. For some reason things didn't work out and he went back to being an employee—this time in a barber shop at the corner of Whitechapel High Street and George Yard.

On October 29, 1889 he married a girl named Lucy Baderski in a German ceremony at St. Boniface Roman Catholic Church in Whitechapel. They had met only five weeks earlier at a Polish social club in the East End. The following year he purchased the barber shop at George Yard where he had been working, and he and Lucy moved into the Tewksbury Buildings on Whitechapel High Street,

The Suspects

almost right next door. Tragedy struck the family on March 3, 1891 when their infant son died of pneumonia.

The Klosowskis were still living in the Tewsbury Buildings four weeks later, when the national census was taken. A seventeen-year-old hairdresser's assistant named Max Storikie lived at the same address. Klosowski and his wife left London shortly afterward, possibly taking a paddle-wheel steamer to Antwerp. When the steamship *S.S. Friesland* set sail from Antwerp for New York in July 1891, among her passengers were a twenty-seven-year-old barber named Severin Klasowsy and his twenty-year-old wife. They claimed to be German nationals. The *Friesland* docked in New York on July 28.

R. Michael Gordon, in his book *The American Murders of Jack the Ripper*, suggests Klosowski might have arrived in New York even sooner. Gordon notes that a thirty-year-old man named Koslowsky was a passenger on the *S.S. Waesland* when she arrived from Antwerp on April 23 after an eleven-day crossing. The man's first name appears to be "Sveri" or "Sverni".

Regardless of when the Klosowskis arrived, they immediately crossed the Hudson and settled in Jersey City, New Jersey. At the time, it housed one of the largest Polish communities on America's east coast. Klosowski rented a store soon after his arrival and was once again in business for himself. He ran a barbershop in the front section, and lived with Lucy in the back room. The arrangement wasn't destined to last.

He had a violent temper, and his wife was the frequent target of his angry outbursts. About six months after their arrival in America, they were in the midst of one of their frequent fights when he suddenly threw his pregnant wife down upon the mattress and pressed his hand over her mouth to keep her from screaming. At that moment a customer walked into the shop and Klosowski got up and went to the front room to wait on him. While he was gone Lucy discovered a large knife hidden under the pillow. A few

CARROTY NELL

days later he told her that if the customer hadn't interrupted, he probably would have cut her throat.

Lucy sailed back to England soon afterward. Klosowski remained in New Jersey for another few months, and then he too returned to London.

Over the course of the next few years he more or less reinvented himself. By 1895 Polish-born Severin Klosowski had become American-born George Chapman, a name conveniently borrowed from a live-in girlfriend who coincidentally had the same name as one of the Ripper victims, Annie Chapman. He also developed a taste for fine clothes and some of the other amenities one doesn't normally associate with a barber.

One day toward the end of 1894, when he and Chapman had been living together for almost a year, he told her that another woman would be moving in with them. Chapman promptly packed up and left only to discover a few weeks later that she was pregnant. When she told him he showed absolutely no interest, and never offered to provide financial help.

A few months later he met an alcoholic named Mary Isabella Spink. She was estranged from her husband, and had recently come into a rather large inheritance. After living together for only a short time, the two began to tell friends they were married. It was a lie. She also gave her new "husband" the bulk of her £500 inheritance. He used some of the money to open a new barbershop, and spent the rest on a sailboat. Mary Spink had one talent Klosowski took advantage of—she could play the piano. Soon Spink was playing piano in the barbershop while he worked. The couple's "musical shaves" became quite popular and the shop prospered for a while only to eventually fail after the novelty wore off. Klosowski then decided to try his hand at something new, and he leased a pub in Bartholomew Square called The Prince of Wales. His temper hadn't improved since his days with Lucy Baderski, and he and Spink fought regularly. Neighbors often heard her crying at night,

The Suspects

and some noticed that she sometimes had severe bruises on her face.

In April 1897 "George Chapman" walked into a chemist's shop in Hastings and purchased a one-ounce bottle of tartar emetic. It was commonly used at the time to worm horses. One of its principal ingredients is a poisonous substance called metallic antimony. If ingested by a human in anything other than a very small amount, it brings on sudden, violent fits of vomiting that expels the poison. A minute quantity however, when administered over a period of time, not only causes excruciating pain, but also invariably proves fatal since it burns through the sensitive tissues of the digestive tract.

James Ruddick, in *Death at the Priory,* his gripping account of the 1876 poisoning of Charles Bravo with metallic antimony, gives a graphic account of the agony a victim suffers. At the inquest into Bravo's death, one doctor testified: "Its caustic nature produces a terrible, lingering death." Another said it was "one of the most painful chemicals in the entire pharmacopoeia."

Shortly after Klosowski's visit to the chemist's shop, Mary Spink began to experience painful cramps, vomiting, and diarrhea. A doctor was called, but he couldn't pinpoint the cause of the ailment. She continued to suffer from agonizing cramps until she died on Christmas Day 1897. Klosowski was at her bedside sobbing. His grief was remarkably short-lived, however, for an hour later he was downstairs tending bar in his pub.

A short time afterward he moved in with Bessie Taylor, a barmaid at the pub. It wasn't long before people began to notice bruises on her face—the telltale signs of Klosowski's abuse. Not surprisingly, she also came down with severe stomach cramps. By that time Klosowski had leased another pub, The Monument, at 135 Union Street in Southwark. He had no idea that a nearby doorway, only eighty-eight ft. away, marked the entrance to the lodging house where Frances Coles had lived in the early 1880s before she

CARROTY NELL

**Severin Klosowski
(a.k.a. George Chapman)**
ca. 1900

Courtesy of Stewart P. Evans

The Suspects

moved to the East End.

As Bessie's condition worsened, Klosowski's cruelty took on a new twist. One of her closest friends often came to visit. Klosowski sometimes feigned a look of sadness and told her that Bessie had just died, and then burst out laughing at her shock and grief. When she came to visit on February 14, 1901, he said that Bessie's condition was "about the same", and that she was resting and shouldn't be disturbed. The woman was furious when she found out later that her dear friend had died the day before.

A few months later Klosowski once again found romance with one of his employees. This time it was with a nineteen-year-old barmaid named Maud Marsh. By late 1901, she and Klosowski were living together. In what was starting to become a pattern, he decided to give up The Monument and try his hand running a nearby pub called The Crown. A fire "of suspicious origin" damaged the interior of The Monument only a few days before his lease was due to expire. Officials suspected, but couldn't prove, that the fire was intentionally set, most likely with the hope of collecting insurance money.

Friends soon began to notice bruises on Maud's face, and she told her sister that her husband had hit her more than once. "He held my hair and banged my head," she said. Shortly afterward, she too began to experience painful cramps.

Maud's mother began to grow concerned when her daughter's condition failed to improve, and she became suspicious when she learned that her son-in-law always prepared and administered the medicine. She told him she was going to call in another doctor. Klosowski must have panicked at the thought of an independent examination, and he gave Maud an overdose of her "medicine" that night. She died the next day, October 22, 1902.

The circumstances of her death were so suspicious that the medical examiner ordered a postmortem examination. That was when doctors discovered a large amount of metallic antimony in her body. "George Chapman" was arrested on October 25. When investigators searched his rooms they soon discovered his true identity. They also found something else that he had foolishly held onto—the label from a bottle of tartar emetic.

Authorities had the bodies of his two previous "wives" exhumed. Unfortunately for Klosowski, one of antimony's side effects is that it acts as a preservative. Neither body showed signs of deterioration, and both contained large amounts of the poison.

The police subsequently charged him with two more murders—Mary Spink and Bessie Taylor. Charles Mathews, the same man who decided to drop the murder charge against James Sadler, was a member of the prosecution team. They must have been confident about the outcome because they decided to bring him to trial on only one of the charges, the murder of Maud Marsh. After four days of testimony during which the defense called no witnesses, the case went to the jury. It took them just eleven minutes to reach a unanimous verdict—guilty!

Severin Klosowski never spoke of the Ripper murders. Shortly after daybreak on Tuesday, April 7, 1903, nineteen days after his conviction, he was hanged at Wandsworth Prison. His body still lies buried in an unmarked grave within the prison walls.

Inspector Abberline had good reason for suspecting him. He more or less matched the sketchy descriptions of the Ripper, he lived close to the murder sites (police officials were almost certain that the Ripper lived in the immediate vicinity of the crimes), and he had some knowledge of anatomy. He often wandered the streets of Whitechapel late at night, and he was known to have battered and beaten several women. In fact, some of the abuse he inflicted on his "wives"—punching them in the face, and grabbing Maud Marsh by the hair and banging her head against a wall—was eerily similar that inflicted on Ellen Calana and Frances Coles. He also killed women—at least three.

The Suspects

Abberline may not have been aware that Klosowski sailed to America by a rather devious route shortly after the murder of Frances Coles, although he must have known that the final letter from Jack the Ripper, the one received on October 14, 1896 with handwriting that bore a strong resemblance to the original letter and card, claimed the writer had been abroad.

Had he been able to look into the future, Abberline would have been even more excited about the likelihood of Klosowski's being Jack the Ripper. In November 2006 Laura Richards, the head of analysis at Scotland Yard's Violent Crime Unit, created what was described as the most accurate sketch of Jack the Ripper ever drawn. She based it on evidence gathered during the investigations into the deaths of the five canonical victims. According to Richards, the man was between five ft., five in. and five ft., seven in. tall, heavyset, and had a prominent moustache. She placed his age somewhere between twenty-six and thirty-five. The drawing, which was first shown on UK's Channel Five, bears an uncanny resemblance to photos of Severin Klosowski!

What makes Richard's profile even more remarkable is that it was created without taking Ellen Calana's statements into consideration. Calana's description of the killer, "He was a very short man, with a dark moustache", meshes perfectly with Richard's profile. Calana added something else to her description—she told investigators the man wore "shiny boots". They would have stood out like a sore thumb in Whitechapel where dirty, scuffed work boots were the norm. One of the witnesses who testified at the 1903 murder trial was a man named Wolff Levisohn. He had known Klosowski quite well around the time of the Whitechapel murders. Here's how he described his friend at that time: "He was a la-de-da back then with his black coat, his high hat, and his *patent leather boots.*"

At first glance, the evidence seems overwhelming. It's important to remember, however, that it is purely circumstantial, and that valid arguments exist that make him appear a rather unlikely suspect.

One of those arguments is his age. He was only twenty-two when the murders began. Most people who thought they saw the Whitechapel murderer placed his age somewhere between thirty and thirty-five. Admittedly, many of those witnesses hadn't gotten a good look at the man's face. Still, very few people mistake a twenty-two-year-old for someone in their early to mid-thirties.

The drastic difference in the pattern of the murders—the change from killing and mutilating strangers selected at random to slowly poisoning women with whom he shared a special bond—remains the greatest stumbling block. Surprisingly, it didn't bother Abberline, who told the reporter from the *Pall Mall Gazette*:

> *"As to the question of the dissimilarity of character in the crimes which one hears so much about, I cannot see why one man should not have done both, provided he had the professional knowledge, and this is admitted in Chapman's case. A man who could watch his wives being slowly tortured to death by poison, as he did, was capable of anything; and the fact that he should have attempted, in such a cold-blooded manner to murder his first wife with a knife in New Jersey, makes one more inclined to believe in the theory that he was mixed up in the two series of crimes. What, indeed, is more likely than that a man to some extent skilled in medicine and surgery should discontinue the use of a knife ... and then, for the remainder of his ghastly deeds, put into practice his knowledge of poisons? Indeed, if the theory be accepted that a man who takes life on a wholesale scale never ceases his accursed habit until he is either arrested or dies, there is much to be said for Chapman's consistency. You see, incentive changes; but the fiendishness is not eradicated. The victims, you will notice, continue to be women; but they are of different classes, and obviously call for different methods of despatch."*

The Suspects

Abberline was a veteran police investigator and an authority on Jack the Ripper. While he had no trouble accepting the change in modus operandi, a great many people today find it just a little too hard to believe.

* * *

The final suspect is a man who, if nothing else, was the most flamboyant of the five. Former Chief Inspector John Littlechild, in his 1913 letter to writer George Sims, added Dr. Francis Tumblety's name to the list.

No one seems to know for certain where Tumblety was born, but most researchers agree on a year—1833. During the late 1840s he lived in Rochester, New York and peddled pornographic pictures to bargemen on the Eire Canal. Soon afterward, in the first of what eventually became many moves that took him to several American, Canadian, and European cities, he traveled to Detroit and began to practice medicine. A self-taught herbalist with no formal medical training, he often wore a military uniform and had a large, prominent, handlebar moustache.

He managed to compile an impressive arrest record over the years on charges that included impersonating an officer, attempting to abort a pregnancy, and prescribing medicine that caused a patient's death. He was even arrested and briefly jailed on suspicion of treason during the American Civil War when he unwisely chose to use the name *Dr. Blackburn* when he registered in a St. Louis hotel. He had no idea that police and private investigators were frantically searching for a Dr. L.P. Blackburn after he was linked to an ill-fated plot to infect Union soldiers with yellow fever by supplying the Army with contaminated blankets. According to some accounts he was also briefly, but mistakenly, suspected of having complicity in the assassination of President Abraham Lincoln.

Francis Tumblety was also a homosexual, and he was arrested in London on November 7, 1888, two days before the murder of Mary Jane Kelly, and charged with indecent (homosexual) assault on two men. He was released on bail soon afterward. He attended a pretrial hearing on November 20, and then abruptly fled to France. From there he sailed for America.

The New York Police soon learned that he was staying in a rooming house in lower Manhattan. Since the indecent assault charges were not considered an extraditable offense, they chose to place him under surveillance and await further developments. It didn't take Tumblety long to discover that he was being watched, and he managed to make his escape. He returned to Rochester for a while, and then moved to Baltimore, Maryland. He eventually settled in St. Louis, Missouri where he died in 1903.

Tumblety didn't care much for women, and he particularly disliked those that he considered low-class. According to one account, he maintained a rather curious collection. A Union Army colonel named Dunham became acquainted with him while he was stationed in Washington during the Civil War. Tumblety was posing as a surgeon. During one visit, the two men happened to walk into Tumblety's office where the colonel noticed a large number of glass bottles containing various specimens. At least a dozen, Tumblety told him, contained uteri from "every class of woman." The significance of such a collection can't be understated in light of the bizarre theory Coroner Baxter expressed at the conclusion of the inquest into Annie Chapman's death. It's important to remember, however, that the incident Colonel Dunham mentioned occurred twenty-five years before the onset of the Whitechapel murders.

On the surface, Tumblety doesn't appear to be a very good suspect. He was fifty-five years old at the time of the murders—at least twenty years older than the killer's suspected age. He was also a very large man, standing almost six ft. tall at a time when the average man's height was about five ft. six. He had one other prominent feature that everyone noticed—an enormous handlebar moustache.

The Suspects

None of the witnesses who thought they saw Jack the Ripper described anyone looking even remotely like him.

Like many of the other police-identified suspects, Francis Tumblety's name will undoubtedly remain on the discussion list as long as there is any interest in Jack the Ripper.

Chapter 18

Was it Jack, or Someone Else?

A surprising turnabout has made its way into the saga of Jack the Ripper over the years—his victim count is widely thought to have gone down. At the time of the Whitechapel murders there was an almost-universal belief that Alice McKenzie and Frances Coles had fallen victim to Jack. The general public thought so, the press thought so, and even a good many members of the police thought so, and that included the Commissioner of the Metropolitan Police and the Assistant Commissioner of the Criminal Investigation Division. James Monro told the Under Secretary of State he thought Jack the Ripper had killed Alice McKenzie; Sir Robert Anderson later forgot he had sent a memo to the Home Office blaming the Ripper for Frances Coles's death. Since then it has become fashionable to exclude McKenzie and Coles from the ranks of the Ripper victims despite the fact that absolutely nothing has been uncovered during those ensuing years that would support that move. Simply put, many modern-day Ripper enthusiasts, or *Ripperologists* as they like to call themselves, don't want them to be Ripper victims. Their killings were too commonplace, too pedestrian to be linked to a legend like Jack.

The first assault on the widespread belief that McKenzie and Coles were Ripper victims came from the various pub-

Was it Jack, or Someone Else?

lic officials who spoke out. Their comments definitely impacted public opinion, especially in the first two decades following the murders. Victorians were more inclined to trust those in positions of authority than we are today, and even though the police officials often contradicted one another, the general public tended to be quite willing to believe them. If a high-ranking police official said there were only four victims, or five victims, that satisfied most people at the time. Jack the Ripper couldn't have killed Alice McKenzie and Frances Coles. If he had, the police would certainly have said so!

Police officials weren't the only ones who influenced public opinion. Authors and writers, particularly those whose books or articles promote a particular suspect, have to take their share of the blame. If someone decides to point an accusing finger at a suspect who committed suicide, or was sent to an asylum, or moved from the area, or for some other reason was no longer in a position to continue his crime spree, they have to expect the inevitable question, "then who killed Alice McKenzie and Frances Coles?" Not surprisingly, they invariably downplay any suggestion that those two murders were linked to Jack the Ripper. Some have solved that dilemma by not even mentioning McKenzie and Coles.

Police officials, authors, writers—yes, they've all played a part—but the main reason for the change in attitude goes a lot deeper, for Jack the Ripper has become a legend, one that continues to attract and fascinate. New books arrive on bookseller's shelves with amazing regularity, many bearing the teasing promise that their pages will finally reveal the identity of the fiendish killer. A few years ago a London museum played host to a Jack the Ripper exhibition that drew near-capacity crowds during much of its six-month run. A large number of those in attendance were from the Greater London area. That's not to say that locals are the only people who still show some interest in Jack the Ripper. For many tourists, a trip to London wouldn't be complete

CARROTY NELL

without joining one of the many Jack the Ripper walking tours that crisscross the narrow lanes and alleyways of Whitechapel every evening.

In the minds of some people, Jack the Ripper has evolved into something larger than life. They want a bit more than just a fiendish killer who terrorized the world's largest city and then vanished, leaving behind a police department baffled and bewildered. They want someone whose string of abominable assaults culminated with one so savage, so horrifying, it couldn't be surpassed.

That's the stuff legends are made of. Melville Macnaughten liked the idea—at least the part about going out with a blaze of glory, although the other part, the baffled police department, came nearer to the truth. The idea still gains favor today even though most investigators scoff at Macnaughten's theory of a climactic killing. The brutality inflicted on Mary Jane Kelly shouldn't come as much of a surprise, they argue, for her room provided the killer with two fortuitous advantages that were lacking at the other murder sites—ample light and ample time. There was practically no likelihood of his being disturbed at Miller's Court.

To some, it just doesn't seem fitting that a legend like Jack would reappear after an eight month hiatus and cut the throat of a rather plain-looking, freckled-faced, middle age woman behind some wagons in a deserted alley. Neither does the idea of his being turned down by his intended victim, forcing him to settle for a substitute in an attack he himself called a "bad one."

Much has changed since Jack stalked the streets of Whitechapel. Several of the police files have gone missing. Pranksters have perpetrated deliberate hoaxes. Assumptions and opinions have been put forth with the same confidence as thought they were proven fact. With the passing of time, the fine line that separates reality from theory has oftentimes become blurred. Rumors are accepted as truth; eyewitness accounts dismissed if they conflict with someone's

Was it Jack, or Someone Else?

preconceived opinion. Under the circumstances it's not surprising that many people today, especially newcomers who rely on Internet chat rooms as their primary source of information, readily subscribe to the belief that Mary Jane Kelly had to have been the Ripper's last victim.

Let's assume for a moment, just for the sake of argument, that they are correct, that Jack the Ripper didn't kill Alice McKenzie and Frances Coles. That means, of course, there were two killers.

When searching for victims, each one chose prostitutes who were drunk or had been drinking, but neither killer ever attempted intercourse. Both struck so suddenly their victims didn't make any sound. Except for the attack on Mary Jane Kelly, where the locale forced the killer to alter his normal routine, both killers crouched or knelt beside their victim's right side while cutting her throat from left to right. Both also knew they had to tilt the victim's head to one side so her blood wouldn't spatter them.

The similarities don't stop there. Neither killer was apprehended, and neither left behind even the slightest clue. From the few accounts of witnesses who thought they had seen the killer, both men more or less answered to the same description.

Does this sound like a likely scenario?

Johnny Cochran, a flamboyant American defense attorney, is credited with making a now-famous remark during the closing arguments of the O. J. Simpson murder trial. Cochran told the jurors, "If it doesn't fit, you must acquit."

Everyone has a right to his or her own opinion, but if someone asked me to accept the supposition that two such virtually-identical serial killers prowled the same tiny, one-square-mile section of East London during one short, thirty-month span, I would have to say, "I'm sorry. In my mind, it just doesn't fit."

CARROTY NELL

EPILOGUE

Frederick Abberline was reassigned from the Whitechapel murders investigation a few months after the death of Mary Jane Kelly. In July 1889 he chanced upon the discovery that some of the highest-ranking officials in government were patronizing a homosexual brothel that employed teenage boys. That opened the door to what has become known as *The Cleveland Street Scandal.*

Abberline retired from the police force in 1892 and later headed the European operation of the Pinkerton Detective Agency. He died at this home in Bournemouth on Dec. 10, 1929 at the age of eighty-six. His remains were interred at Wimbourne Cemetery, the same cemetery where Montague John Druitt lies buried.

Sir Robert Anderson retired from the Metropolitan Police in 1901 and was knighted the same year. In 1910 he published his autobiography, *The Lighter Side of My Official Life*. He died of heart failure in Kensington on November 15, 1918. He was seventy-seven years old.

Albert Bachert was back in the news two years after his failed attempt to serve on the coroner's jury that investigated Frances Coles's death. On March 7, 1893 he was

CARROTY NELL

found guilty of defrauding a local charity of some bread and flour, and was sentenced to three months in prison at hard labor. *The Times* described him as a "known agitator in the East End" in their coverage of that trial. He apparently left England not long afterward. His name doesn't appear on any subsequent records.

Wynne Baxter's career as a coroner spanned more than thirty-five years, and continued until World War I when he presided over the inquests into the deaths of eleven German spies. In 1907, ten years before his retirement, he mentioned that he had already presided over more than thirty thousand inquests. He passed away in 1920 at his home in Stoke Newington at the age of seventy-six. The law firm he founded is still in existence.

James Coles spent the rest of his life in the St. Olave's Union Workhouse. He died there of "senile decay" on February 20, 1903 at the age of eighty-three.

Mary Ann Coles drifted back into obscurity after her brief moment in the limelight following her sister's death. Efforts to trace her whereabouts after 1891 have proven unsuccessful.

Selina Coles never left the Leavesden Asylum in Watford. She died of tertiary syphilis on April 23, 1897 at the age of forty-one, her body and mind ravaged by a long struggle with the disease. Her remains were interred in the asylum's cemetery on East Lane. She had been institutionalized for most of her adult life.

Charles Cutbush, the former Executive Superintendent of Scotland Yard who Melville Macnaughten mistakenly believed was the uncle of the suspect suggested in a series of articles in the *Sun*, had been retired from the Metropolitan Police two and a half years when those articles appeared.

Epilogue

He continued to suffer from the severe headaches and chronic depression that cut short his police career, and he took his own life on March 5, 1896 in the kitchen of his home in Lambeth. He was fifty-two years old.

Thomas Cutbush, the subject of the articles in the *Sun* that prompted Melville Macnaughten to pen his famous report, was committed to the Broadmoor Criminal Lunatic Asylum in Berkshire on April 15, 1891. He died there of chronic kidney disease on July 5, 1903, a few days after his thirty-seventh birthday. The release of his medical records in November 2008 caused a brief resurgence of interest in his candidacy as a suspect.

William Fryday never stopped believing that the couple he saw in the doorway on Royal Mint Street were the victim and her killer. Two decades later he was still driving a wagon for the Great Eastern Railway. He married a girl named Harriet Gatrell a year after the murder, and they settled in Islington where they raised two daughters. He died in 1943 at the age of seventy-two.

Charles Guiver, the night watchman who ordered Tom Sadler to leave Spitalfields Chambers a short time before the murder, and then again shortly afterward, collapsed and died at the same lodging house on the evening February 25, 1891, only a few hours after Frances Coles's funeral service. He was thirty-four years old. The circumstances at first appeared to be suspicious, but his death was eventually attributed to natural causes.

Henry Winfield Hora continued to take an active part in the charitable activities of his former parish, St. Botolph's Church in Aldgate, until he retired and moved to Gloucestershire. He died there on May 24, 1904 at *Upmeads*, his home on Cleve Hill in Cheltenham. He was seventy-five years old, and left an estate valued at almost £21,000 (the

CARROTY NELL

equivalent of approx. £2 million, or US $3.1 million, in 2012).

Aaron Kosminski, the favorite suspect of former Assistant Commissioner of the C.I.D. Sir Robert Anderson, and former Metropolitan Police Superintendent Donald Swanson continued to suffer from deteriorating mental health. He was transferred from Colney Hatch to the Leavesden Asylum on April 19, 1894, and remained there for the rest of his life. He died on March 24, 1919.

George Lusk faded from the limelight after the dissolution of the Whitechapel Vigilance Committee. Twenty years later he was still working as a builder, specializing in theatre renovations. He died in Poplar in 1919 at the age of eighty.

Sir Melville Macnaughton was knighted in 1907, and forced to retire six years later when his health began to fail. In 1914 he published his memoirs, *Days of My Years*. He passed away at his home in London on May 12, 1921 at age sixty-seven.

John McCarthy, the landlord of McCarthy's Rents, still owned the property in 1909 when a prostitute named Kitty Ronan was murdered in the room directly above the one formerly occupied by Mary Jane Kelly. He died in 1934 and was buried in St. Patrick's Roman Catholic Cemetery in Leydonstone, not far from the grave of Kelly, his former tenant. His great-granddaughter, Kay Kendall, was a popular film actress in the 1950s. She was thirty-three years old and married to actor Rex Harrison when she died of leukemia in 1959.

Kate McCarthy and Thomas Fowles, the couple William Fryday mistook for the victim and her killer, were married at the Church of The English Martyrs on Prescott Street in Whitechapel on February 4, 1893. The church is about six

Epilogue

hundred feet from the Chamber Street entrance to Swallow Gardens. Neither Kate nor Thomas appear on subsequent UK census records.

Michael Ostrog, one of the three suspects named by Melville Macnaughten, returned to England in 1890 after completing his sentence in a French prison. He spent part of the following year in a mental hospital in Surrey. He was twice charged with petty theft during the 1890s, and in 1900 was jailed for four years for stealing a microscope from a London hospital. He dropped from public view after his release from prison in 1904.

Dr. Frederick J. Oxley, who thought the knife James Sadler supposedly sold was far too small to make the deep cuts in Frances Coles's throat, was back in the news seven years later when he testified on behalf of a woman seeking damages from a baker after she fell through an unsecured sidewalk cover outside his shop and tumbled into the coal bin. Oxley told the court it was his professional opinion that the shock of the fall caused the woman to contract bronchitis. The judge laughed at him and refused to accept his view. Oxley went on to serve as a Major in the Army Medical Corps during World War I. He died on July 30, 1950 at the age eighty-three at his home at Epping, Essex.

Dr. George Bagster Phillips served as a police surgeon for the Metropolitan Police Department's Whitechapel Division for more than thirty years. He died of a cerebral hemorrhage on October 27, 1897 at his home on Spital Square in London. He was sixty-three years old.

James Sadler's trail seems to have grown cold after his move to Camberwell. In January 1896 a James Sadler of Canning Town was fined for assaulting a married couple who had lodged in his home but left without paying their overdue rent. When the couple returned to pick up their

CARROTY NELL

belongings, Sadler struck the man several times and then slapped the woman in the face even though she was holding a baby in her arms. Three years later a James Sadler of Nottingdale, described as a general dealer, was jailed for two months at hard labor after being convicted of beating and kicking his common-law wife of seven years. Newspaper accounts didn't give either defendant's age, nor did they mention the murder in Swallow Gardens. That makes it seem doubtful that either of the two individuals was the man arrested for the murder of Frances Coles.

Sir Henry Smith learned that he had been appointed a Knight Commander while he was reading his morning newspaper one day in 1897. He resigned from the London City Police four years later, and in 1910 he published his autobiography, *From Constable to Commissioner*. In it, he mentioned that he was a cousin of Robert Louis Stevenson. He died in Edinburgh, Scotland on March 2, 1921 at the age of eighty-five.

Ernest Thompson continued to question whether he had made the right decision when he chose to stay with Frances Coles instead of chasing after the footsteps he heard on Chamber Street. He was still working out of the Leman Street Police Station in 1900 when he was fatally stabbed in the neck in the early morning hours of Saturday, December 1, while trying to quell a disturbance in Whitechapel. He was thirty-two years old, and the father of four small children. The youngest was only three months old. Nearly twenty-five hundred uniformed Metropolitan Police officers attended his funeral services at Bow Cemetery.

Appendix

CARROTY NELL

Appendix 1

The Witnesses

Known witnesses who testified at the Inquest into Frances Coles's death

Saturday, February 14 (evening session)

Metropolitan Police Constable Ernest Thompson
Metropolitan Police Constable Frederick Hyde
Metropolitan Police Constable George Elliott

Tuesday, February 17

James Coles, father of the deceased
Mary Ann Coles, sister of the deceased
Peter Hawkes, assistant at his mother's hat shop on Nottingham St.
Charles Guiver, night watchman at the Spitalfields Chambers lodging house
Samuel Harris, a resident of the Spitalfields Chambers lodging house

Friday, February 20

Anne Shuttleworth, wife of the owner of Shuttleworth's

CARROTY NELL

Eating House
William Steer, head barman at The Bell public house
Sarah Treadway, wife of the landlord of the Marlborough Head public house
Sarah Fleming, deputy at the Spitalfields Chambers lodging house
Metropolitan Police Constable William Bogan
Frederick Session, a security guard at the St. Katherine Docks
Henry Sutton, a security guard at the St. Katherine Docks
John Dooley, a laborer at the St. Katherine Docks
Charles Treadway, landlord of the Marlborough Head public house on Brick Lane
George Peakall, landlord of the Melbourne Chambers lodging house
Metropolitan Police Sergeant Wesley Edwards
Metropolitan Police Constable Frederick Hyde, recalled
Solomon Guttridge, an employee of the Great Northern Railway
Michael Redding, an employee of the Great Northern Railway
Metropolitan Police Inspector James Flanagan
Metropolitan Police Constable Arthur Sharp
Joseph Richards, the manager of a coffee house
William Fewell, night porter in the receiving room of the London Hospital
Helen Cooper, the London Hospital nurse who dressed Sadler's wounds

Monday, February 23

Stephen Longhurst, the manager of a coffee house
Charles Littlewood, a waiter employed by Stephen Longhurst
Frederick Smith, a waiter at Lockhart's on Tower Hill

The Witnesses

Joseph Haswell, night manager at Shuttleworth's Eating House
Duncan Campbell, a resident of the Sailor's Home on Well St.
Thomas Robinson, a marine store dealer
Edward Delaforce, superintendent at the Tower Hill Shipping Office
Edward Gray, deputy superintendent at the Tower Hill Shipping Office
Metropolitan Police Chief Inspector Donald Swanson, C.I.D.
James Thomas Sadler (his statement to Chief Inspector Donald Swanson was read to the jurors)
Metropolitan Police Detective Sergeant Don
Metropolitan Police Sergeant Ward
Dr. Frederick J. Oxley, M.R.C.S.
Dr. George Bagster Phillips, M.R.C.S.

Friday, February 27

Metropolitan Police Sergeant George Bush
Edward Gray, recalled
John Johnson, deputy at the Victoria Chambers lodging house
Thomas Johnson, a resident of the Sailor's Home on Well St.
Florence Davis, a barmaid at The Swan public house
Metropolitan Police Inspector Henry Moore, C.I.D.
Metropolitan Police Detective Inspector Edmund Reid
Ellen Calana, an acquaintance of Frances Coles
William Fryday, an employee of the Great Northern Railway
Kate McCarthy, a resident of 42 Royal Mint St.
Thomas Fowles, the fiancé of Kate McCarthy

Appendix 2

The Statement

James Sadler's Statement Given to Chief Inspector Swanson on February 14, 1891

I am a fireman and am generally known as Tom Sadler. I was discharged at 7 p.m. on the 11th inst. from the steamship *Fez*. I think I had a drink of holland's gin at Williams Brothers', at the corner of Goulston Street. I then went, at 8:30 p.m., to the Victoria Home. I then left the Home and went into the Princess Alice opposite, and had something to drink. I had no person with me.

While in the Princess Alice, between 8:30 and 9 p.m., I saw a woman (whom I had previously known) named Frances. I had known her for 18 months. I first met her in the Whitechapel Road, and went with her to Thrawl Street, to a lodging house and I stayed with her all night, having paid for a double bed at the lodging house. I don't remember the name of the lodging house where I then stayed with her. I think I then took a ship, the name of which I do not remember. I did not see this woman again until I saw her in another bar of the Princess Alice, and recognizing her, I beckoned her over to me. There was nobody with her.

The Statement

She asked me to leave the public house, as when she had got a little money the customers in the public house expected her to spend it amongst them. We left the Princess Alice, and went round drinking at other public houses. Among other houses I went into a house at the corner of Dorset Street, where another woman named Annie Lawrence joined us. Frances stopped me from treating this woman, and we then went to White's Row chambers. I paid for a double bed, and we stayed the night there. She had a bottle of whisky (half-pint), which I had bought at Davis's, White Swan, Whitechapel. I took the bottle back yesterday morning, and the young woman (barmaid) gave me twopennyworth of drink for it.

Frances and I left White's Row Chambers between 11 and 12 noon, and we went into a number of public houses, one of which was the Bell, Middlesex Street. We stayed there for about two hours drinking and laughing. When in the Bell, she spoke to me about a hat, which she had paid a shilling for a month previously. We then went on the way to the bonnet shop drinking at the public houses on the way. The shop is in White's Row or Baker's Row, and I gave her the half-a-crown, which was due for the hat, and she went into the shop. She came out again and said that her hat was not ready; the woman was putting some elastic on. We then went into a public house in White's or Baker's Row, and we had some more drinks. Then she went for her hat and got it; and brought it to me at the public house, and I made her try it on. I wanted her to throw the old one away, but she declined, and I pinned it on to her dress. Then we went to the Marlborough Head public house, in Brick Lane, and had some more drink. I was then getting into drink, and the landlady rather objected to Frances and me being in the house. I can't remember what the landlady said now. I treated some men in the house. I can't say their names. I had met them previously in the same house. From there I had an appointment to see a man Nichols [sic] in Spital Street, and I left her there to see Nichols, arranging to meet her again at a public house - where I cannot say now, and I have forgotten it. We came down Thrawl Street, and while going down a woman with a red shawl struck me on the head and I fell down, and when down I was kicked by some men around me. The men ran into the lodging houses, and on getting up I found my money and my watch gone. I was then penniless, and I then had a row with Frances, for I thought she might have helped me when I was down. I then left her at the corner of Thrawl Street without making any appointment that I can remember. I was downhearted at the loss of my money, because I could not pay for my bed.

I then went to the London Docks and applied for admission, as I wanted to go aboard the steamship *Fez*. There was a stout sergeant inside the gate and a constable. They refused me admission, as I was too intoxicated. I cannot remember what hour this was, as I was dazed and drunk. There was a Metropolitan Police officer near the gate, a young man. I abused the sergeant and constable because they refused me admission. There were some dock labourers coming out, and they said something to me, and I replied abusively, and one of the labourers took it up, saying, "If the policeman would turn his back he would give me a good hiding." The policeman walked across the road, across Nightingale Lane, towards the Tower way, and as soon as he had done so the labourers made a dead set at me, especially the one who took my abuse. This one knocked me down and kicked me, and eventually another labourer stopped him. I then turned down Nightingale Lane and the labourers went up Smithfield way. I remained in Nightingale Lane for about a quarter of an hour, feeling my injuries. I then went to the Victoria lodging house in East Smithfield, and applied for a bed, but was refused, as I was so drunk, by the night porter, a stout, fat man. I begged and prayed him to let me have a bed, but he refused. To the best of my belief I told him I had been knocked about. He refused to give me a bed, and I left and wandered about. I

The Statement

cannot say what the time was. I went towards Dorset Street: I cannot say which way, but possibly Leman Street way. When I got to Dorset Street I went into the lodging house where I had stopped with Frances on the previous night, and found her in the kitchen, sitting with her head on her arms. I spoke to Frances about her hat. She appeared half-dazed from drink, and I asked her if she had enough money to pay the double bed with. She said she had no money, and I told her I had not a farthing, but I had £4 15s. coming to me. I asked her if she could get trust, but she said she could not. I then went to the deputy and asked for a night's lodging on the strength of the money I was to lift the next day, but I was refused. I was eventually turned out by a man, and left Frances behind in the house.

I then went, to the best of my belief, towards the London Hospital, and about the middle of the Whitechapel Road a young policeman stopped me and asked where I was going, as I looked in a pretty pickle. I said that I had had two doings last night, one in Spitalfields and one at the docks. I said I had been cut or hacked about with a knife or bottle. Immediately I mentioned the word knife he said, "Oh, have you a knife about you?" and then searched me. I told him I did not carry a knife. My shipmates, one Mat Curley and another named Bowen, know that I have not carried a knife for years. The policeman helped me across the road towards the hospital gate. I spoke to the porter, but he hummed and hawed about it, and I began to abuse him. However, he did let me in, and I went to the accident ward and had the cut in my head dressed. The porter asked me if I had any place to go to, and I said no, and he let me lay down on a couch in the room where the first accidents are brought in. I can give no idea of the time I called at the hospital. When he let me out, somewhere between six and eight o'clock in the morning, I went straight to the Victoria Home, and begged for a few halfpence; but I did not succeed.

I then went to the shipping office, where I was paid £4

CARROTY NELL

15s. 3d. Having got my money, I went to the Victoria, Upper East Smithfield, and stayed there all day, as I was miserable. The furthest I went out was the Phoenix, about 12 doors off. I spent the night there and I was there this morning. I had gone to the Phoenix this morning to have a drink, and I was beckoned out and asked to come here (Leman Street) and I came.

As far as I can think, it was between 5 and 6 that I was assaulted in Thrawl Street at any rate it was getting dark, and it was some hours after that that I went to the London Docks. I forgot to mention that Frances and I had some food at Mr. Shuttleworth's, in Wentworth Street.

My discharges are as follows: - Last discharged 11-2-90 in London ship *Fez*. Next discharge 6-9-90, London. Next 15-7-90, London. Next 27-5-90, Barry. Next 1-10-89, London. Next 2-10-88, London. Engaged, 17-8-86; next, 5-5-87; engaged, 24-3-87, London.

The last I had seen of the woman Frances was when I left her in the lodging house when I was turned out. The lodging house deputy can give you the name. The clothes that I am now wearing are the only clothes I have. They are the clothes I was discharged in and I have worn them ever since. My wife resides in the country, but I would prefer not to mention it. The lodging house I refer to is White's Row, not Dorset Street. It has a large lamp over it. Passing a little huckster's shop at the corner of Brick Lane and Brown's Lane I purchased a pair of earrings, or rather I gave her the money and she bought them. I think she gave a penny for them.

Appendix 3

The Interview

Interview with James Sadler that appeared in the *East London Observer* on March 28, 1891

SADLER - HE IS FOUND ILL AND POVERTY STRICKEN IN A SHADWELL COFFEE HOUSE. HE ALLEGES PERJURY ON THE PART OF WITNESSES, AND COMMUNICATES SOME IMPORTANT INFORMATION.

James Sadler, who was, a few weeks ago, within an ace of being committed for trial for the most recent of the Whitechapel murders, has not by any means improved his worldly position since the time of his discharge.

There was no denying that fact, as the veteran sporting M.C., Joe Farrell—who, the *Observer* man in quest of copy considered the safest company in such a mission—stopped suddenly in one of the dirtiest and dingiest parts of Shadwell, and knocked at the door of a not altogether inviting-looking coffee shop bearing the legend of "Good Beds."

There was somebody else at the door when we got

CARROTY NELL

there. He was a docky, evidently in search of a bed for the night. He looked somewhat suspiciously at us visitors, and at last ventured on "What d'ye want, mates?"

"Is Sadler in?" queried Joe.

"Yes," replied the docky. "But he's in bed and mortal queer. Shares the same room with me. D'ye want to see him?"

We intimated that we did, and procuring a candle that led a precarious kind of existence in a crazy candlestick, he led the way up the rickety stairs to what he euphemistically called, "the second floor front."

It was a small and dingy room, dimly lighted up by the fitful candlelight, containing four single beds with the scantiest of coverings, a superannuated looking wash hand stand—and little besides. There was only one bed occupied at the time—the one by the window, and looking out into the dingy street below. It was a restless occupant that the bed contained, for the counterpane and sheet were performing some curious evolutions as they were tossed and tumbled by the man underneath them.

"He's feverish mate," says the docky, as he deposits the candle he has brought up on the rickety washstand. "Better not disturb him much."

Then he leans over the bed and tells its occupant that there's somebody to see him.

"Somebody to see me?" asks a voice from beneath the clothes, and Sadler—for it is he—sits half-up in bed.

He is wearing a grey check flannel shirt, with a red checked scarf round his throat. His features are pretty well known to the public now—thanks to the unenviable notoriety he gained during the time of his incarceration in Leman Street Station and Holloway Gaol. They are massive, not by any means unintelligent, and are set off by heavy eyebrows and a thick, dark brown beard, extending from the chin.

The sudden movement brings on a painful fit of coughing. When it is over, we explain our mission.

The Interview

"So you've found me out down here," says Sadler, in a deep and not unpleasant voice. "You newspaper fellows are as smart as detectives. I came down here partly to get rid of the eternal talk, talk, talk, about that wretched affair, and partly—and he smiles cynically—because beggars mustn't be choosers."

"You've got a nasty cough?" the *Observer* man begins.

"Yes," says Sadler, as he applies his mouth to a bottle of medicine standing near by. The police have just about done for me over this affair. Up to that Saturday morning when I was taken in charge at Leman Street, I had always enjoyed good health. For thirty-five years I've been a hard workingman, and haven't had much time to get ill. Twenty-five years of that time I've been at sea. The rest of the time I've been employed as a docker here; and another bit of time I've put in at the Australian diggings. I've gone through all kinds of hardships, but the time I spent in the cells and gaols of this civilised country—and the cynical smile is apparent again—over this murder business has just about finished me up."

"But how was that. You were not treated as an ordinary criminal?"

"No; perhaps it would have been better for me if I had been. When I was taken to Leman Street Station on the Saturday morning, I was put into a draughty, cold, anteroom. During the time I was there, up to the Sunday night, I had to get in and out of all kinds of changes of clothes—some of them damp, and others positively wet—for the purposes of identification. Then, on the Saturday night I got for my bed a plank—worse than that of a prison cell. Add to that the journeyings in that draughty 'Black Maria' that I had to do between Holloway and Arbour Square, then remember that I was still suffering from the knocking about I received on the night of the murder, and I think that'll explain why you find me like this now."

"You've seen a doctor, I suppose?"

"Yes, I was taken in by a friend last night to see Dr.

CARROTY NELL

Kay, in the Commercial Road. He said I was suffering from bronchitis, and when he felt my ribs he said that I was worse than I thought, and wanted me to go to the hospital at once."

"You were treated alright in Holloway?"

"Yes, I've nothing to complain of there, except what I've to complain of all through the case, that the police, and everybody in their employ, were dead against me, and meant to have me if they possibly could. They tried to get me to incriminate myself in any way they knew how to. What do you think they did in Holloway?"

The newspaperman confessed his ignorance of Holloway and Holloway's ways.

"Well I hadn't been in there long before the Governor and the Chaplain, and half a dozen justices—I suppose they were—came along to where I was.

" 'How do you feel now Sadler?' says the Governor.

" 'Very sore; especially about the ribs,' says I.

" 'Ah, but I don't mean that,' says the Governor. 'I mean, how do you feel in your mind?'

" 'Right enough,' says I. 'Why should I feel otherwise?'

" 'Don't you feel uneasy about that murder?' says he.

" 'Uneasy,' says I. 'Why should I feel uneasy? I've done nothing that I need feel uneasy about.'

" 'Ah,' says he, 'but what about the knife, Sadler? You know you were drunk on the night. Now tell me, don't you think you did the murder while you were drunk, and didn't know what you were doing?'

" 'The story about the knife,' I says, 'is an infernal lie of Duncan Campbell's, and if I ever get out I shall have him prosecuted for perjury.'

"But," puts in the reporter, "you know Campbell swore most positively as to buying the knife from you. Further than that, he identified you. How are you going to get over that?"

"It's my firm belief," says Sadler, rising up in bed on his excitement, "that Duncan Campbell was in the pay of the

The Interview

police."

"That's a very serious statement to make. How are you going to prove it?"

"Easy enough; and in this way. You may recollect that after I had received that cut in the head from that woman in Thrawl Street or Flower and Dean Street—I don't know which it was now—I turned round to Frances, the murdered girl. She had stood by and hadn't lifted a finger to interfere, although I will say this for her, that she warned me from going down the street. She said it was full of thieves, who would think nothing of robbing a drunken old sailor like me. But I wasn't going to be put off going down that street. I said, 'I've travelled nearly all over the world, and in all kinds of company, and I've never yet turned back on anything. I ain't a-going to fence that street.' That's how I came to go down there. Well, after I had been struck on the head with that blunt knife, or bottle, or whatever it was, and after Frances hadn't lifted a finger to save me, I of course turned to her. 'You're a pretty pal,' I said, 'to see me knocked about in this way and never to do anything for me.'

" 'How could I, Jim?' she says. 'You know if I'd lifted a finger for you I should have been marked by three people, and they'd pay me out when they got the opportunity.'

"I see the force of her argument now, poor girl. But I was drunk at the time, and felt mad like.

" 'I'll go down to the ship,' (that's the "*Fez*," the boat I was engaged on) 'and stay there the night now,' I said.

"Well you may remember that when I get down to the dock gates I was set upon by some dockers, while the policeman at the gates turned his back the other way. I hear, by the way, that he's got shifted over that job, and serve him right. Well, I was so knocked about in the ribs, and my head where it was cut felt so bad, that I walked back to Whitechapel towards the hospital. Just near the hospital I met a policeman. You can guess that I looked a pretty scarecrow at that time, what with being drunk, and groan-

CARROTY NELL

ing away over my ribs, and the blood all running down my head.

"That, it seems, was after the murder, and the policeman knew of it, and was on the look out for anybody suspicious, though I hadn't heard a word about the affair, and didn't know anything of it for hours after.

" 'Hullo,' says the policeman, 'what's the matter with you?'

" 'I've been out and knocked about,' I says.

" 'Why, your head's all over blood,' says he; 'let's look if you've got a knife about you.'

" 'I haven't got a knife,' I replied. 'I never carry one.' "

"Indeed, now that I come to think of it, I remembered the night before—on Thursday night—when I was in one of the public houses along with Frances, and wanted to cut a bit of hard tobacco, we had to search all over the place for a knife to cut it with.

"However, the policeman searched me, and it's a good job he did, for he can now prove that what I say is true. He felt all over my pockets and even down to my sea boots.

" 'No you haven't got a knife,' says he. 'And now you'd better get into the hospital and have that wound of yours dressed.' "

"Now, if you remember, Duncan Campbell swore that I went over to his shop on the Friday morning and sold a knife to him because I said I wanted the money to get drink. In the first place, as I say, I hadn't got a knife to sell, in the second, I didn't want a drink, or if I did want it, I had the money to buy one, and I also had a bottle that I had left twopence on the night before, and that I could have got back if I wanted, and then, in the third place, I never saw Duncan Campbell at all. I never saw Duncan Campbell in my life till he came down to Leman Street Police Station to identify me. I don't want to see him again, because if I do, there's bound to be a row, and I suppose the police will say, 'look what a violent temper that man's got. It only proves that he did the murder.' At the same time, a man can't have

The Interview

his neck pretty nigh put into the rope with an infernal lie like that without wanting to have his own back from the man who tried to swear his life away."

"But do you seriously mean to tell me," queries the newspaper man, "that you never saw Duncan Campbell until the time that he identified you?"

"Never," cries Sadler, as he again starts up in bed in his excitement, and there's a world of conviction about his tone that carries the impress of truth with the assertion.

"Then how do you account for his identifying you in the Leman Street Police Station as the man who sold him the knife?"

"I'll tell you all about that, and I think that after you've heard what I've got to say, you'll agree with me that Campbell was all along aided and abetted by the police, if he wasn't in their pay. The day that Campbell came to identify me, I was brought out and placed in a line with a lot of other men. There were several of the police there at the time. Campbell came in and went twice along the line without picking out anybody—although goodness knows he might have easily enough picked me out for I was wearing my cap at the time, which was all covered and clotted with blood, and my eyes were all swollen and bruised with the knocking about I'd received.

"Then one of the police came and stationed himself right opposite where I was standing and looked straight at me with his eyes. Campbell was standing by him just at that time.

" 'Can't you recognise him?' says the policeman—and he was looking as hard as he could at me all the time.

"Then Campbell, he, of course, looked towards where I was standing, too; but even then he didn't seem quite sure. So he goes all along the line of men again and lifts off their hats one by one. At last, when he comes to mine, and sees the blood on the cap and the wound on the head, he says 'That's the man.' That's how Campbell identified me, although I'd never seen him and he'd never seen me in my life before.

"But didn't you complain of the irregular manner in which this identification business was carried out?"

"They didn't give me an opportunity. As soon as Campbell says, 'That's the man,' they hurried me off to the cells and placed me in custody. But after I was discharged I went to Inspector Moore and complained to him about it. I told him that I meant to prosecute Campbell for perjury. 'Oh,' says he, 'you'd better not. You weren't taken to the Central Criminal Court. If you were, and Campbell had repeated his evidence there, you might have had ground, but I don't think you'd better take proceedings now.'

"But I understand," remarked the reporter, "that you do intend to take proceedings against certain newspapers?"

"Yes, my solicitors, Messrs. Wilson and Wallace, are taking proceedings against, I think, about half a dozen newspapers for publishing that villainous, lying, and scandalous so-called interview with my wife during the time when I was charged with the crime. The first action will be against the Daily Telegraph. That comes on, I think, next Thursday, and if the judgment goes against that paper the others will be proceeded against."

"But excuse me for saying so—you don't look exactly like a flourishing sort of a man who could afford to employ solicitors in an expensive law suit."

"You're right there. I'm just about on my beam ends now. I've scarcely got a penny to bless myself with, and only last Saturday I was out looking for a job among the Thames steamboats for the Easter Holidays, but they said I wasn't fit for work of any kind—and I quite believe it."

And Sadler takes up his medicine bottle again and applies himself to it.

"Then who are paying the expenses of the legal proceedings—if it's a fair question?"

"I'm not quite sure, but I think I have to thank the Star for that, and also for paying for the barrister who defended me during the inquest and my hearings at the police court."

The Interview

"Of course, those statements alleged to have been made by your wife in that interview of which you complain—the statements, I mean, about your meeting her in Aldgate when you were disguised, and about your knowing all about the previous murders—were false, then?"

"False, lying, and scandalous," cries Sadler. "It's true that I met her once after I had come from sea, some years ago, somewhere in East London—I forget where just now—but as for being disguised—well, it's such rubbish that I don't care about talking of it. I haven't got the patience for it. As to knowing anything about the other murders, if you'll believe me, I don't think there's a man in London who can read, who knows less about those other murders than I do. I was at sea most of the time when they occurred, and I had other things to think about than them when I was on shore."

"But how do you account for a woman—and more that all, for your wife—making statements of that kind which were likely to place you in a very serious position?"

"I can't make it out. I don't believe she ever said any such things. There was no ill-feeling between us that I am aware of. It is true we are separated, but that was because our tastes didn't exactly suit each other. She was always too fond of dress, and of flirty ways for me. I, on the other hand, was always a hard workingman, always willing to do what I could for a living, and never shirking my share of duty. But I always treated her well. Whenever I came home from sea, the very first thing I did when I got my wages was to send down her money to 3, Skinner Street, Chatham—that's where she lives. On the Friday of the murder I sent her down £2."

"And about Frances, the murdered woman. Had you known her long?"

"Yes; off and on, for some time past. I stayed with her when I came home the voyage before last. She was always a quiet, inoffensive kind of girl, and we always got on well together. There was never a shilling difference between us.

CARROTY NELL

When I first knew her she was a very reserved kind of girl, keeping herself to herself, and never mixing with any other women of her class. When I came home last time, though, I found her very much altered so far as her position went. She had come down in the world like they all do in time, but even then, she hated the women with whom she had to associate. Many a time on that Thursday night when she was murdered, and when we were going from one public house to another, drinking, she would say to me, 'Don't go into that bar, Jim. There's a lot of rough characters there. I don't like them, and if they see me with you they'll want a share of your money.' She was rather weak minded in that way."

"Have you any theory of your own about the murder, Sadler?"

"It is as much a mystery to me a it is to everyone else. The only thing that can make me account for her being at the place where she was found murdered is this. You may recollect I told you a little while back that after the row we had in Thrawl Street or Flower and Dean Street, when I was attacked, I told her I was going back to the ship to stay the night. I believe that she was hard up, and that, knowing she was always welcome to share in any money I ever had, she was on the way to the '*Fez*,' where she expected to find me."

"During the time you were drinking with her on Thursday night, did she ever hint to you or tell you that she was going to meet anybody that night?"

"Never. I don't believe she ever intended to meet anybody."

"Just one question more. You may remember that at the time you were before the magistrate at Arbour Square you complained of the way in which you were treated in the matter of food. Was they any foundation for that complaint?"

"Plenty. On that particular day at seven o'clock in the morning I had a couple of slices of bread and butter for my

The Interview

breakfast—nothing more. A little after two o'clock on the same day I was dragged before the magistrate. I had had nothing to eat all that time, and I think you will agree with me there was plenty of time between seven in the morning and two in the afternoon for those two slices to get down. I didn't know whether or not I was to have anybody to defend me, and thought I should have to fight my own case. More than that I knew that all the police were against me, and I felt that I wanted all my wits about me if I was going to get off. It wasn't the way exactly to enable a man to defend himself from so serious a charge, to keep him without food all that time, was it? But after I left the dock I was treated all right as regards food in the Arbour Square Station."

And with that the reporter found his way down the rickety stairs again and so into the murky streets below.

CARROTY NELL

NOTES AND SOURCES

Foreword

xiii The August 27, 1883 explosion that decimated the island of Krakatao was heard almost three thousand miles away, making it the loudest noise in recorded history. The resulting tsunamis reached the west coat of Africa. Dust particles that were blown skyward continued to color sunsets for years afterward.

Chapter 1 -- Swallow Gardens

3 Several writers have stated that Ernest Thompson was twenty-seven at the time of the murder in Swallow Gardens. His December 1900 Death Certificate however, issued only two months before the tenth anniversary of that crime, noted his age as thirty-two.

Chapter 2 -- A Gruesome Discovery in George Yard

10 "people of the poorest description" – *East London Observer,* August 11, 1888.

CARROTY NELL

Chapter 4 -- "I Won't Be Long"

32   Chapman's injuries were described in detail in *The Lancet*, September 20, 1888.

Chapter 5 -- The Double Event

38   "as dull and lonely a spot as can be found anywhere in London" – *The Daily News*, October 1, 1888.

44   The account of the journalist who was forced to seek refuge in the Southwark Police Station while attired in women's clothing appeared in the October 8, 1888 edition of *The (North Yorkshire) Northern Echo*.

Chapter 7 -- Castle Alley

68   Alice McKenzie's burial details – *Penny Illustrated Paper*, August 3, 1889.

Chapter 8 -- "She's Known As Carroty Nell"

80   **"The supposed work of Jack the Ripper,"** warning transmitted by telegraph from Leman Street at 3:05 on the morning of the murder - *Lloyd's Weekly*, February 22, 1891.

81   The activities that took place in Swallow Gardens on the night after the murder – *The Daily News*, February 14, 1891.

Notes and Sources

Chapter 9 -- Rumors, Hearsay, and Misinformation

87 **"a married woman named Hawkins"** – *Lloyd's Weekly*, Feb. 22, 1891

88 William Fryday's account of his visit to the mortuary was also included in the February 22 edition of *Lloyd's Weekly*.

93 The interview with Rev. Robinson appeared in the February 14 edition of the *Pall Mall Gazette*. Robinson is perhaps best known for his staunch opposition to displaying the crucifix in Anglican churches.

94 The report that Frances had worked as a domestic appeared in the February 16 edition of the *Pall Mall Gazette*.

Chapter 10 -- Frances Coles

95 Details of James Coles's early years courtesy of Mr. Paul Goodman of Folkestone, Kent

98 BMD Birth Records for the Coles children:

Selina
4th qtr. 1855, St. Olave District, Vol. 1d, pg. 50

Frances
4th qtr. 1859, St. Olave District, Vol. 1d, pg. 47

James Jr.
4th qtr. 1862, St. Olave District, Vol. 1d, pg. 3

CARROTY NELL

99 The description of 3 White Lion Court and the November 4, 1843 inquest into the death of Ann Galway appeared in *The Condition of the Working-Class in England in 1844* by Frederick Engels.

101 James Coles was described as a cripple in *Lloyd's Weekly* on February 22, 1891.

103 Details of Frances's job at James Sinclair & Sons appeared in the February 17, 1891 edition of *The Daily News*.

104 Winfield Hora & Co. information from *The Lancet*, February 18, 1860, and the *Business Directory of London*, 1884. Published by J.S.C. Morris, London.

104 Winfield Hora's role in the Parochial Charities - *House of Commons Papers*, Volume 12, 1882.

106 The interview with Frances's foreman at Winfield Hora & Co. appeared in the February 17, 1891 edition of *The Daily News*.

106 **"a Christian mission on Commercial Road"** – *Western Mail*, February 17, 1891.

107 **"had worked as a packer for nine years"** – *The Star* (Saint Peter Port, Guerney, Channel Islands), February 17, 1891.

113 BMD Death Record of James Coles Jr.:

2nd qtr. 1889, St. Olave District, Vol. 1d, pg. 119

114 **"She used to bring different men to the house to sleep with her."** remark by Charles Guiver,

Notes and Sources

watchman at Wilmott's – *Lloyd's Weekly*, February 22, 1891.

118 The report of Frances's meeting with her former landlady at Wilmott's appeared in the *East London Advertiser* on February 21, 1891.

Chapter 11 -- Friday, the 13th

120 **"quite imposing by 1891 standards"** The height of the average adult male in 1880s England was 171 cm, or five ft., seven inches according to *Making a long story short: a note on men's height and mortality in England from the first through the nineteenth centuries* by Stephen J. Kunitz, *Medical History*, July 1987.

123 **"You need new underwear more than you need a new bonnet."** – *Birmingham (England) Daily Post*, February 16, 1891

123 Several published reports claim that Frances told Sadler she had given a one-shilling deposit on a hat, and he agreed to pay the balance. Those reports are based on the statement Sadler gave to Chief Inspector Swanson on February 14, 1891. That statement is reproduced in the Appendix. Sadler appeared confused when he made his statement, and he placed several events in the wrong time sequence. The testimony of Peter Hawkes, who waited on Frances and sold her the hat, contradicts Sadler's account.

124 Sarah Treadway's account of James Sadler's condition – *Hampshire Advertiser*, February 21, 1891.

CARROTY NELL

132   "he'd give her a half crown" – *The Dundee Courier & Argus,* February 17, 1891.

Chapter 12 -- "You Are Hereby Charged …"

135   "in a maudlin condition from drink" – *The Morning Post,* February 14, 1891.

137   The suggestion that Frances might not have been a Ripper-victim because she was too good-looking appeared in *Lloyd's Weekly* on February 22, 1891

143   Mrs. Sadler's refusal to speak to reporters – *Belfast Newsletter,* February 20, 1891

143   "threats of lynching and tearing the prisoner to pieces were made" – *New York Times,* February 17, 1891

147   Sadler's letter to his union – *Blackburn Standard,* February 21, 1891

Chapter 13 -- Mr. Baxter's Inquest

153   "He had received a letter" – At the time of the Coles Inquest, London residents received seven mail deliveries a day according to *Victorianlondon.org.*

153   "Honored Sir, The enclosed is Mr. Bachert's letter" – *Lloyd's Weekly,* February 22, 1891.

153   "horses that are engaged in shunting have to go backwards and forwards through it" – the Great Northern Railway kept their wagons at the

Notes and Sources

freight depot on Royal Mint Street, but their stables were on Chamber Street. Swallow Gardens was the shortest route between the two.

159   The *Belfast Newsletter* and the *Bristol Mercury & Daily Post* were among the newspapers that carried Mary Ann Coles's alleged statement that her sister Frances had a daughter.

178   **"appeared to have been rather imaginative"** – *Birmingham Daily Post*, February 28, 1891.

Chapter 14 -- Rest In Peace

184   Details of Frances Coles's burial location and confirmation that it was reused years later courtesy of Toni Slade, Manager at the East London Cemetery.

Chapter 15 -- Upon Closer Examination

190   **"a slight cut, not even dangerous"** – Central News Agency dispatch, February 14, 1891.

194   **"had been coming to visit twice a week"** – Central News Agency dispatch, cited in the *Western Mail*, February 17, 1891.

Chapter 16 -- Total Disagreement

201   **"but he did visit the murder site in Swallow Gardens"** – *The Times*, February 14, 1891

CARROTY NELL

201 "he stopped by the Leman Street Police Station" – *Western Mail*, February 17, 1891

209 "a much more lenient view of our failure to find Jack the Ripper" – *Pall Mall Gazette*, November 4, 1889.

211 Inspector Edmund Reid's comments appeared in the April 23, 1910 edition of the *Morning Advertiser*.

Chapter 17 -- The Suspects

227 "He held my hair and banged my head," – *The Complete History of Jack the Ripper* by Philip Sugden.

Epilogue

243 "the shock of the fall caused the woman to contract bronchitis" – *The Lancet*, December 17, 1898.

244 "was reading his morning newspaper" – *The Times*, March 4, 1921.

BIBLIOGRAPHY

Begg, Paul, Martin Fido, and Keith Skinner, *The Complete Jack the Ripper A to Z*, London, John Blake (2010)

Begg, Paul, *Jack the Ripper, the Definitive History*, Harlow, Pearson (2005)

Clack, Robert and Philip Hutchinson, *The London of Jack theRipper, Then and Now*, Derby, Breedon (2007)

Cullen, Tom. A, *When London Walked in Terror*, Boston, Houghton Mifflin (1965)

Engels, Frederick, *The Condition of the Working-Class in England in 1844*, London, George Allen & Unwin Ltd. (1943)

Evans, Stewart P. and Keith Skinner, *The Ultimate Jack the Ripper Companion*, New York, Carroll & Graf (2001)

Evans, Stewart P. and Donald Rumbelow, *Jack the Ripper:Scotland Yard Investigates*, Stroud, Sutton (2006)

Fishman, William J., *East End 1888*, Philadelphia, Temple University Press (1988)

Goldsmid, Howard J., *Dottings of a Dosser*, Gloucester, Dodo Press (reprint, 2009)

Gordon, R. Michael, *The American Murders of Jack the Ripper*, Guilford, CT, Lyons (2003)

Harkness, Margaret, *Toilers in London*, London, Hodder and Stoughton (1889)
Horsler, Val, *Jack the Ripper*, Kew, The National Archives (2007)
Jakubowski, Maxim and Nathan Braund (eds.), *The Mammoth Book of Jack the Ripper*, New York, Carroll & Graf (1999)
Jones, Richard, *Uncovering Jack the Ripper's London*, London, New Holland (2007)
London, Jack, *The People of the Abyss*, New York, Macmillan (1903)
Morley, Christopher J., *Jack the Ripper: A Suspect Guide* (E-Book) (2005)
Odell, Robin, *Ripperology*, Kent, OH, Kent State University Press (2006)
Picard, Liza, *Victorian London*, London, Weidenfeld & Nicolson (2005)
Ruddick, James, *Death at the Priory*, New York, Atlantic Monthly Press (2001)
Rumbelow, Donald, *The Complete Jack the Ripper*, New York, Signet (1975)
Shelden, Neal, *The Victims of Jack the Ripper*, Knoxville, Inklings (2007)
Smith, Henry, *From Constable to Commissioner*, Ann Arbor, University of Michigan Library (reprint, 2010)
Sugden, Philip, *The Complete History of Jack the Ripper*, London, Robinson (2006)
Williams, Montagu, *Later Leaves*, Boston, Houghton, Mifflin & Co. (1891)

INDEX

Aarons, Joseph 51, 52
Abberline, Frederick 60, 200, 204, 206, 207, 213, 220-222, 228-231, 239
Adam, Hargrave 209
Anderson, Isabel 202
Anderson, Sir Robert 62, 136, 137, 208-211, 217-219, 239, 241
Andrews, Walter 64, 65, 67
Arnold, Thomas 46, 54, 76, 84, 145, 190, 200

Bachert, Albert 151-153, 156, 157, 239
Baderski, Lucy 222, 224
Badham, Edward 64
Barnett, Joseph 56, 58
Barrett, Thomas 11, 12, 14
Baxter, Wynne 22, 23, 32, 33, 39, 59, 60, 148-181, 193, 194, 232, 240
Beck, Walter, 54
Blackwell, Dr. Frederick 38-40
Bogan, William 164, 166-169, 179, 248
Bond, Dr. Thomas 55, 56, 67, 210
Boswell, Francis 199
Bowen, Frederick 142, 253
Bowyer, Thomas 53, 54, 57
Bravo, Charles 225
Brown, Dr. Frederick G. 46, 50
Brownfield, Dr. Matthew 209, 210
Bulling, Tom 35

Cadosch, Albert 29
Caine, Michael 213
Calana, Ellen 131, 132, 134-136, 138, 141, 174, 175, 191, 228, 229, 249
Campbell, Duncan 140, 142, 170-172, 174, 178, 197, 248, 258, 260-262
Carney, Mary Ann 95, 96, 100
Chandler, Joseph 26
Chapman, Annie (girlfriend

CARROTY NELL

of Severin Klosowski) 224
Chapman, Annie (victim) 27-34, 136, 173, 189, 190, 200, 203, 215, 232
Chapman, George (Severin Klosowski) 206, 207, 221, 224, 226, 227, 230
Chapman, John 28
Churchill, Winston xvi, 209
Clark, Dr. Percy 212
Cochran, Johnny 237
Coleman, Frances (alias) 83
Coles, Frances xvii, 79, 83-86, 90-93, 95-110, 112-115, 117-120, 122-137, 140, 144, 145, 148, 149, 152, 153, 156-161, 163, 164, 167, 169, 174, 175, 177-182, 184-194, 201, 206, 209, 211, 225, 228, 229, 234-236, 240, 242, 250-254, 259, 260, 263
Coles, James 83, 84, 94, 95, 98-101, 108, 114, 117, 158, 159, 194, 240
Coles, James Jr. 98, 103, 113
Coles, Mary Ann 92, 95, 96, 103, 106, 113, 115, 119, 137, 158-160, 182, 193, 194, 240, 247
Coles, Selina 92, 95, 96, 100, 102, 103, 113, 193, 240
Collier, George 13, 180
Connolly, Mary Ann 14
Conway, Thomas 47, 48
Cooper, Helen 248
Cox, Henry 207, 222

Cox, Mary Ann 59
Cross, Charles 17, 18
Curley, Mathew 142, 253
Cutbush, Charles H. 202, 240
Cutbush, Thomas 201-205, 241

Davis, Florence 249
Davis, John 25, 26
Delaforce, Edward 171, 172, 249
Diemschutz, Louis 36, 37, 39
Dooley, John 166, 248
Drew, Thomas 20
Druitt, Ann 215
Druitt, Montague John 203, 215-217, 238
Dunham, Col. 232

Eddowes, Catherine 47-52, 100, 136, 139, 189, 190, 200, 203, 220
Edwards, Wesley 87, 166-169, 179, 248
Elliott, George 76, 155, 168, 189, 247
Evans, John 28
Evans, Stewart P. 15, 21, 31, 41, 49, 57, 66, 75, 82, 85, 105, 129, 141, 208, 212, 226, 275

Fewell, William 168, 169, 248
Flanagan, James 76, 77, 135, 248
Fleming, Sarah 91, 114, 130, 138, 163-165, 248
Fowles, Thomas 145, 176,

Index

177, 242, 249
Franklin, Margaret   67
Fryday, William   87-89, 144-147, 175-177, 241, 249
Gilbert, Sir W. S.   xii, 110-112
Gold, Eliza   50

Goldsmid, Howard   107, 108, 275
Gordon, R. Michael   223, 275
Goodman, Paul   269
Gray, Edward   249
Guild, Thatcher Howland   112
Guiver, Charles   108, 114, 127, 128, 130, 161-163, 241, 247
Gull, Sir William   212

Hague, Mrs.   115, 118, 122
Halse, Daniel   46
Harkness, Margaret   106, 275
Harris, Charles   138, 161, 162, 247
Harrison, Rex   241
Haswell, Joseph   130, 131, 169, 170, 248
Hawkes, Peter   124, 160, 247
Hebbert, Dr. Charles   210
Holland, Ellen   22
Hora, Henry Winfield   103, 104, 106-110, 158, 159, 194, 241, 270
Hutchinson, George   58-60, 136

Hutchinson, Philip   79, 275
Hutt, George   50
Hyde, Frederick   74, 76, 155, 166-168, 179, 247, 248
Johnson, Florence   202
Johnson, John   249
Johnson, Thomas   174, 249

Kelly, John   47, 48
Kelly, Mary Jane   53-61, 63, 67, 109, 136, 173, 188, 190, 200, 203, 207, 209, 210, 217, 231, 236-238, 241
Kendall, Kay   241
Killeen, Dr. Timothy   11, 12
Klosowski, Severin   xi, 136, 206, 207, 222-229
Kosminski, Aaron   204, 208, 217-220, 242

Lamb, Henry   38
Lawende, Joseph   139, 140, 219, 220
Lawless, H. H.   163, 171, 174- 176, 180
Leary, John   12
Levisohn, Wolff   229
Lewis, Sarah   59
Lincoln, Pres. Abraham   231
Littlechild, John   212, 231
Llewellyn, Dr. Rees   18, 19, 22, 23
Long, Alfred   46
Long, Elizabeth   29
Lushington, Godfrey   137
Lusk, George   51, 52, 242

MacDonald, Roderick 59, 60
Macnaughten, Sir Melville 201-204, 207, 208, 215-221, 236, 239-242
Mansfield, Richard 213
Marsh, Emily 51, 52
Marsh, Maud 206, 227, 228
Mathews, Charles 157, 158, 160-164, 166-168, 173-175, 180, 228
Matthews, Henry 137
Maxwell, Caroline 61
Maybrick, James 213
McCarthy, John 53, 242
McCarthy, Kate 145, 146, 175-177, 242, 249
McCormack, John 65, 67
McKellar, Dr. Alexander 210
McKenzie, Alice 65-68, 136, 151, 189, 190, 211, 234-236
Mizen, Jonas 18
Monro, James 63, 68, 201
Moore, Henry 107, 115, 131, 141. 174, 176, 177, 193, 205, 206, 249, 262
Murray, James 81, 83, 107
Mylett, Rose 209, 210

Neil, John 18
Nichols, Mary Ann 19-22, 24, 26, 32, 51, 108, 136, 188-190, 200, 203
Nichols, William 20
Norris, Ann 13

Ostrog, Michael 204, 220, 221, 243
Oxley, Dr. Frederick 76, 89, 170, 172, 179, 187, 243

Packer, Matthew 42, 43
Paul, Robert 18
Phillips, Annie 48
Phillips, Dr. George B. 26, 27, 32, 56, 61, 64, 67, 76, 77, 89, 170, 172, 173, 187, 188, 190, 212, 243
Pizer, John 24
Prater, Elizabeth 59, 61

Redding, Michael 248
Reeves, John 9-11
Reid, Edmund 64, 137, 174, 211, 249
Richards, Laura 229
Richardson, John 29, 30
Robinson, Rev. Arthur J. 92
Robinson, Thomas 140, 171, 249
Ronan, Kitty 241
Ruddick, James 225, 276
Rumbelow, Donald 208, 275, 276
Ryder, Elizabeth 65

Sadler, James T. 87, 112, 113, 120-125, 127-130, 138-144, 146-149, 152, 157, 160-164, 166-175, 177-180, 197-199, 228, 242, 249-265
Sadler, Sarah 120, 143, 198, 199
Sharp, Arthur 168, 178,

Index

248
Shuttleworth, Anne 123, 163, 165, 247
Simpson, O. J. 237
Slade, Toni 273
Smith, Frederick 169, 248
Smith, Sir Henry 211, 244
Spink, Mary 224, 225, 228
Spratling, John 19
Stanley, Edward 28
Steer, William 163, 247
Stevenson, Robert Louis 243
Storikie, Max 223
Stride, Elizabeth 40, 41, 43, 136, 156, 189-192, 200, 203, 220
Stride, John 40
Sugden, Philip 189, 209, 219, 221, 276
Swanson, Donald 43, 139, 140, 198, 200, 217-220, 249

Tabram, Henry 13, 14
Tabram, Martha 13-17, 19, 22, 188-190, 221
Taylor, Bessie 225, 228
Thain, John 18
Thick, William 24
Thompson, Ernest xxi, 3-5, 7, 8, 69, 73, 74, 76, 88, 153, 154, 156, 166, 173, 191, 192, 244, 247
Treadway, Sarah 123, 124, 163, 247
Tumblety, Francis 212, 231-233
Turner, William 14

Victor, Prince Albert 212
Victoria, H.R.H. Queen xiv, 212

Warren, Charles 30, 46, 54, 92, 205
Watkins, Edward 37, 38
Watts, Elizabeth 39
White, Stephen 42
Whitehead, James 53
Williams, Montagu 116, 198, 276

CARROTY NELL

ABOUT THE AUTHOR

John Keefe is a graduate of Boston College. He has maintained an avid interest in the Whitechapel murders for more than twenty years. Many consider him the foremost authority on victim Frances Coles. The first edition of *Carroty Nell* was published in 2010. Mr. Keefe and his wife live near Boston, Massachusetts.

CARROTY NELL